THE LAST WORD ON. . .

Cool Names
"MAX—like his pinochle-playing partners Sam and Jake—suddenly became hip."

Classic Names
"HOPE is too high-minded to be corrupted, and is such a lovely classic name that it deserves all the attention it gets."

Tired Names
"BRAD—despite the appeal of current heartthrob Brad Pitt—is still out on surfin' safari with Chad, Todd, and Scott."

Sophisticated Names
"KAY wears bias-cut satin evening gowns and fox jackets and goes to nightclubs where there are miniature lamps on each table and everybody smokes."

Up-and-Coming Names
"CHESTER: A comfortable, solid, teddy bear of a name that we would place in the so-far-out-they-could-be-on-their-way-back-in category."

Impossible Names
"HORTENSE: No!"

Don't even *think* of naming your baby before checking out *The Last Word on First Names!*

The
LAST WORD
on FIRST
NAMES

The Definitive A-Z Guide to the Best and Worst in Baby Names by America's Leading Experts

LINDA ROSENKRANTZ and PAMELA REDMOND SATRAN

St. Martin's Paperbacks

THE LAST WORD ON FIRST NAMES

Copyright © 1995 by Linda Rosenkrantz and Pamela Redmond Satran.

Cover photograph © Penny Gentieu/Tony Stone Images.

Library of Congress Catalog Card Number: 94-42081

ISBN: 0-312-96106-5

Printed in Canada

St. Martin's Press hardcover edition/March 1995
St. Martin's Press trade paperback edition/March 1995
St. Martin's Paperbacks edition/June 1997

10 9 8 7 6 5

For

JOSEPH LEOPOLD,

OWEN REDMOND,

and

WILLA FRANCES

Our thanks to Hope Dellon, Molly Friedrich, Jenny Notz, Thomas Duncan Dunsmuir, Karen Shapiro, Fifi Rivera, Marilen Cadabos, Christopher Finch, and Dick Satran.

ABOUT THE AUTHORS

∿∿∿∿∿∿∿∿∿∿∿∿∿∿∿∿ ◉ ∿∿∿∿∿∿∿∿∿∿∿∿∿∿∿∿

LINDA ROSENKRANTZ is the author of the novel *Talk* and coauthor of *Gone Hollywood* and *SoHo*. The former editor of *Auction* magazine, she now writes a weekly syndicated column on collectibles and also contributes to numerous national magazines. She currently lives in Los Angeles with her husband and daughter.

PAMELA REDMOND SATRAN is a columnist for *Parenting* magazine and also writes a syndicated newspaper column on working parenthood. Her essays and articles appear frequently in *Working Mother, Glamour, Redbook,* and other national magazines. She is the author of a book on style and a novel, and lives outside New York with her husband and three children.

Together, the authors have written the bestselling *Beyond Jennifer & Jason,* and a series of books on British names, Irish names, and Jewish names.

INTRODUCTION

∿∿∿∿∿∿∿∿∿∿∿∿∿∿∿∿∿∿∿∿∿ ◉ ∿∿∿∿∿∿∿∿∿∿∿∿∿∿∿∿∿∿∿∿∿

In the introduction to our first guide to naming your baby, *Beyond Jennifer & Jason,* we stated our feelings about baby naming dictionaries in no uncertain terms. We hated wading through endless pages of archaic names. We hated trying to find some real-life meaning in literal definitions like "flaming hill" for Brandon. And we hated discovering that, of a book's ten thousand advertised names, seventy-eight were deviant spellings of Carly.

Our belief was that parents—and babies—deserved something that was smarter, savvier, *better* than that. To make the best name choice for your child and yourself, you need a name book that's more honest than your friends and hipper than your parents, that tells you what names signify right here and now, not merely in ancient Greece.

Beyond Jennifer & Jason gave parents one inventive tool for divining those real-life meanings of names. That book turned conventional name dictionaries inside out and approached baby naming from a completely new direction, organizing names into subjective categories—trendy names and traditional names, biblical names and creative names—that addressed parents' real-life concerns and desires.

The Last Word on First Names may look more traditional than our first book, but we think you'll find it's just as innovative. The classic A to Z format lets us examine thousands of names in light of the questions that burn in the heart of every parent in search of the perfect name. How popular is this name, and how will that affect my child? What are other people going to assume about my son or daughter, about our family, based on this name? What's the downside of names I like? What are some wonderful names I may not have thought of?

To answer those kinds of questions, we have drawn on sources as far-ranging as the Bible and the atlas, old movies and current TV shows, foreign baby naming guides and academic journals, name popularity lists and celebrity gossip sheets. There is no rigid format: We include a name's origins and literal meanings if they provide relevant information, foreign versions and variant spellings if they offer interesting options; if they don't, we don't. Only once did a name strike us speechless, and then our advice boiled down to a single word: No!

One note: Within the text, names that do not have listings of their own are printed in all capital letters. Those that *do* have their own, more complete listings elsewhere in the book are in upper and lower case.

And one caution: Please don't be miffed if you look up your own name (as many people feel impelled to do) and find that we've said something less than positive about it. Our advice focuses on choosing a name for a child born at this time, and a name that may be perfectly sound and suitable for a thirty-three-year-old parent—Pam or Linda, say, or Alan or Gary—just doesn't have the same appeal for a child of today.

As always, you've got to consider context. Where you live, what you do, who your ancestors were, and who you hope your child will become all play an important part in determining which name is best. Tallulah Belle Willis, for example, Hollywood child of Bruce and Demi, will fit right in with little Sawyer Spielberg and Wolfgang Van Halen. On your block, the atmosphere might be a tad more conservative.

Choosing the right name from all the thousands of possibilities can seem like an overwhelmingly daunting decision. We hope that at the ultimate moment, when your pen is poised above your newborn baby's birth certificate, this book will give you more confidence, a steadier hand, a feeling that you've chosen a name you love nearly as thoroughly and unconditionally as your unnameably wonderful child.

The
LAST WORD
on FIRST
NAMES

GIRLS' NAMES

A

ABIGAIL. Abigail, a name that has moved far in and out of fashion and up and down the class scale over the centuries, has a somewhat quaint and straitlaced image today, which works to give it a singular charm. In the Old Testament, Abigail—which means father's joy in Hebrew—was the wife of King David, renowned for her beauty, wisdom, and powers of prophecy; later, it became a slang term for a lady's trusted maid-confidante. Its two considerably more relaxed nicknames, Gail and ABBY (or ABBIE), have taken on lives of their own. Gail is rarely used these days, but ABBY has popped up on both the cast and character lists of such shows as *L.A. Law* and *Knots Landing*. The only problem might be that your own darling Abby gets referred to as "dear."

ABRA. A soft, sensitive biblical name most widely used in seventeenth-century England, and reappearing in the book and movie *East of Eden*. But while the name itself has a good deal of creative charm, a child named Abra will certainly tire of hearing people say "Cadabra" and, during those sensitive pubescent years, "Abra, like a bra. A bra, get it?"

ACTON. An ambisexual surname name, à la Taylor, Kenyon, Parker, et al., of the kind that has become so popular for girls in recent years. While Acton is less melodious and considerably more severe (it sounds like a steel town) than some of its counterparts, it does have the admittedly obscure distinction of having been the masculine pseudonym (Acton Bell) of one of the Brontë sisters.

ADA, ADAH. Ada pronounced Ay-dah is a Germanic name that was popular in this country a century ago and still feels too great-grandmotherly to be ready for revival. Pronounced Ah-Dah, it's a Nigerian Ibo name meaning "firstborn girl." Spelled Adah, it's a completely different Old Testament name, actually the first female name mentioned in Genesis after Eve. We think both Ah-Dahs feel more fresh and interesting than Ay-dah. The Irish AIDAN has begun to be used for girls, including Faith Daniels's baby daughter.

ADANNA. This is an appealing name used by the Ibo people of Nigeria. It means "father's daughter."

ADELAIDE, ADELE, ADELIA, ADELINE. Think of Adelaide as one of the hot new place-names, and suddenly it doesn't sound quite as fusty and musty as it otherwise might. The Australian city was named for the popular nineteenth-century British "Good Queen Adelaide," the wife of William IV. All in all, though, we prefer the gentler-sounding Adeline, celebrated in turn-of-the-century barbershop harmonies as "Sweet Adeline," a name definitely starting to be rediscovered. And while Adele is lost in fashion limbo, parents who wish to honor an ancestral Adelaide might want to consider ADELA—a final *a* seems to make almost any girl's name sound more fashionable these days— or the even fresher-sounding Adelia, which gains in contemporary appeal because it sounds like the stylish Amelia, or maybe because writer Delia Ephron has made a form of the name familiar.

ADINA, ADENA. In the Bible, this is a male name, but it has come to be used exclusively for girls and, even then, infrequently. The name's major flaw: It sounds made up, as if you rearranged Scrabble letters until you hit on a euphonic combination.

ADORA. Is Adora a real name? Not in the sense that Anne and Catherine and Elizabeth are real names. Rather, like CHERISH and Darla, it's a term of endearment fashioned into an ultrafeminine first name.

ADRIENNE, ADRIANA. Adrienne is a name with a lot of substance and dignity—except to those who might still overidentify it with Rocky's cry, "Yo! Adrienne!" But as with many other names, the version ending in *a* (think of Joanna vs. Joanne, Diana vs. Diane) is more fashionable now anyway, and Adriana could make a pretty choice for parents who don't shy away from the dramatic.

AFRICA. As a name, there are two Africas. One is an ancient Irish name well used by medieval royalty—there is even an Irish St. Africa. The other, more usual form is a place name that refers to the continent and is gaining in popularity as a first name along with its compatriots Dakota, Savannah, Chelsea, and even that other favorite continental choice, ASIA. Africa, however, stands out from the place-name crowd because of its significant meaning for African-Americans and its real history as a personal name. AFRIKA is an alternate spelling, but it seems a tad disrespectful, like *"Amerika."*

AGATHA. The name Agatha summons up visions of mauve silk, needlepoint footstools, filigreed brooches clasped to high collars. It's a name that's long been covered with cobwebs, except when Agatha Christie mysteries are dramatized on public television, but adventurous parents may want to dust it off and restore it to prominence in their families. Popular in the Middle Ages, Agatha is the name of the patron saint of firefighters and nurses.

AGNES. Maybe it's the harsh *ag* sound, but Agnes, like Agatha, is another of those quintessentially old-fashioned names that's been relegated to the attic for years. Some may see it as a terminally ugly name that deserves to remain in storage; other parents may find charm and style in its very clunkiness. And while Agnes sounds infinitely hipper and more graceful pronounced the French way (on-yez) that's a bit pretentious for an American child, and no one looking at it on paper would say it that way anyhow. Believe it or not, for four hundred years, Agnes was one of the three most common English girls' names (together with Elizabeth and Joan), and was even in the Top 50 in this country a century ago. Scottish parents have liked the name so much they devised a backward version: SENGA. The Scots also use the nicknames NESSIE and Nessa, while the Welsh prefer NESTA.

AIDA. This melodic name is largely associated with the title character in the Verdi opera, an Ethiopian princess enslaved in Egypt, who dies to save her people.

AILEEN. This variant of Eileen (both of them are Irish forms of Helen) enjoyed fifteen minutes of fame when child actress Aileen Quinn starred in the movie version of *Annie*. But it seems a flyaway name, with no meat in either its flimsy *A* beginning or its dated *-een* ending. Other Gaelic names with a similar feel and a bit more texture include Scottish place-name AILSA and nickname AILIE.

AISHA. Aisha (pronounced I-ee-sha) is one of the more popular African-American girls' names—Stevie Wonder, for one, used it for his daughter. It derives from both the Swahili and Arabic cultures and means "life." Aisha was also the name of the prophet Mohammad's chief wife. Alternate spellings include AYISHA and ASHA (pronounced Ah-sha) and, less authentically, AYEESHA—the spelling Mick Jagger and Jerry Hall chose as the third name for their daughter Georgia May.

AISLING. Almost unheard of here, this name is very popular among modern Irish parents, who also use its phonetic spelling, ASHLING, as well as the more correct Gaelic one, AISLINN. Any variant of Aisling may be an interesting, if challenging choice for Irish-American parents who are attracted to the sound of the ubiquitous Ashley, but want something more original.

AKIBA. This African name has a melodic sound and energetic image.

ALANA. This feminine form of Alan probably would have retreated to near-obscurity along with other offbeat versions of male names— DONALDINA, RICHARDA—had it not been for the tagalong fame of Alana Hamilton Stewart, ex-wife of both George and Rod. ALANNA is one alternate spelling, another is ALANNAH, as in rock singer Alannah Myles.

ALBERTA. In the days of Queen Victoria, when she campaigned hard for the use of her beloved consort, Prince Albert's, name in any form, Alberta did come into fairly common use, as did such rarer examples as ALBERTINE and ALBERTINA. None of them is a name likely to appeal to a parent of today. ALFREDA is similarly out.

ALEX, ALIX. In the last decade or so, this name has definitely broken away from its longer-form parents and established an identity of its own—smart, efficient, slightly boyish, and hip. For a while there, it seemed as if every movie heroine fitting that description was an automatic Alex—Glenn Close in *Fatal Attraction*, Cher in *The Witches of Eastwick*, Debra Winger in *Black Widow*, Jane Fonda in *The Morning After*, Jennifer Beals in *Flashdance*. And in fact there may be many more baby Alexes than the unsuspecting parent might guess. While no single form of the name might make the Top 20, taken together all versions of Alex (including Alexandra, Alexis, etc.) often hit the Top 5! Alix is a more contemporary-looking spelling and ALYX is still another version, this one chosen by newsperson Faith Daniels for one of her daughters.

ALEXANDRA. Alexandra, like its twin brother Alexander, is in many ways the quintessential eighties Yuppie name: upwardly mobile, combining a classic pedigree with high fashion appeal. If Ralph Lauren designed names as well as clothes, Alexandra would surely be at the top of his line. And while there is something about the name that indicates you're trying a bit too hard to be tasteful and elegant, it does have an impressive background and is well used to this day by royals and the upper crust. Celebrities including Jessica Lange and Mikail Baryshnikov, Dustin Hoffman, and Christopher Reeve have all chosen Alexandra as a name for their daughters. Other stars have given their children names from among the legion of Alexandra variants and diminutives: the very popular ALEXA (Christie Brinkley and Billy Joel), ALEXANDRIA (Keith Richards and Patti Hanson), ALEXIA (Rod and Alana Stewart), and the appealing Italian alternative, ALESSANDRA (Andy Garcia). The Spanish form, ALEJANDRA, makes many states' Hispanic Top 10 list. ALEXANDRINA was the real first name of Queen Victoria; other variations include ALEXANDRINE, ALEXINA, and ALEXINE. Zandra is a more unusual diminutive.

ALEXIS. While Alexis is often considered a form of Alexandra, it is in fact a separate name in its own right. With Greek roots, this once-male name, brought into the American consciousness as a girl's name by actress Alexis Smith (born Gladys) in the forties, is now almost exclusively feminine. Unfortunately, its strong, upscale image has been somewhat tarnished by its association with the over-the-top Alexis Carrington character played by Joan Collins on *Dynasty*, the soap opera that put a tacky spin on many a perfectly good name. In Texas, Alexis is the number five name for African-American girls.

ALICE. A classic name, and an extremely pretty one, Alice is high on the list for stylish parents in Britain but has not yet made the leap here. Perhaps the name's classic and innocent Alice in Wonderland image, primary in the minds of British parents, is sullied here by those of the long-suffering Alice Kramden on *The Honeymooners* or the diner waitress Linda Lavin character on the sitcom *Alice*, or even punk rockers Alice Cooper and Alice in Chains. Whatever the reason, American parents, in our opinion, are too often neglecting a name with an illustrious history and a great deal of charm.

ALICIA, ALYSSA. Where Alice has failed, its little sisters Alicia (the classic version, and the real name of Jodie Foster) and especially Alyssa have succeeded. Alyssa, the spelling favored by the majority of parents these days, ranks in the Top 20 in many states all on its own, and when the name's myriad other variations and spellings—ALISSA, ALISHA, ALYSHA, ALYCIA, ELISSA, ILYSHA ad infinitum—are tallied, it climbs securely into the Top 10. Considered for its sound alone, Alicia is a beautiful, feminine name, but it has been bastardized to the extent that it's losing much of its character. Like a wildly popular hit song ("Don't Worry, Be Happy" comes to mind), it has been heard so often and imitated so frequently that its intrinsic appeal has gotten lost within the cliché.

ALISON, ALLISON. Alison has been very much around from the time of *Peyton Place* (the mid-sixties) to the current *Melrose Place*. Another derivative of Alice that has far surpassed the original in popularity, this medieval diminutive with a Scottish accent is still en vogue to the point of overuse. The only reason Alison doesn't show up on more popularity lists is that, like Alicia, it has so many spelling variations that each is often counted as a separate name and the cumulative mass is seldom given its full weight. And the more upwardly mobile you are, the more likely it is that you (and your child) will encounter a legion of little Alisons: According to research by Harvard sociologist Stanley Lieberson, Alison is second only to Emily in names favored by highly educated mothers. While the alternate (and perfectly acceptable) spelling ALLISON is in fact used more often than the original, other variations—ALLYSON, ALYSON, ALISSAN on down—will only confuse your child's life.

ALLEGRA. The quintessential ballet dancer's name—musical with Italianate allure—Allegra can be a triumph of a name for a child who is able to live up to its promise. But a name with such a powerfully graceful image can prove a burden, too. The call is yours; just be aware of your own expectations when contemplating such a choice.

ALLIE, ALLY, ALI. Allie is a cute, tomboyish name of the type that became a rage in the sixties—à la Jody, Kerry, Jamie et al.—and received a further fashion boost from *Love Story*'s Ali (born Alice) Mac-Graw. Actress Ally Sheedy helps keep the name before the public eye, as did the sitcom *Kate & Allie*. While such ambisexual nickname names are no longer fashionably used on their own, Allie is a good option to keep in mind should your Alexandra or Allegra prove more of a tree climber than a toe dancer.

ALMA. Rather solemn and soulful, Alma is one of those names, like Bertha or Esther, that enjoyed a burst of popularity around the turn of the century and now seems the province exclusively of elderly great-aunts, although it still is current in some Latino families. But while it seems in general too flat-footed to spring back to center stage, parents with special Almas in their backgrounds (it has roots in Hebrew, Latin, Spanish, and Celtic), may want to consider giving it their own personal style revival.

ALTHEA. A poetic, almost ethereal name found in Greek myth and seventeenth-century verse, Althea comes from the Greek meaning "wholesome" or "healer." It won honors in the 1950s via the champion tennis player, Althea Gibson.

ALYSSA. See ALICIA.

AMA. Ama, alternately spelled AMMA, is a name and/or word in several African cultures, meaning, alternately, "a female born on Saturday," "happy," and "beloved." Ama. A. Aidoo is a respected Ghanaian writer. AMARA, which was the word for "paradise" in ancient Abyssinia, has a related sound and can also be used as a girls' name.

AMABEL. A very old name, meaning "lovable" in Latin, that has long since been surpassed by its derivatives Mabel and Annabel. Prettier than the former and more distinctive than the latter, Amabel is a name we think might deserve a second look.

AMANDA. A name so popular it approaches number one in several states, Amanda was among the romantic-sounding names—Jessica, Samantha, Vanessa—that rocketed to stardom in the eighties and continue to enjoy widespread favor today. Their appeal is rooted in nostalgia for a gentler time. Despite its trendiness, Amanda is a certifiable classic—it appears in a play as early as 1694, and was prominent among saints and eighteenth-century literary heroines. Amanda later made a big hit in Noel Coward's 1930 play, *Private Lives*, as well as the name of Katharine Hepburn's character in the 1949 film, *Adam's Rib*. In the end, if you don't mind—or find an advantage in—giving your child a name she'll share with peers throughout her life, you couldn't make a prettier choice than Amanda. Or you might, as John Malkovitch did for his daughter, use the lovely French version, AMANDINE.

AMBER. Fifty years ago, Amber was lifted from the list of nineteenth-century jewel names by the notoriety of the then-shocking novel, *Forever Amber*. And it is still the only one of that group to enjoy real popularity these days, making the Top 20 hit list in many states. Its problem, compared with a more classic popular name like, say, Amanda, is that Amber is also somewhat offbeat, a factor that tends to link a name forever to its period of popularity. Just as most Shirleys were born in the thirties and forties, most Ambers will probably be born between

1975 and 2000. A twist that might make the name more outstanding: Use the Italian version, AMBRA.

AMELIA. Amelia's star is definitely on the rise as a stand-in for its cousins—Amanda, Emily, Amy, Melissa, Melanie—that have become a tad overused. Amelia does sound newer and more interesting than those names right now, but we can't promise that it still will in a decade. Introduced by Henry Fielding for the heroine of his eponymous 1751 novel, the name was further popularized in eighteenth-century England by Princess Amelia. Its connection to aviation (and feminist) heroine Amelia Earhart only adds to its recipe for success. The Italian version, AMALIA, will undoubtedly remain fresher but will also require that your child pronounce, spell, and explain the name endlessly throughout her life. EMILIA is a nineteenth-century form occasionally used today.

AMERICA. America is probably one place-name that is too firmly attached to the earth—to our corner of it, anyway—for widespread use, even though it was a given name for girls as well as boys as far back as Colonial times. An eighteenth-century marker in the same New Hampshire graveyard where writer Willa Cather is buried lists the name "Caroline America"—an inventive idea for the parent in search of a middle name with meaning.

AMY. Sweet and well-loved (exactly as its French meaning signifies), Amy rocketed to popularity in the late-nineteenth century along with the names of the other Louisa May Alcott *Little Women* (Amy was the artistic one), fell from favor, then burst onto the scene again in the 1970s, when parents were turning back to basic names like JESSIE, Maggie, and Molly. Now, after a twenty-year run, Amy is definitely ready for another respite. AIMEE, the original French version, is sometimes used here, but it does seem a bit affected. Other names—all similar in feel if not directly related to the original—to consider if you find the name Amy appealing but want something more unusual: the Hebrew name AMARIS; AMICA, an ancient Roman name still occasionally found in Italy; and AMINTA, an Italian adaptation of an ancient Macedonian royal name. AMIAS, also a male name, is attractive and spirited when used for girls. AMITY, with its references to friendship and harmony, might be considered as a virtue name, though its connection to *The Amityville Horror* may frighten off some parents.

AMINA, AMINAH. The name of the mother of the prophet Mohammad, Amina is well used among Muslims everywhere, and is especially popular among the Hausa of West Africa, while AMINATA is a popular name in Senegal.

ANAÏS. An unusual, creative name that means "graceful" in Hebrew. It is largely associated with the colorful Paris-born American novelist and diarist, Anaïs Nin, so choosing this name for your child will definitely brand you as a Nin devotee.

ANASTASIA. An elegant and luxuriously romantic name that may seem too rich for some parents' taste, Anastasia's greatest claim to fame is in relation to the "lost" daughter of the last czar of Russia, whose story has been told and retold in books and movies. An old Greek name and also the name of an ancient saint, the patron saint of weavers, Anastasia was popular in medieval Britain and in Ireland, as well as in Russia. We think it deserves another look: It would certainly prove a worthy substitute for overused favorites such as Alexandra or Amanda. Stacy is the usual, but way too wispy, nickname. STASIA or STACIA, pronounced with an *-ah* sound, is a more substantial choice.

ANDREA. Andrea has three different pronunciations, each of which projects a different image. The most prevalent and familiar, ANN-dree-a, is the one that has been moderately popular since the 1940s, and can pretty much sound like the girl next door, as do the nickname forms of ANDI or ANDIE (as in MacDowell). Pronounced ON-dree-a, as it is on *Beverly Hills 90210*, it becomes a bit more affected, while On-DRAY-a pushes it over the edge into the exotic. Originally the Italian male form of Andrew, which means "strong and valiant" in Greek, Andrea is found throughout most European cultures, for one sex or the other, while in the United States, it continues to hover near the bottom of the list of Top 50 names for girls. Variations include the Scottish ANDRENA and the arty ANDRA.

ANGEL, ANGELA, ANGELINA, ANGELICA. Angel first appeared as a male name in Britain in the seventeenth century, until the Puritans came along and deemed it presumptuous, shunning it along with angel names Gabriel, Michael, and Raphael. The name persisted for both men (the hero of Thomas Hardy's *Tess of the d'Urbervilles* is named Angel Clare) and women, although it was still considered too loaded ever to become a favorite in English-speaking countries. Much more popular for girls was first the Italian diminutive Angelina, followed by Angela, the most well used version of the name through most of the twentieth century—particularly in Italian-American families. Now, however, Angela is the one that, along with diminutive ANGIE, feels terminally dated, while the more poetic Angelica, because of its association with actress Anjelica Houston and the character Anjelica Devereaux on *Days of Our Lives*, is by far the hippest form of the name. Other variations worth consideration include the German ANGELIKA, the Spanish ANGELITA, the French ANGELINE (the full name of Angie Dickinson) and ANGELIQUE (a character on *All My Children*). One caveat: If you stick with the original Angel, you'll be under some pressure to make sure she is one.

ANIKA. Some of the most interesting names span widely divergent cultures, and so it is with Anika/ANNIKA, which is both African and Scandinavian. Anika (pronounced Ah-NEE-ka) is a modern African-American name as well as an eighteenth-century slave name that undoubtedly derives from the African name ANNAKIYA (pronounced Anna-kee-a), which means "sweet face" in Hausa. Spelled ANNIKA (pronounced ANN-e-ka) the name is a Scandinavian diminutive for Anne. But spellings and pronunciations get mixed up, and Anika and ANNIKA can seem like the same name. Fortunately, it's a good one.

ANN, ANNE. Originally, Ann was the British form of this name and Anne the French one, but that distinction was muddied as long as five hundred years ago and now which spelling you use is simply a matter of taste. The versions have switched places many times in the fashion parade: In 1900, there were ten times as many Anns as Annes, but after Princess Anne was born in 1950 that proportion flipflopped so that now Anne is the widely preferred spelling. The heroine of *Anne* *of Green Gables* pronounced the Ann spelling "dreadful" and said the *e* made the name more distinguished, a feeling most people today share. But the spelling argument is largely academic these days because not many parents are choosing either Ann or Anne for their daughters. Where once the name was seen as elegant in its simplicity, today it's viewed by many as plain and drab, with parents instead favoring the diminutive Annie or the fuller Anna over the one-syllable form. It no longer even has stature as a middle name, with parents rejecting harmonious "bridge" names like Ann and Lee in favor of middle names with more personal meaning. The Spanish diminutive ANITA and the French ANNETTE (which will always conjure up The Mickey Mouse Club and beach-blanket movies to some boomers)—both popular at one time—now join the Annes as style outcasts.

ANNA. Anna, the original Latin and Greek variation on the biblical Hannah, has always been well used throughout Europe, from Russia to Italy, from Spain to Roumania. The Old World quality that made it unpopular in the United States in the all-American fifties is exactly what parents of today like about the name Anna. It's classic and simple, yet has an exotic, Anna Karenina–style charm. Anna is also a favorite with parents in search of a name that will bridge their different cultures: When she is Jewish and he's Hungarian, when he's a Wasp and she's Italian, Anna is often the perfect compromise name. Anna has authentic American history, also; it was the favored form of the name here from 1850 until 1900, when Ann took precedence. Yet however perfect the name Anna is on all these fronts, parents who are considering it should be aware that it is already very popular and certain to remain so for many years.

ANNABEL. Annabel made the news in the eighties when Queen Elizabeth deemed it "too Yuppie" for the royal baby who became Princess Beatrice. And she did have a point: Annabel, the name of the ultimate trendy Swinging London disco, is a bit self-consciously cute, a tad upscale but-we-still-have-a-sense-of-humor. Still, it's a melodious and lively name with much intrinsic appeal; you expect an Annabel to be engaging before you even meet her. Originally a bastardization of Amabel and well used since medieval times in Scotland, Annabel also recalls the romantic Edgar Allan Poe lyric, "Annabel Lee." It was chosen for her daughter by Lynn Redgrave. Variations include ANABEL, ANNABELLE, ANABELLE, ANNABELLA, and ANABELLA. Whichever version you use, it's important to distinguish Annabel from the combo names that were faddish in the fifties: ANNAMARIA, ANNEMARIE, ANNALISA, and the German ANNELIESE. Although the first pair are still found in some traditional Italian-American households, as a group they seem as outmoded now as Billie Jo.

ANNIE. This friendly pet form of Ann was in style a century ago and is again favored as a name in its own right, having been celebrated over the years in song ("Annie Laurie," "Annie"), comic strip ("Little Orphan Annie"), folklore (Annie Oakley, born Phoebe), and film (*Annie Hall*). It strikes a nice old-fashioned-but-jaunty chord that appeals to today's parents—including Glenn Close, Kevin Costner, and Jamie Lee Curtis, who made it their choice. Our one caveat: Cute as the name is for a little girl, it might seem too childish or casual for a twenty-five or forty-five-year-old. Do your daughter a favor and present her with an alternative as a future option, inscribing a more formal version of the name—Anne, Anna, or even Annabel or Anastasia—on her birth certificate.

ANTHEA. Like Althea, this is a pastorally poetic Greek name used by creative-minded Brits but totally neglected here. In ancient Greece, the name, which means "lady of the flowers," was bestowed as a title on Hera, Queen of Olympus.

ANTONIA. Stronger than most feminizations of male names, perhaps reflecting the pioneer spirit of Willa Cather's *My Antonia*, this name has been quietly used by stylish parents over the past few decades or so, and we think it deserves wider circulation. It is absolutely imperative, however, to only use the Antonia form of this name. The French variations ANTOINETTE or ANTONETTE and diminutives TONIA, TONYA, or TONI all take the name markedly downscale.

ANWEN. An undiscovered Welsh name, more unusual than Bronwen but with the same serene feeling. ANWYN is a spelling alternative, though the -wyn ending is used, in Wales, only for male names.

ANYA. Anya, here in its phonetic spelling, is one of those evocative pan-European names that occurs in various forms (and derives from disparate roots) throughout Europe and sounds exotic but not weirdly so to the American ear. Pronounced as either "on-ya" or "an-ya," ANYA is the form most often found in Russia, Poland, and other East European countries, while ANJA is the spelling usually preferred in Germany, and AINE is the Gaelic form popular in Ireland.

APRIL. Taken from the springtime month and first used as a proper name less than one hundred years ago, April is one of those names that's neither fashionable nor extremely unfashionable but exists in some seasonless style limbo. TV-nostalgia buffs will remember it from the Stefanie Powers character, April Dancer, on *The Girl from U.N.C.L.E.* and soap opera fans will be acquainted with April Stevens on *The Young and the Restless.* The French AVRIL, an accepted form in England for the past fifty years, seems affected here; it is sometimes confused with the more interesting AVERIL, a form of an early saint's name.

ARABELLA. A lovely, feminine name whose lilting rhythm does not betray its medieval roots, Arabella has been well used over the centuries among Scottish and British royalty. Rarely heard here but an equal in every way to the mega-modish Isabel and Isabella, Arabella deserves serious consideration by parents in search of a name with both a respectable pedigree and contemporary appeal.

ARAMINTA. An eighteenth-century British invention that is still used occasionally in England, and so enchanting it's positively ripe for the plucking by any parent with a taste for the exotic. The short form is MINTA. Added attraction: Araminta was the given name of abolitionist heroine Harriet Tubman.

ARIADNE. A Greek name somewhat more familiar in its *d*-less forms, the French ARIANE and the Italian ARIANNA. While they are all graceful names with the foreign flavor fashionable now, they seem a bit precious, a tad showy, in a way many other exotic names do not. Maybe that's because Ariadne in any version is a name that allows no margin for error: Parents who choose it must be absolutely certain their child will be gorgeous and sylphlike, and that level of confidence seems presumptuous. In Greek lore, Ariadne was the daughter of the Cretan king of Minos who helped the Athenian hero Theseus find his way out of the Labyrinth. Other variations with modern possibilities: ARIANA and ARIANNE.

ARIEL. We can't think of any other name that's quite as delicate and ethereal as Ariel, with its varied spectral connections. Ariel was a water spirit in demonology, an air spirit of medieval fable, and the male sprite in Shakespeare's *The Tempest*. Apart from that, it is an Old Testament place-name—used in the Book of Isaiah as another name for Jerusalem—and is frequently found in Israel for both boys and girls, not to mention its tie to poet Sylvia Plath's revelatory work of that name. But for kids today, these centuries of tradition were swept away when Disney adopted the name for its own Little Mermaid. Now that the animated Ariel has entered the American vernacular, some parents may consider the name too closely tied to the cartoon character to be used for a real live child, while others will overlook that connection and choose Ariel for its lovely sound. Related options: ARIELLA, ARIELLE, ARIELA, ARI, and ORIEL.

ARLENE. A name that sprang from an early nineteenth-century opera, *The Bohemian Girl* (in which it was spelled ARLINE), to the Top 50 list of girls names in this country in the 1940s, the period of actresses Arlenes Dahl and Francis. The popularity of Arlene was undoubtedly boosted by that of its cousins Eileen, Colleen, FRANCINE, et al. But now it and all the other *-een* names are seriously out of favor. ARLENA, ARLETTE, and ARLETTA are less common but equally dated variations.

ASHANTI. An African tribal and place-name used as a first name for both boys and girls by some African-Americans. Other possibilities are the variants ASHANTA and ASHANTE.

ASHLEY. Now the number one girls' name, or close to it, in most states, Ashley is a name that seems to have been propelled to popularity to a great degree by a soap opera character: the beautiful, ambitious Ashley Abbott, who debuted on *The Young and the Restless* in 1982. Originally a British place-and-surname, Ashley became a boys' first name about a century ago, making a deep impression via the sensitive Ashley Wilkes character in *Gone with the Wind*. Its ambisexual image was undoubtedly one factor that attracted droves of parents to Ashley, though the name very quickly became almost exclusively feminine, and does indeed have a sound that is soft and pretty, certainly another ingredient in its success. But unless Ashley is the name you love far above all others, or you like the idea of giving your child an extremely popular name, we advise you to steer clear of this choice from now on. The world has all the Ashleys it needs, even one whose father is Howard Stern. And, lest you believe an inventive spelling will make the name stand out, it also has more than its quota of girls named ASHLEIGH, ASHLEE, ASHLIE, and ASHLEA.

ASIA. One of the most popular of the trendy place-names, Asia is already on some Top 20 lists and promises to keep moving up over the next several years. With a sound as exotic as its image, the phonetic spelling—AJA—is sometimes used.

ASTRID. A Scandinavian royal name meaning "divinely beautiful," Astrid has never truly assimilated into our culture in the way that, say, Ingrid did. Still, it's an attractive name and, with the renewed interest in ethnic names, might be worth consideration by parents with Norse roots or those who have simply enjoyed a holiday among the fjords. Variations and nicknames include ASTRI, ASTA, and ATTI. The short forms ASSA and ASSI are out for obvious reasons.

ATALANTA. This name of a beautiful and fleet-footed huntress who refused to marry unless she could find a man who could outrace her is heard occasionally among the British nobility and gaining some small measure of attention here as an ersatz place-name. ATLANTA, as in Georgia, will undoubtedly be used more often simply because it's more familiar. ATLANTIC and ATLANTIS are other related, though somewhat hippie-sounding, options.

ATHENA. The name of the Greek goddess of wisdom, as well as of fertility and arts and crafts, could gain in appeal for enlightened parents who particularly prize intelligence as a quality in their daughters.

AUDREY. The actress Audrey Hepburn (born Edda) lent her unparalleled glamour and glow to this otherwise-plain name, which, believe it or not, derived from the Old English AETHELTHRYTH. Moderately popular from the twenties to the fifties, Audrey was the name of the heroine and the villainous plant in *The Little Shop of Horrors* and a book by Frank DeFelitta, *Audrey Rose*. AUDRA is a variant that was occasionally used in the sixties.

AUGUSTA. It means "venerable" in Latin and, today Augusta seems to be the quintessential great-great-aunt name. Still, it does possess a certain fussy charm and could even be conceived as fashionable when considered as one of the revived Frances-Charlotte-Violet-type ancestor names. In ancient Rome, Augusta was a title conferred on the wives and female relatives of emperors. Variants include AUGUST (recently used by country singer Garth Brooks for his daughter), which is hip in a more obvious way, and AUGUSTINA or AUGUSTIA, which seem too dusty to bother shining up. Augusta might also be considered a place-name: It's the capital of Maine as well as a city in Georgia. Another place-name that's more recognizable and certainly more groovy: Austin, originally a shortened version of Augustine and still used primarily for boys, but interesting for girls, too. The spelling Austen makes it a surname name, honoring Jane.

AURELIA. This richly evocative name was one of the most common in the Christian inscriptions of the Roman Empire, but is rarely heard in modern life, even if Maria Shriver and Arnold Schwarzenegger did use it as a middle name for their daughter Christina. Still, it and variants AURALIA and AURIEL, which was a Roman slave name, have possibilities for the adventurous parent.

AURORA. With its mythic, fairy-tale aura, Aurora seems almost too theatrical and airy a name for real life. In mythology she was the beautiful Roman goddess of the dawn, whose tears turned into the morning dew, and also the mother of Memnon, whose African army helped the Trojans at the battle of Troy. In later literature, Aurora appeared as the heroine of both a Lord Byron and an Elizabeth Barrett Browning poem, the princess in Disney's *Sleeping Beauty* and even the Shirley MacLaine character in *Terms of Endearment*. With all that, a parent with a flair for the dramatic might want to consider Aurora or its French form AURORE, keeping the short form AUREA and even the nickname Rory in reserve for down-to-earth occasions.

AUTUMN. A season name, with only a bit more weight than Summer or Spring. Unconventional in a hippie-ish sort of way, but prettily so, Autumn, along with Summer seems to be catching on with some parents.

AVA. A name with a certain residue of black-and-white forties glamour, thanks largely to screen icon Ava Gardner. More recently, it's been used for the Marilu Henner character on TV's *Evening Shade*, and was chosen for his little girl by actor Aidan Quinn—who may have been thinking also of the Gaelic form of the name popular in Ireland, pronounced the same but spelled AOIFE.

AVERY. One of the surname names that sprang to prominence in the 1980s, Avery stands out from the rest as the name of TV's Murphy Brown's (male) baby—given more than its share of publicity thanks to then-Vice President Dan Quayle. It should be noted, however, that he was named after his fictional grandmother, and the name Avery does have a distinctly feminine lilt.

AVIVA. A Hebrew name, very popular in Israel, that means "spring," connotes youthfulness and freshness, and is often given to girls born in that season.

AZIZA. Aziza is a familiar name in four different languages: Hebrew, Arabic, Kiswahili, and Somali. A common name in Egypt, it's also one that will allow a child to both fit in and stand out in American culture. The two z's give it a zippy feel, but it's also easy to spell and pronounce.

B

ⅿⅿⅿⅿⅿⅿⅿⅿⅿⅿⅿⅿⅿⅿ ◉ ⅿⅿⅿⅿⅿⅿⅿⅿⅿⅿⅿⅿⅿ

BAILEY. This lively last-name-first name was one of the earliest female examples to appear on the media, when *WKRP in Cincinnati* debuted in 1978 with the character Bailey Quarters as a member of the radio station's staff. Perhaps because it's free of that upwardly striving Waspy image à la PEYTON and PORTER and Carter, it remains among the more attractive and energetic of the genre.

BAMBI. What parent, enamored of the Disney fawn, could fail to find this name endearing? But just as the four-legged Bambi grew up to be Prince of the Forest, so too will your little Bambi age while her name remains eternally rooted in childhood. Bambi may be cute, but the name sounds far too helpless, too vulnerable, too negligible for a girl of today, much less for a woman of the future.

BARAKA. A Muslim name meaning "blessing" which can be similarly translated in Kiswahili, Baraka is a native African name that has already gained some popularity among African-American parents.

BARBARA. The current image of this name is very much reflected by Barbara Bush: grandmotherly, silver-haired, and out of the public domain. A sad but inevitable fate for a name that was second only to the immovable Mary in 1925, and was still hanging on at number seven twenty-five years later. An ancient Greek name meaning "a foreign woman" (the feminine version of "barbarian"), it originally related to the cacophony of indecipherable sounds that sounded to the nonconversant like Ba-Ba. Barbara was also the name of a well-known medieval saint, patroness of mathematicians, engineers, architects, carpenters, and firemen, as well as a protector against thunder. As Barbara faded, most of its nicknames went with it—BARB, BABS, BOBBIE, et al., leaving only the eternally nubile BARBIE, which, despite her many careers, from astronaut to doctor, has still become a euphemism for bimbo. BARBRA Streisand dropped one letter and came up with a version that is uniquely hers. As for the French form, BABETTE, it might have remained as mere Eurofluff had it not been for the admirable, strong-minded heroine of the film *Babette's Feast*. Still, even devotees of that movie would admit that, as names go, there's a world of choices with more character than Babette.

BATHSHEBA. The Puritans used this name of a famed biblical beauty, wife of King David and mother of Solomon, and there was a Thomas Hardy heroine with that name in *Far from the Madding Crowd*, but it's hard to imagine it for a modern baby in this country, although pet names BASHA or BATYA might be more manageable. We also occasionally hear the short form, SHEBA, as in The Queen of and Come Back, Little . . ., but parents would do well to remember that, in the latter case, Sheba was a dog, and the name is still used far more for pets than people.

BEATRICE, BEATRIX. Beatrice, which means "one who brings happiness," was locked firmly in the attic until Fergie and Prince Andrew dusted it off and restored it to the realm of possibility when they bestowed it on their first little princess. Popular in the Middle Ages, Beatrice was revived by the British Pre-Raphaelites in their restitution of all things medieval, reaching the Top 40 in this country in 1900. Beatrice also has a long and splendid literary history, both as Dante's beautiful guide through Paradise, who becomes the symbol of spiritual love, in *The Divine Comedy* and the clever and witty heroine of Shakespeare's *Much Ado about Nothing*—portrayed by Emma Thompson in the recent film. Beatrice is the Italian and French form of the original Beatrix, a livelier version which we slightly prefer and not only for its associations with Beatrix (born Helen) Potter, creator of Peter Rabbit. The final *X* is near-irresistible, adding a playful element to the name's imposing history. Both versions have a legion of variants and nicknames including: BETTRICE, BEATA, BEA, BEAH, BEBE, TRIXIE, and TRISS.

BEDELIA. Familiar almost solely through its connection to the wacky series of children's books about Amelia Bedelia, the literal-minded maid, Bedelia, also spelled BIDELIA, is a nickname for girls named Bridget in Ireland, but one that might stand perfectly well on its own.

BELINDA. Belinda has the feel of an invented name but actually carries a long and impressive history. It comes from the Latin meaning "beautiful snake" (coined at a time when snakes were a sacred symbol of wisdom and immortality) and, indeed, Belinda does seem to have more serpentine charm than the blander (if more popular) Melinda. In Babylonian mythology the goddess of heaven and earth, Belinda was introduced to England in the eighteenth century when Alexander Pope used it for the heroine of his satirical poem, *The Rape of the Lock.* A contemporary bearer is singer Belinda Carlisle.

BELLE. This favorite of a hundred years ago has been infused with new life as the name of the popular and spirited heroine of Disney's *Beauty and the Beast* and also as a nickname for the très chic Isabel and variants. Dan Aykroyd and Donna Dixon combined this name's fashion revival with the craze for place-names by calling their daughter Belle Kingston. It also serves as a sweet, stylish middle name, as in Tallulah Belle, daughter of Demi Moore and Bruce Willis. Belle's own variant, BELLA, which had a slightly Grandma-ish residue, is also pretty and gaining in popularity.

BERENICE, BERNICE. Since most Bernices were called BUNNY or BINNIE or BERNIE anyway, the world will hardly notice that this old Greek name has faded out of fashion.

BERNADETTE. A solid, attractive, feminine but strong name that was once the exclusive property of Catholics, as a result of the fame of St. Bernadette Soubirous of Lourdes, whose experiences of seeing visions of the Virgin Mary starting at the age of fourteen were portrayed in novels and a 1943 movie. Bernadette Peters is a contemporary bearer of the name. And the related BERNADINE was celebrated in an old Pat Boone song.

BERTHA. Poor Bertha is thought of as the ultimate ugly name, calling to mind a pasty complexion, orthopedic shoes, and mounds of ungainly flesh. Its association with Big Bertha, the nickname given to Germany's enormous guns used in World War I, made the unattractive connection official.

BERYL. One of the gem names that surfaced around the turn of the twentieth century, but was never as popular here as it was in Britain, Beryl retains a small measure of dash thanks to adventurer, aviatrix, and author Beryl Markham. BERRY is a more modern sounding but less substantial substitute.

BESS, BETH. These two pet names of Elizabeth (Beth has also stood in for BETHEL) have long been used on their own. Beth was a softer, more starry-eyed and sensitive alternative to Betty and Betsy a few decades ago, having been long associated with the tragic sister in *Little Women*. Bess, although it is older, manages to sound fresher, despite onetime ties to Queen Elizabeth I, known as "Good Queen Bess," and Gershwin's operetta, *Porgy and Bess*.

BETHANY. This appealing, underused name, whose rhythms make it a perfect substitute for the ubiquitous Brittany, is one of the primal place-names, Bethany being the village where Jesus stayed at Lazarus's home on his way to Jerusalem.

BETTY, BETSY. Two more long-running nicknames for Elizabeth, with disparate images, both of them faded. Betty was hugely popular in the Betty Boop twenties, reaching number four in 1925, when it was the all-American girls' name blanketing the country. Until the fifties, it was the typical name for the typical girl, like the older daughter (also called "Princess") on the typical fifties sitcom, *Father Knows Best*. Hep Bettys of the era often had their names combined with such single-syllable extenders as Jo, Ann, and Lou. The BETTE version came in with Bette Davis and has been perpetuated by Bette Midler. Betsy goes back in this country to the days of Betsy Ross and was a perkier, younger-sounding alternate to Betty. It has a bit more life left in it today than Betty does. Yet another version is BETTINA, a name used by Danielle Steel in her novel, *Loving*.

BEULAH. This name—mentioned in the Bible as a name for Israel and sometimes taken as a reference for Heaven—was fatally damaged by being stereotyped as a black maid's name, initially in Mae West's famous line, "Beulah, peel me a grape," and then in the early fifties TV series of that name, the first to star an African-American performer—Ethel Waters, later replaced by Louise Beavers.

BEVERLY. More visible now as part of the name of a wealthy California community than as a girls' name, Beverly (also used for men in England) was much heard here from the twenties through the fifties—too recently to allow for a revival.

BIANCA. An exotic but not eccentric name brought to prominence by Nicaraguan Bianca Jagger, who has managed to remain before the public eye since her divorce from Mick and whose glamour has inspired many a baby Bianca. Biancas of the past have included characters in *Othello*, *The Taming of the Shrew*, and its takeoff, *Kiss Me Kate*, and a more contemporary one on the soap opera *All My Children*.

BIJOU. A highly distinctive French name meaning jewel. The plural version BIJOUX was chosen by John Phillips and Genevieve Waite for their daughter. Warning: We have also known of poodles, and even one horse, with this name.

BILLIE. Billie is a friendly, tomboyish name that far predates the Jamies and Caseys that came along in the late sixties. It also has a country feel like, say, LULU or Pearl, that might appeal to some sophisticated parents, combining the homespun charm of twig furniture with the reverse chic of old linoleum. There have been several notable Billies in the past that you might consider worthy of honor: jazz immortal Billie Holliday (born Eleanora), the not-so-dumb-blonde, Billie Dawn, in *Born Yesterday*, and tennis great Billie Jean King. In the present, Carrie Fisher named her baby Billie Cathryn, and there is also a prominent Billie in *Days of Our Lives*.

BLAIR. Isn't Blair the snobby rich girl? That seems to be the character who always gets this name in sitcoms (e.g., *The Facts of Life*) and soaps. Blair was one of the first upwardly mobile androgynous names to hit the big time—followed by Whitney, Morgan, Ashley, and company—but now its "I'm-climbing-as-fast-as-I-can" image seems sort of dated. Compatible companions for Blair would be BLAINE (the name of Donald Trump's socialite sister-in-law) and Blake.

BLANCHE. Blanche instantly evokes its own stereotype, that of the classic faded Southern belle, à la Blanche DuBois (*A Streetcar Named Desire*) and Blanche Devereaux (*The Golden Girls*). Originally a nickname for a blonde (it means "white" in French), Blanche was extremely popular a century ago, and some upscale parents are beginning to look at it again as a more plainspoken alternative to Bianca. BLANCHETTE is another more feminine, French version.

BLOSSOM. Blossom might have remained a completely wilted flower if the TV series of that name, with its exuberant eponymous teenaged lead character, hadn't at least put it before the public. We don't really foresee it gaining any ground, though; parents attracted to the name's flowery qualities have many other choices—Rose, Daisy, Violet, Flora, take your pick—that will almost certainly stay fresher and brighter over time.

BONNIE. The Scottish really do say "bonnie" to mean "pretty," thus the roots of this name. *Gone with The Wind* gave the name Bonnie a big push when Scarlett and Rhett used it for their daughter (her full given name was Eugenie Victoria, but she had "eyes as blue as the bonnie blue flag"). Bonnie's last moment in the limelight came in the late sixties, with the film *Bonnie and Clyde*, about outlaw Bonnie Parker, and is still visible via singer Bonnie Raitt, but it's been out of the fashion loop for decades, as have the related BONITA and BENITA.

BRANDY. If names are destiny, we hate to think of what the future has in store for all the little girls called Brandy. While the name might be cute and saucy, it doesn't give your offspring much to aim for.

Variant spellings—BRANDI, BRANDEE, BRANDIE—may take your mind off the liquor, but ultimately only make matters worse.

BREE. Jane Fonda won an Academy Award for playing a character with this name in the 1971 *Klute*, which spawned a limited contingent of young Brees. You may find appeal in the name's sophisticated yet upbeat image but we must warn you against the cheesy spelling: BRIE.

BRENDA. Brenda had long been a name that symbolized some form of outdated glamour, summoning to mind a faded forties B movie star or well-publicized debutante, or the intrepid vintage comic strip reporter, Brenda Starr. Then, the name was revived to some measure by the infamous character Brenda Walsh of *Beverly Hills 90210*, the Alexis Carrington of her generation. But now, Brenda's gone, though the related, more modern, BRENNA seems to be moving up fast on the hit parade.

BRETT. The dashing and seductive Lady Brett Ashley of Ernest Hemingway's *The Sun Also Rises* was a captivating enough character to warrant giving a child her name. Although some may find it a tad affected, Brett combines a pleasingly brisk androgyny with a distinctly feminine softness, and has found a new identity in sitcom star, Brett Butler.

BRIANA, BRIANNA. Although the epidemically popular Briana sounds like a recent invention, the name actually appears in Edmund Spenser's sixteenth-century poem, *The Faerie Queene*. But the fact that it sounds so made-up works against Briana, in our opinion, relating it to other spun-sugar creations like Brandy and Brittany. Before 1985 Briana didn't even appear in most naming dictionaries, making it a name with a lot more style than substance. Now, Briana/Brianna is the second most popular name for African-American girls in some states, such as California and Pennsylvania. Its countless variants include BRIANE, BREEANNA, BRYANNE, ad almost infinitum, with the shortened BRIA/BREA (chosen by the Eddie Murphys) running a close second to the original. But Briana's best attributes—a certain strength combined with a melodic quality—can be found in other names with more history and meaning and a more durable brand of style. The up-and-coming BRENNA, for instance, which is an Irish Gaelic name, might be one substitute worth considering. Parents who like Briana's exotic quality might want to think about names like LILIANA or MARIANA, Bronwen or Bryn or Bryony. And those using it to honor a Brian, might want to choose BRENNAN, or maybe even—why not?—Brian itself.

BRIDGET, BRIGITTE. A century ago Bridget was the Irish cook fresh off the boat from County Cork. By 1950 she had transmogrified into a sex kitten, à la Bardot. But Bridget has survived both those stereotypes to become more wholesome as well as more upwardly mobile, more stylish and more ethnically authentic than the shopworn Colleens and Caitlins, Eileens and Erins. Hot young actress Bridget Fonda bolsters the name's new au courant image; singer Sting gave it the star-stamp-of-approval by choosing it for his young daughter, Brigitte Michael. Bridget is the Anglicized form of the name of an ancient Celtic goddess, a saint (also called St. Bride) who was the patroness of Ireland, as well as patron saint of poets and healers. Irish variants and nicknames include BRIGIT, BRIGID (the spelling used for the devious character Brigid O'Shaunessy in Dashiell Hammett's classic Sam Spade story, *The Maltese Falcon*), BRIGHID, BIDDIE, BRIDIE, and BEDELIA. Scandinavians use BIRGITTA, BIRGITTE, BRIGITTA, BIRGIT, BRITT, BRITA, BRITTA, and BITTAN. The French version is BRIGITTE, so powerfully publicized by Mlle Bardot, who was born Camille.

BRITTANY. Although Brittany is, of course, a place, the wild popularity of this name does not seem to be tied directly to the craze for place-names. Brittany has more in common with names like Tiffany and Ashley than with Dakota or, well, PARIS: Its popularity suffuses every layer of society and its appeal is more mainstream than offbeat. But, like Tiffany and Ashley, Brittany, on virtually every Top Ten list, has become overused to the point of cliché. As have its batallion of variant spellings, including BRITTNEY (a best-seller in its own right), BRITNEY, BRITENY, BRITNI, BRITENY—can we please stop now?

BRONWEN. Bronwen is one of the best-known of the traditional Welsh girls' names, although it's still so seldom heard that it retains an exotic ring. A real winner. The common alternate spelling, BRON-WYN, is incorrect if you want to preserve this name's ethnic integrity as well as its sexual identity: Welsh female names end in *-wen*, with only male names getting the *-wyn* spelling. Similar in sound but different in meaning—it means "beautiful raven"—is BRANWEN, famous in legend as a figure in the romance of Sir Tristram.

BROOKE. Brooke might have been just another surname name, à la Paige or Courtney, had it not been for Brooke Shields (actually christened Christa), who took the name from quietly fashionable to ultra-trendy. Admittedly a pretty name, but one that's loaded down with all manner of sophisticated baggage you might not want to force a small girl to carry. It has been the soap opera name of our age, from the time Brooke Hamilton appeared on *Days of Our Lives* in 1975 and Brooke English debuted on *All My Children* the following year, through the current Brooke Logan on *The Bold and the Beautiful*. More distinctive would be BRYCE, the name Ron Howard chose for his oldest daughter.

BRYN, BRYONY. Two appealing names rooted in nature. Bryn is a Welsh name meaning "hill" and Bryony is the word for a kind of climbing vine, from the ancient Greek meaning "to grow luxuriantly." The latter can be found on invitation lists for parties to be held in Knightsbridge, Belgravia, and other posh London enclaves.

C

CAITLIN. The Irish and Welsh form of Kathleen, Caitlin was a boom name of the eighties, rocketing from obscurity (America first heard it as the name of the wife of doomed poet Dylan Thomas) to the height of popularity in the space of a decade. Today, Caitlin is even more widely used than most people realize, climbing into the Top Ten when you consider all its spelling variations. Though Caitlin is the Gaelic form and the only authentic version of the name, KAITLYN and KATELYN are becoming more common than the original. Other spelling twists abound: On official rosters we've seen KAITLIN, CAITLYN, KAITLYNN, and KATELIN, and we know it doesn't end there. But no matter how you spell it, nothing about the name Caitlin is creative anymore.

CALISTA, CALLISTA. This unfamiliar gem, a Greek name meaning "most beautiful," was used by actor David Carradine for his daughter. Its shortened form, CALLA, which is also pretty in a lilylike kind of way, has appeared on the soap opera *The Guiding Light*. CALLIE, heard recently as the first name of *Thelma and Louise* writer Khouri, is a bouncy short form.

CAMERON. Gone are the days when you could receive a birth announcement for a Cameron and be sure it was for a boy. This Scottish male name is now one of the hottest girl's names going. Example: Jim Carrey's sultry costar, Cameron Diaz, in *The Mask*.

CAMILLA, CAMILLE. Both these names, the ancient classic and its French pet version, would make excellent choices, accessible but by no means ordinary. Camilla, the frillier of the two, was associated in Roman myth with a swift-footed huntress who, according to Virgil, was so fast that she could run over a cornfield without bending a blade of corn. As for Camille, at one time just the sound of the name used to start people coughing, recalling the tragic "Lady of the Camellias" heroine portrayed by Greta Garbo in the vintage film. But that image has certainly faded sufficiently now for the name to be safely, and successfully, used.

CANDACE. Candace, originally the name of a dynasty of Ethiopian queens mentioned in the New Testament, would be more obscure than it is were it not for the popularity of actress Candice Bergen. Because of her current visibility, choosing this somewhat dated name now may peg you as a very serious *Murphy Brown* fan. CANDICE is the variant spelling; far-too-sugary CANDY, the most prevalent nickname sometimes, unfortunately, is used on its own.

CANDIDA. This ancient name—it was used in the Roman Empire, and also for several saints—became known in the modern world through the George Bernard Shaw play of that name, whose heroine was one of his most delightfully sympathetic creations. Rarely heard today, Candida could make a solid yet original choice—though some may find it more familiar as the name of an infection than as one for a child.

CARA. Cara, which means "dear" in Italian, is popular by association with similar-sounding names—Kyra, Kerry—that have been in fashion for the last few decades, though Cara itself has never gone over the top to full-blown trendiness. Its diminutives include CARINA, CARISSA, and CARITA, all more decorative but ultimately as insubstantial as the original. Cara and variants can all acceptably but less appropriately be spelled with Ks.

CARLA. Except on reruns of *Cheers*, this somewhat severe feminization of Carl has rarely been heard for years now. Neither have such gussied-up variants as CARLENE, CARLEEN, CARLINE, or CARLINA. The one respectable member of the group is CARLOTTA, the Italian form of Charlotte, that has some exotic charm and style. CARLY, on the other hand, is quite another story. Not that long ago, Carly Simon seemed to be the sole owner of her first name. Now, though, after it has had considerable exposure on soap operas, (*Loving, Days of Our Lives*), the land is rife with little girls named Carly—and CARLI, KARLY, CARLEIGH, KARLEE, ad infinitum. Enough already! Today's Carly is tomorrow's Shirley.

CARMEL, CARMEN. Carmel itself, the name of a mountain in Israel associated with the Blessed Virgin, is rarely heard, although families favoring ethnic names do use the Italian CARMELA, and its diminutives CARMELITA and CARMELINA. More substantial and less limited, although it is the Spanish version, is Carmen, associated with the sensuous tragic heroine of Bizet's opera.

CAROL. There must be thousands of new mothers (and maybe even grandmothers) named Carol, but perhaps only a handful of new babies.

We've left this once semiandrogynous favorite of our own parents behind along with diaper pins and car beds. Ditto its variants CAROLE, CARROLL, and CARYL, though the German CAROLA retains some modern charm.

CAROLINE. A traditional favorite revived by taste-conscious contemporary parents who had been exposed for years to the privileged lives of Caroline Kennedy and Princess Caroline of Monaco, Caroline might be considered a Yuppie name by some. If so, it's also a name with an impressive royal pedigree and a composed, capable image. Caroline is stylish (especially when pronounced to rhyme with wine) but not trendy, feminine but not prissy. You could circumvent the Yuppie aspect of the name by changing it to CAROLINA, which gives it a Latinate/place-name spin. CAROLYN, which was very popular from the twenties to the sixties, accomplishes the same end, but takes the name way down-market. An attractive nickname for all of the above, used much more in England, is CARO.

CARRIE. This Little-House-on-the-Prairie–type pet form of Caroline was a hit in 1875 and again a century later, despite the chilling effect of the Stephen King book and movie, released in 1976. At this point we'd stay stick to the original: Carrie is too reminiscent of the sixties nickname names—RICKI, Jody, et al.—that seem as dated now as go-go boots.

CARSON and CARTER. Two upscale Waspy surnames that sounded a lot fresher a few years ago than they do now. The friendlier Carson (via frontiersman Kit, and "Heeeeere's Johnny"), also has a distinguished connection to writer Carson McCullers (born Lula). Carter, on the other hand, could conjure up visions of Little Liver Pills or children's underwear.

CASEY. When Casey bounced onto the scene in the late sixties, it had the twin appeal of traditional Irish flavor combined with an energetic and new, modern androgyny. Though Casey is a common surname in Ireland, it's not often used as a first name there, and never for girls. With its folkloric associations, it's an American adaptation, made famous by mythologized (but very real) train engineer Casey Jones, the poem "Casey at the Bat" and even, to a lesser extent, colorful Hall of Famer Casey Stengel. Casey has the distinction of being one of the handful of ambisexual names that has managed to hang onto its masculine edge while gaining feminine appeal.

CASSANDRA. Cassandra is one of the few Greek mythological names that still reverberates with its ancient aura, that of a prophetess cursed with the fate of not being believed. In spite of that, Cassandra has been undergoing a major revival of late, showing up in the Top 50—and even the Top 25—in some states. It combines the initial *K* sound so popular today with the feminine formality of other fashionable names such as Alexandra, Amanda, and Melissa. One celebrity Dad who chose it for his daughter is Charlie Sheen. The nickname CASS may still be too tied to the unfortunate Mama (who was born Ellen), but CASSIE is cute and provides a down-to-earth alternative to the name's full and somewhat imposing version.

CASSIDY. If Kathie Lee Gifford can do for her daughter's name what she did for her son Cody's, then Cassidy is bound to be found on popularity lists before long.

CATHERINE. Catherine, together with its other standard English forms Katherine, Katharine and Kathryn, is one of the oldest, best-known and most widely used girls' names in the Western world. In all its variations, Catherine has remained among the Top 25 girls' names in America all during the twentieth century, and has been well used throughout history for saints (one of whom, Catherine of Alexandria, is the patron saint of philosophers, students, craftsmen, nurses, and librarians), queens, and commoners alike. Catherine has also been associated with some of the great romantic heroines of literature, including Heathcliff's love in *Wuthering Heights* and the passionate nurse, Catherine Barkley, in Hemingway's *A Farewell to Arms*. In recent years, parents have preferred the *K* spellings, partly as an ode to style icon Katharine Hepburn and partly because they relate most directly to the nickname Kate, the fifties favorite, CATHY, having worn out its welcome. While Catherine/Katherine is too classic ever to be trendy, it is today an extremely popular name, often undercounted in official polls because of its many variant spellings. Taken together, all forms of Catherine actually rank number one in some states. If you're opposed to using Catherine on the grounds that it's overused, it may be worth exploring some of the name's foreign versions and nicknames. Some of these are: CATERINA (Italian), CATALINA (Spanish), KASIA (Polish), KATINKA or KATYA (Russian), or KATJA (German). The Scottish CATRIONA and the Irish CAITRIONA both seem more appealing before you realize they're pronounced like Katrina, which has no Celtic flavor at all. By the way, trivia note: if you are wondering why all these interchangeable *C*s and *K*s: When the name was introduced into Anglo-Saxon Britain by the Crusaders, Catherine was spelled with a *C* because *K* did not yet exist in the English alphabet.

CECILIA. Cecilia seems like one of those quintessentially Catholic names that sounds incomplete without the word *saint* before it. And indeed, Cecilia was the name of a popular saint, designated the patroness of musicians because she supposedly sang to God while the musicians played at her wedding. This feminine form of Cecil, most popular at the end of the nineteenth century and beginning of the twentieth, has a delicate, lacy feel that just might appeal to modern parents. This quality is shared by some of Cecilia's variants—CECILE, CECILY, and CICELY—which also sound to the American ear like the ultimate British upper-crust names, slightly old-fashioned and very genteel, summoning images of pale pink cashmere, tea in a flowered china cup, dainty cucumber sandwiches. Cecily has been naturalized to the point of becoming a soap opera character—Cecily Kelly on *All My Children*.

CELESTE. Celeste is a softly pretty and somewhat quaint name with heavenly (celestial) overtones. It also has a forties kind of feel, like Celeste Holm, or Queen Celeste of Babar's elephant kingdom. But Celeste has never been popular enough to truly be in style, so it's never really gone out. You couldn't call it a cutting edge name now, or even a comer, although it has appeared recently on *Beverly Hills 90210*, but that may be exactly the secret of its appeal. Both its French diminutives, CELESTINE and CELESTINA, have a certain fey charm.

CELIA. Although it is often mistaken for a diminutive of Cecilia, Celia is actually a much older name which, lacking that extra, extravagant syllable, feels more energetic and modern. Celia is sprinkled all through Elizabethan literature—Shakespeare is sometimes credited with introducing it in *As You Like It*, and it was to Celia that Ben Jonson penned the immortal line, "Drink to me only with thine eyes." CELINE is a French derivative, and CEIL is a friendly short form.

CHANEL and CHANTAL. The venerable designer Coco's surname has been revived for use as a first name along with the short boxy jackets, fake pearls, and chained purses she made famous. Unfortunately, the name Chanel doesn't have quite the style or timeless quality of the clothes, though its melodiousness, plus the popular *Sha-* sound, have been appreciated by some parents. The same is true of CHANTAL, which may not be as famous a name as Chanel, but as a first name is definitely more authentically French.

CHARIS. Pronounced as Karis, this is the name of one of the Three Graces of Greek mythology. The Welsh CERYS sounds the same, and is similarly unfamiliar here. If you're attracted to names with the trendy hard *C* sound—as in Caitlin, Kayla, Caroline, Carly—but want something further off the beaten track, Charis should definitely be on your short list.

CHARITY. Charity is one of the Big Three among the "abstract virtue" names, along with the more frequently used Hope and Faith, and the one of which the Bible says "but the greatest of these is charity." These names in general have begun to sound fresh again today, and Charity also has a pleasing *Y*-ending rhythmic sound as well as a kind-hearted, generous association. If the name's image is a bit *too* generous for you—i.e., "Sweet Charity," Shirley MacLaine's hooker with a heart of gold—you might want to pursue alternative virtues: Felicity, VERITY, and sisters.

CHARLOTTE. Charlotte is an ultrafashionable baby name in England (number one in 1991, and still going strong) but, while it's definitely been rediscovered here, it hasn't yet made its way onto the popularity charts. Charlotte has somewhat the same image and pedigree as Caroline—they're both classic names long favored by royals (Princess Caroline of Monaco's daughter is named Charlotte) and carry a manicured, socially conscious air today. Charlotte has had some disparate associations in the past, from novelist Charlotte Brontë to the gallant spider in E. B. White's children's classic, *Charlotte's Web*, to the grotesqueries of *Hush Hush Sweet Charlotte*. Contemporary parents who have chosen the name include Sigourney Weaver and singer Rickie Lee Jones. Aside from these classic feminizations of Charles, there are some more recent inventions, such as CHARLENE (as represented by Charlene Tipton of *Dallas* fame and the character on *Designing Women*) and CHARLAYNE, which definitely do not convey the same patina of class. If you're honoring a relative named Charles, our advice would be to stick with Charlotte.

CHARMAINE and **CHARMIAN**. These two names seem similar but actually have little in common. Charmaine (pronounced with a *Sh*-sound) was popularized in the twenties by a theatrical character and song, while Charmian (which derives from the Greek word for "joy" and can be pronounced either with a *K* or *Sh* sound) was used by Shakespeare for the faithful, kind-hearted servant of the Egyptian queen in *Antony and Cleopatra*. Unfortunate association to both names: Charmin bathroom tissue.

CHASTITY. If your name is Cher, it may be okay to name your child Chastity. Otherwise, don't.

CHELSEA. Chelsea was just another semihip quasi-trendy place-name until we got a president who'd bestowed it on his daughter (inspired by a lyric in a Judy Collins song). Now it's a semihip ultratrendy name, à la Hillary. Actually, though, it's kind of surprising to note how long ago the name started being used. In the late sixties, there was a Chelsea Brown on the old *Laugh-In* show, and Jane Fonda's name in *On Golden Pond* (1981) was Chelsea as well, while Chelsea Reardon appeared on *The Guiding Light* later in the eighties.

CHERRY. The poor girl named Cherry will suffer mightily from embarrassment come puberty and the inevitable barrage of jokes from her male classmates. If you value your child's psychological well-being, steer far clear of this name and its variations—CHERI, CHERIE (Marilyn Monroe's name in *Bus Stop*), the whole bowl. Other related names present different problems. CHER is one of the all-time great one-person names, and CHERYL and CHERILYN are as firmly cemented in the pre-Beatles sixties as panty girdles. The more substantial French version is CERISE.

CHEYENNE. Along with other cowgirl-boy place-names like Sierra and Dakota, Cheyenne is galloping wildly across the country. The name of a Native American tribe, as well as the capital of Wyoming, (in addition to Marlon Brando's notorious daughter) Cheyenne runs the risk of rapidly exhausting all its energy.

CHINA. Long predating the current place-name craze, a pair of the more daring pop singers of the sixties and seventies used this name for their daughters, Grace Slick choosing the conventional spelling, Michelle Phillips going further afield by spelling the name CHYNNA. Both versions are a lot less far-out and more acceptable today.

CHLOE. Much more dynamic than most of the other old Greek-based romantic literary names of the seventeenth-century, Chloe, which is a springtime name symbolizing new growth, has emerged as a very fashionable real-life option, chosen for their daughters by such celebrities as Candice Bergen and Louis Malle, and Olivia Newton-John. Chloe is also the real name of Nobel Prize writer Toni Morrison, whose first book mistakenly carried her nickname (for middle name Anthony) on the title page. Since one of us has chosen it for her own child, we can give it a very personal stamp of approval. But do be warned: Chloe is no longer as offbeat as some first-time parents might think.

CHRISTINA, CHRISTINE. Pristine and crystal-clear, these are a pair of centuries-old, multicultural, long-popular names whose roots and offshoots have become nearly too numerous and complex to untangle. The earliest forms of the name are probably CHRISTIAN (a female name in medieval times) and CHRISTIANA, both beautiful and more distinctive than any of the later versions of the name. Christina, originally an abbreviated form, became a royal name in Sweden and Spain, and is more fashionable today than the French Christine, which was popular here from the forties to the seventies, being the tenth most popular name for girl babies in 1970. Over the past several years, the trendiest forms of the name have been the Scandinavian Kristin and Kirsten, although they too are beginning to fade. Still, taken together, all Chris-versions push the name to number one in some states. Variant spellings and pet forms of the name, many of them used as names in their own right, abound. CHRISTIE became popular via model Christie Brinkley, and CHRISSY with the wiggly *Three's Company* character. CHRISTA is a German pet form that has a certain charm, and KIRSTY, or KIRSTIE, is a Scottish diminutive found as often in Abilene as Aberdeen. CHRISTABEL and CHRISTMAS are oddball distant relatives of the name. Please note: The *K*s and *Ch*s are theoretically interchangeable, and "creative" spellings of all these names have proliferated. But we feel that the variations are numerous and confusing enough without starting to spell Christine (as one minor star did) KHRYSTYNE.

CINDY. The omnipresent Cindy Crawford is single-handedly keeping this sixties nickname name alive. It was originally a pet form of CINDERELLA (yes, that really was a name), LUCINDA, and Cynthia.

CLARE, CLAIRE, CLARA, CLARISSA. Clare is a name that seemed to be gliding toward high-fashion status in the tradition-conscious eighties, but never quite made it here the way it did in England. We consider that a plus, because today Clare remains one of those special names that combine familiarity with distinction, straightforward strength with feminine softness, historical depth with modern simplicity. Although Clare, as in the medieval saint (who was made the patron saint of television in 1958 because of her reputed power to see events at a distance), and in Clare Huxtable, supermom of *The Cosby Show*, is the original spelling, the French version—Claire—is the one favored today. Clara, a variation that was popular in this country at the end of the nineteenth century, sounds old-fashioned and quaint—it's the name of Heidi's wheelchair-bound friend—though not prohibitively moldy. The daintier CLARISSA, long a well used name in its own right, might sound equally antique were it not for the cable TV hit teenage show, *Clarissa Explains It All*. The Irish form CIARA (pronounced keer-a), and the Italian CHIARA (kee-ah-ra) are two more options. One we do not recommend is CLARICE, maybe because we can still hear Hannibal Lecter hissing it at Jodie Foster in *The Silence of the Lambs*.

CLAUDIA. Like other feminizations that had long been relegated to the attic—Olivia, for instance, and Clementine and Theodora—Claudia has been retrieved, spruced up, and is now ready for a reappraisal. Straightforward but soft, with a hint of ancient Roman splendor, Claudia is in that category of distinctive, classic, yet slightly offbeat names favored by parents who are not afraid of being a little different. The actress Michelle Pfeiffer chose the name Claudia for her daughter. Chic French versions are CLAUDIE (pronounced Cloudy) or just plain CLAUDE (yes, it's really used for girls), but both CLAUDINE and CLAUDETTE seem to date back to the Jean Claude Killy-Yvette Mimieux era. A fact to forget: In Wales, Claudia is a name closely related to Gladys.

CLEA. This pretty, unappreciated name, was given to the chief female character in Lawrence Durrell's *Alexandria Quartet*. Its longer form, CLEANTHA, would make an interesting choice as well.

CLEMENTINE. Forget the song: Clementine is one of the most appealing names around. In England, where people do not automatically say "Oh my darling" when they hear it, Clementine (the name of Mrs. Winston Churchill) is particularly fashionable and popular for well-born young ladies. There, they sometimes pronounce it Clementeen—which might help sidestep the unfortunate association here. We also like CLEMENTINA, again pronounced with the long *e*, as in teena, the name of America's first female publisher, Clementina Ride. CLEMENCY, which leans toward being a Puritan virtue name, along the lines of Faith, Felicity, and COMFORT, is interesting, too. CLEMENTIA, however, sounds like it might be a gynecological problem.

CLEO, CLIO. Cleo is short for CLEOPATRA and is pronounced the same as Clio, who was the Greek muse of history. Both are ancient names with modern spirit and that great *o* ending. Cleopatra itself, on the other hand, would almost certainly prove a bit much.

CLOTILDE, CLOTILDA. This name—while well used in France— sounds "cloddy" to the American ear. And the German CLOTILDA makes an even duller thud.

CLOVER. The fact that this perky, plucky botanical name has not gotten anywhere disproves the theory that all soap opera names automatically go on to real-world popularity, as this one has been seen regularly on both *The Young and the Reckless* and *One Life to Live*. Others in this unsuccessful category include CRICKET and CALLIOPE.

COLETTE. The French novelist Colette, who wrote under her surname (her first was Sidonie), is a feminist heroine and the inspiration for her name's newfound stylish status. Parents may also want to consider using the name's French long form, NICOLETTE.

COLLEEN. Colleen is the Irish word for girl and, while considered a quintessentially Irish name in countries outside of Ireland, you won't be finding it in County Cork. Today, along with other *een* period names (Maureen, DOREEN), and other inauthentic Irish names (Erin, Shannon), Colleen sounds passé. A parent in search of an Irish ethnic name would do better to examine genuine Gaelic choices, such as Maeve or MAIRE.

CONSTANCE. This name has taken on an icy and forbidding matriarchal image, just as it was portrayed on *The Colbys*, for example. Although it has been around for centuries, being an early Christian name that was adopted by the Puritans as a virtue name, often in the form of CONSTANT or CONSTANCY, Constance is far from being a favorite among modern parents.

CONNOR. Soap operas are crawling with Connors, and one of them happens to be a female. Add in the trends toward surname names and fresh Irish choices and we expect to see playgrounds full of little girls named Connor (and CONOR and maybe even CONNELLY and CONNERY) in the near future.

CONSUELO. This sophisticated Spanish name works well with Anglo surnames and is often found in international social columns. Meaning "to console, or comfort," it was used by George Sand for the title and leading character of a novel about a beautiful Venetian singer.

CORA, CORINNE, CORAL. A fairly basic, grandmotherly name, Cora is not as dated as Dora, not as soigné as Nora, not as pretty as Laura. The name was probably invented by James Fenimore Cooper for the heroine of his novel, *The Last of the Mohicans*, written in 1826. One of its French diminutives, which is an attractive name in its own right, is Corinne, while the more unusual CORINNA belonged to an ancient lyric poet, one of the earliest known female writers, who was reputed to be a beauty as well. The modern nickname name COREY, which is also an Irish surname, is bouncy in a sixties cheerleader kind of way. Coral may come from the variant CORALIE, but it makes more sense to think of it as a nineteenth-century gem name.

CORDELIA. The name of King Lear's youngest and only loyal daughter is one with backbone as well as style. Cordelia's appeal is that of the somewhat formal, grownup-sounding names that have come back into favor since the eighties as an antidote to all the invented and fly-by-night names common from the sixties onward. Among that group, Cordelia, which means "daughter of the sea," is certainly one of the loveliest options.

CORNELIA. In ancient Rome, Cornelia was considered the paragon of womanly virtues, and, like Cordelia, it is a handsome name with an excellent pedigree. But it does have the downside of the nickname CORNY.

COURTNEY. Courtney, like its sisters Brooke and Paige, Morgan and Blair, is a mega-fashionable androgynous name with a thick upper crust—a bit too thick, perhaps, for these less pretentious and prosperous times. An aristocratic British surname that was used as a first name for boys a hundred years ago but now has become almost exclusively female, it has been on the girls Top 25 list for several years now, has been seen on a couple of soap operas, and we're afraid it has nowhere to go but down.

CRYSTAL. When the "jewel-name" fad took hold around 1900, Crystal, then a male name in Scotland and the north of England, was drafted into the movement. After being quietly used for most of the century, it rose in popularity as a member of the *Dynasty* clan—although Mrs. Carrington opted for the nouveau riche Krystle spelling—and reached the Top 10 in some states in the eighties. But it has now slipped from its peak, after being branded as tacky à la Tiffany, and being attached to one of the supporting players on working-class *Roseanne.* Nowadays, its old turn-of-the-century companions like Pearl and Ruby seem a lot classier by comparison. Needless to say, imitation Crystal—KRYSTLE, CRISTAL, or any other spelling variation parents can invent—has even less worth than the original.

CYNTHIA. One of the classical names—it's an alternate appellation for the Greek moon goddess Artemis—given by plantation owners to slaves in the early nineteenth century but not widely popular in the United States until the 1950s—Elizabeth Taylor was a glowing fifteen-year-old Cynthia in a 1947 film. It has faded from sight once again, though using the nickname CIA instead of the now-hackneyed Cindy (or, much worse, CYNDI or CINDI) makes it sound more modern.

D

〰〰〰〰〰〰〰〰〰〰 ◎ 〰〰〰〰〰〰〰〰〰〰

DAHLIA. A flower name used occasionally in Britain (especially in novels) that is a bit affected—its sound is reminiscent of dah-ling—for modern American tastes. DALIA is a variant.

DAISY. Daisy is one of the flower names bursting into full bloom again in recent years after nearly a century of lying dormant. Originally a nickname for Margaret (the flower was the symbol of Santa Margherita), Daisy is now very current in Britain, and American parents are beginning to agree that it sounds fresh as a daisy, too. Also, if you're honoring a loved one named Margaret, Daisy is a great nickname solution, more inventive than the eighties' favorite Maggie. The name has had a colorful history, portrayed as the innocent Daisy Miller in the Henry James novel, as Daisy Buchanan, the hero's object of desire in *The Great Gatsby*, in the 1890s song "Bicycle Built for Two" ("Daisy, Daisy, give me your answer true . . ."), as the sexy blonde and barefoot Daisys in *L'il Abner* and *The Dukes of Hazzard*, and finally as the older Daisy in *Driving Miss*. . . . Cable talk show host Daisy Fuentes is a contemporary bearer, and actress Markie Post used the name for her daughter.

DAKOTA. The most fashionable of the fashionable western place-names, Dakota is popping up everywhere for girls as well as boys. Melanie Griffith and Don Johnson certainly heated up the name's image when they gave it to their daughter a few years back—about the same time, incidentally, that actress Melissa Gilbert used it for her son. Celebrity types have since galloped on to less developed lands in search of names for their daughters, from MONTANA (Woody Harrelson) to KENYA (Nastassja Kinski and Quincy Jones) to CAIRO (model Beverly Peele). Crowd-shy parents might consider doing the same.

DALE. Dale is one of the original ambisexual names, famous for both the female Dale Evans (born Frances) and the male Dale Carnegie as far back as the forties. In baby naming, this counts as ancient history, which helps give Dale a measure of depth and a pleasing patina. As with many ambi- names that survive over the years, Dale has become almost the exclusive property of girls.

DAMARIS. A New Testament name that was a favorite among the Puritans but has become near obsolete now, Damaris might be worth resurrection by parents in search of an unusual biblical name that nevertheless remains on the safe side of weird.

DANA. Just when the aura of Dana Andrews had faded and Dana seemed to be a completely female name, along came *Wayne's World's* Dana Carvey. But since all its other current well-known bearers— Dana Delaney of *China Beach*, the Sigourney Weaver character, Dana Barrett, in *Ghostbusters*, Dana Lambert on *As the World Turns*—are women, Dana is still a safe bet for a girl.

DANIELLE. This French feminine of Daniel was one of the trendiest names of the seventies, remained on the pop charts through the eighties—helped along by the unremitting stream of best-selling novels from Danielle Steel—but has now just about burned itself out. The Italianate DANIELLA or DANIELA may be a marginally more stylish option for those wanting to honor an ancestral Daniel or carrying an undying torch for the name, but it too is beginning to sound shopworn, as is the nickname DANI. A fresher French choice might be DELPHINE; an Italian, ORIANA.

DAPHNE. When the writers of *Frasier* sought a recognizably English name for the character of Dad's companion, what they came up with was Daphne, which to many Americans does seem quintessentially British, and upper-class at that. Its roots are classical—in Greek mythology, Daphne was a nymph who was saved from an over-amorous Apollo by having the gods transform her into a laurel tree. It was first used in modern times as a slave name, as many classical names were. It does have two unfortunate nicknames, DAFF (DAPH) and DAFFY.

DARIA, DARA. These two pretty but rather spineless names do have a few interesting references in their backgrounds. Daria was a Greek woman who became an early Christian martyr, while Dara, a male name in the Bible, was also the Persian angel of rivers and rain, and is now the name of a daughter of Gregory Hines. Both names are sometimes used as female versions of Daryl or Darren, but with the inspiration of actress Daryl Hannah, who needs a variant? DARYL and DARREN (and all spelling variations thereof) are now perfectly acceptable for girls.

DARCY. An Irish surname (originally d'Arcy) now used as a first name for both girls and boys, Darcy is a delicate name that unfortunately sounds neither Irish nor distinctive enough to pack any real power. DARBY is a similar kind of name, worn by Julia Roberts in the film, *The Pelican Brief*.

DARLA, DARLENE. Darla was the only female Little Rascal, and the name's dimpled image is about as dated as the original versions of those movies. The same can be said of Darlene, which came on a bit later, but enjoyed much greater popularity, being on the Top 50 list all through the fifties. It lives on now in the character of Darlene Conner, the rebellious, intensely realistic middle child on the *Roseanne* show.

DAVINA. Davina sounds a lot more exotic and interesting than what it really is: a Scottish feminine form of David. It's not too bad, if you want to honor an ancestral David, and at the very least a far sight better than DAVIDA or (we swear we've heard it) DAVETTE. The spelling DIVINA takes the name into a more celestial realm which may prove a burden if your child dares ever be less than divine.

DAWN. Dawn was first used in the nineteenth century, but it didn't become a superhot name until about 1970, parents responding to the impression it created of sunrise and a fresh new day. But it always had a bit of a goody-goody image, except perhaps when combined with a tough last name, as in the case of movie executive Dawn Steel. Now dawn has broken, and the forecast for the name is cloudy at best. For the parent still enchanted by Dawn's golden image, Aurora would make both a more classic and brighter choice, or, a little further afield, Zora (Arabic for dawn) or Roxana (the same word in Persian). Actress Dawnn Lewis of *A Different World* and *Hanging with Mr. Cooper* added a new but not improved spelling to the pot.

DEBORAH. There have been so many Debbies, Debbys, and Debras over the past several decades that the beauty and meaning of the original name have been all but lost. The fifth most popular girls name in 1950 and still hanging on at number thirteen in 1970, Deborah today doesn't even make the Top 50. But in addition to having a lovely sound, and feeling fresher, at this point, than the classic but overused Sarah and Rachel, Deborah has the further modern appeal of a strong Old Testament heritage—Deborah was a poet, judge, and heroic prophet who first predicted that the Israelites would win their freedom from the tyrannical Canaanites, then led a successful revolt that helped accomplish it, celebrating the victory in a famous song of triumph. Because of this, parents in search of Old Testament names with character may be the first to revive Deborah. Just remember: Absolutely the only way to go with this name is as Deborah—not DEBRA or that perennial cheerleader, DEBBIE. The only permissible alternative: Parents with strong ties to Israel may want to use the Hebrew version, DEVORAH.

DECIMA. This name of the Roman goddess of childbirth would be reserved for a tenth child in the days when huge families were common; today, it could be used for one born in October, the tenth month of the year. Warning: Other kids might be quick to point out the similarity to the word *decimate*.

DEIRDRE. Unfortunately this strong Celtic name often has the phrase "of the sorrows" attached to it, because of the tragic fate of the character in Irish legend, retold in the works of Yeats and Synge. If that doesn't bother you, consider Deirdre as an authentic Irish Gaelic name that has managed to become familiar here without losing any of its ethnic identity. Please note: While spelling variations of Deirdre abound, the one here is the most authentic.

DELIA. A rich and appealing name with Southern overtones, Delia was another appellation for the moon goddess Artemis, who was born on the Greek island of Delos. A favorite of the eighteenth-century pastoral poets—and much stronger than most of those names, like Phyllis and CHLORIS—it later was used as a nickname for Cordelia and ADELIA and such. In the same family are DELL and DELLA.

DELILAH. Delilah has never managed to move much beyond its biblical image as a seductive temptress, and even a twenty-first century Delilah will doubtless have to battle assumptions and jokes sparked by people's perceptions of the name. Too bad, because Delilah is one of the most haunting female names in the Bible—sexy, yes, but also melodic and strong and somehow modern. If you love the name so much you find it irresistible, you can pray your little Delilah has the fortitude to withstand everyone asking her where Sampson is, or hiding the scissors when she comes into the room. There has long been a Delilah on *One Life to Live*, and the vibrant rhythms of Tom Jones's trademark song, "Delilah," are familiar to all of us. LILAH is an appealing nickname, DELILA is a variant spelling and DALILA (pronounced da-lee-la) is an unrelated but equally attractive Swahili name meaning "gentle."

DELTA. Sort of a semiplace-name, the richly evocative Delta has strong ties both to the South and to the tabloids, largely via headline-making Delta Burke, late of *Designing Women*.

DEMETRIA. In Greek myth this is the name of an earth mother goddess of fertility and the harvest, and in Hollywood, it's the full name of Demi Moore.

DENISE. One of the Frenchified names that became enormously popular in the fifties and sixties (reaching number fifteen in 1960), Denise is far out of the loop now. It was last heard from as the name of the in-again, out-again daughter played by Lisa Bonet on *The Cosby Show*.

DESIRÉE. It's hard to imagine why any parent would name a daughter Desirée. Its sexiness borders on the salacious, and giving it to a child would only invite a lifetime of sleazy come-ons and nasty presumptions. Early Christians, on the contrary, often used it for a longed-for child— the object of their desire, and it was also known as the name of Napoleon's great love before he became emperor. The Pilgrims used the English form, DESIRE, which is more unusual but no less suggestive. If you find the idea of an ultrafeminine, blatantly attractive-sounding name appealing, consider options—from Angelica to Gabriella to Sabrina, even to MONIQUE—that move beyond sex to a softer sensuality and beauty. Trivia Tidbit: Desirée was Lucille Ball's middle name, and the first name of her mother.

DEVON. One of the loveliest of place-names, evoking the beautiful county of dramatic seacoast and vast moors in southwest England, Devon is probably still used most often for boys but its strength is by no means exclusively masculine, as evidenced by the soap opera character Devon Shepherd on *All My Children*. Although Devon is the proper spelling, DEVIN is also used.

DIANA, DIANE. Anyone who has picked up a magazine in the last ten years is more than familiar with the name Diana—the Princess of Wales and estranged wife of Britain's Prince Charles is surely more tied to it now than is the old Roman goddess of the moon and the hunt. This still-appealing name undoubtedly was an enormous influence on the trend toward *a*-ending versions of names that might also end with an *e*. Where Diane and Joanne and Christine were once by far the favored forms, (Diane was on Top 25 popularity lists from 1940 to 1960), today they're far surpassed by Diana, Joanna, and Christina. Spelling variants of Diana and Diane are legion and include DIANNA, DIANNE, DYAN (as in Cannon), even DIAHANN (Carroll). Variations DEANNA and DEANNE haven't really been hot since Deanna Durbin (born Edna May) introduced them. DIONNE, like singer Dionne Warwick, is actually an unrelated mythological name, stemming from either Dionysius or DIONE, Zeus's consort and Aphrodite's mom. DIANTHA, a flower name in Greek myth, is one of the more interesting exotic-sounding Greek variants. Somewhat demeaning nicknames for all the above: DI, DEE, and DEE DEE. Another Di name, DIAMOND, has recently come into play. There were sixty-five of them born in Pennsylvania in 1993.

DINAH. One of the most appealing and least used of the mainstream Old Testament female names—probably shunned because of an old slave-name stereotype, having appeared as such in *Uncle Tom's Cabin*. We hope that finally parents will feel free to use this vivid name again for their contemporary girls. Besides its biblical roots—Dinah was the beautiful daughter of Leah and Jacob—this name was also a favorite of the Puritans and appeared in novels by Laurence Sterne and George Eliot. It was also adopted by two wonderful singers, Dinahs Shore (born Frances) and Washington (born Ruth). The related DINA was the name of the Guardian Angel of Wisdom and the Law, and is also, along with DENA and when pronounced dee-na, a nickname for such abominations as BERNADINA.

DIXIE. A saucy waitress-showgirl name, Dixie can also be considered a place-name, although it won't be found on any map, being a generic title for the whole of the American south. Actress Dixie Carter added to the name's Southern image in TV's *Designing Women* a few seasons back.

DOLLY. From the sixteenth century on, there have been Dollys, one of whom (spelled DOLLEY) was among our most famous First Ladies, Mrs. Madison, and another who became successful enough to build her own Dollywood. But we think Dolly is definitely too cutesy for a child born into this postfeminist age.

DOLORES. A Spanish name related to the Virgin Mary (in Latin countries she is known as Santa Maria de los Dolores—the lady of sorrows), developed at a time when Maria itself was considered too sacred to use, Dolores is now pretty much depleted of power. Once upon a time, however, it was the height of sexiness, the name of the exotic Mexican-born star, Dolores Del Rio, and the mother name of seductive pet forms Lola and LOLITA.

DOMINIQUE. Ever since the dramatic character of Dominique Devereaux, as played by Diahann Carroll, stormed onto the set of *Dynasty* in 1984, this name has taken off like a rocket, particularly among African-Americans—it was number ten on California's African-American popularity list in 1993. Other, perhaps more stylish forms today include DOMINICA or, as actor Andy Garcia used for his young daughter, the original no-longer-for-boys-only DOMINIC or DOMINICK.

DONNA. Literally "lady" in Italian, Donna was the perfect ladylike Donna Reed–show period name for the fifties and sixties. And there were plenty of namesakes: Donna was in the Top 10 in 1964. Nowadays, we'd be more likely to associate it with the emancipated clothes of Donna Karan or the more notorious Madonna than as a prospective baby name.

DORA. Starting as a pet form of Theodora, Dora emerged as a name on its own in Charles Dickens's *David Copperfield*, where she was the pretty but impractical first child-wife of the hero. The name suffered for years from the stigma inherent in the title of the long-running comic strip, *Dumb Dora*—created by Chic Young who would go on to produce *Blondie*, about a young flapper who wasn't really dumb after all (the last line in the strip was usually "She's not so dumb!")—but that didn't do the name any good. Today, Dora continues to lag far behind the ever-more-popular Nora and Laura, and isn't likely to catch up soon.

DORCAS. A classic name—both the Romans and the Puritans favored it and Shakespeare used it as well—that's pretty much out-of-bounds today because of its unfortunate relationship to the word *dork*.

DORIS. As heavy-footed as it sounds to us now, Doris seemed the very paragon of grace, when it was part of a group of *s*-ending names (Phyllis, Frances, Iris) at the height of fashion in the twenties, and it got another shot of life when it was attached to the perky Doris Day in the fifties. In classical mythology, Doris is the daughter of Oceanus, god of the sea, a nymph who gave birth to fifty beautiful golden-haired sea nymphs. No wonder the name sounds tired.

DOROTHEA, DOROTHY. Dorothy has left Kansas and Oz and become a Golden Girl, living in retirement with friends Blanche and Rose in Miami. It did have a good run though—it was the sixth most popular girl-baby name in America in 1900, third in 1925, and still in the Top 25 in 1940. Today it is the more flowing, romantic Victorian-sounding Dorothea—and its inverse Theodora—that are being embraced. Dorothea has had a long literary tradition, prominent most recently as the idealistic heroine, Dorothea Brooke, in the *Masterpiece Theater* production of George Eliot's *Middlemarch*. The revival of Dorothea (and Theodora) is sure to breathe new life into some old nicknames: THEA, for one, as well as DORRIE or DORY. DORIA, Dora, and even the originally male DORIAN (seen in female guise on *One Life to Live* since 1979) may get some attention, and the Hebrew name DORIT is very popular in Israel. Forms of the name nearly certain to remain on the shelf: DOT and DOTTY, DORINDA, DOREEN, and especially DODIE and DODO.

DREW. This elegant, formerly male surname name was brought into the female camp by actress Drew Barrymore, who comes by it legitimately—it is a name that has been in her famous acting family for generations.

DULCIE, DULCY. Though it sounds as if it might have been invented a few decades ago, Dulcie was actually a common female name during the Roman Empire, as were fancier versions DULCIA and DULCITIA. Dulcy was later found in the American South, particularly among African-Americans, and we think it is probably too lightweight for parents to want to revive.

DUSTIN and DYLAN. This is an age when parents are getting tired of feminizing boys' names and are beginning to appropriate the originals for their daughters. These are two of the latest examples, in the air since Debby Boone called one of her twin girls Dustin a few years ago. Female Dylans are more common: Adopted daughter Dylan was at the center of the Woody Allen-Mia Farrow custody trial; Sean Penn and Robin Wright also have a daughter named Dylan, and needless to say there has been one on a soap opera—*Santa Barbara*. Dylan and Dustin's real problem: They're trying so hard to be cool that they're not. An alternate spelling (which would take it into the realm of surname names): DILLON.

E

EBONY. A fashionable color name—Amber, GRAY, and Scarlett are others from this group—Ebony is especially popular among African-American parents, who have also been choosing another name celebrating blackness—Raven. In use since the 1970s, Ebony was the tenth most popular name for African-American girls born in Texas a couple of years ago, and remains in the Black Top 10 nationwide, appreciated both for its strong, energetic sound and rich, polished associations. The only caveat: If you name a child Ebony, do not be tempted to call her sister Ivory—or to give siblings any of the other color names, for that matter. Way too cutesy for modern sensibilities.

EDEN. A place-name, at least for those who believe in the concept of Paradise, Eden strikes an appealing balance between the Big Country Dakotas and MONTANAS and the ultraexotic ASIAS and KENYAS.

EDITH. Edith is one of the oldest surviving Anglo-Saxon names, overidentified these past few decades with Edith Bunker, Archie's incorruptible but sometimes confused wife. As her fame fades and that of Edith Wharton, novelist of recent *Age of Innocence* attention, brightens, Edith may once again seem an attractive, if conservative, choice. And EDIE has some nickname appeal.

EDNA. Edna is one of those names that, until what seemed like a few minutes ago, felt so terminally dowdy that no one could imagine a parent choosing it for an innocent modern baby. But with the enormous upswing in names that honor family members, Edna—along with dozens of other similar choices ranging from Adeline to Zelda—might be pulled along in the slipstream. This would certainly follow the hundred-year rule, in which names often come back into style after a century. Although it might not sound it, Edna is a biblical name, that of the mother of Abraham, first of the prophets, and was enormously popular in this country in the last half of the nineteenth century. The name has roots in both Greek and Hebrew: The Hebrew "ednah," which means "delight," also relates to Eden, a name option for those who want to honor Grandma Edna but seek something more contemporary-sounding than the original.

EDWINA. Edwina becomes a much more attractive name when pronounced like Edwin, rather than Ed-weeeee-na. Then it takes on a mauve-tinted Victorian charm, summoning up lacy shawls fastened with carved cameos. It had quite a different image in the cult favorite, *Raising Arizona*, in which Holly Hunter was a police officer named Edwina, and usually called Ed.

EGYPT. Whatever currency this name has can be laid to a single source: the talk-show host soap opera character Egypt Masters, on *Loving*. This well may have contributed to the rise of place-names in general.

EILEEN. An Irish form of Helen that was among the Top 10 of 1925 and still remained stylish in the fifties, Eileen's star has fallen far. It does seem, from this viewpoint, like a slim name, at a time when modern parents quite reasonably want more texture, depth, and substance for their daughters. Other Irish-accented names that might provide those qualities include Sinead or ONORA.

EITHNE. A Gaelic name very popular among Irish parents, also spelled ETHNA but perhaps best known here in the phonetic spelling of the name of haunting singer ENYA (who was christened Eithne). EMER (pronounced as ever) and ETAIN (pronounced eden) are two other Gaelic choices well used in modern Ireland, but all might prove too exotic for an ordinary American child.

ELAINE. Being featured on a hot TV show—*Seinfeld*—has done nothing to heat up the image of this dated name, which was at its most recent heyday in the World War II period. Originally an Old French form of Helen, Elaine, "the lily maid of Astolat," was one of the shining heroines of the Arthurian legends, the princess who fell in love with Sir Lancelot and became the mother of Sir Galahad. Nowadays, the more stylish spins on this name are ELENA, the Spanish and Italian form that's pronounced as ELAINA, and the Hebrew ELANA, which means "tree" and may also be spelled ILANA. ELIANA is another very pretty Hebrew name close to the name ELIAS or ELIHU and also spelled ELIANE or ELIANNA.

ELEANOR. Eleanor was one of the first of the old-fashioned, no-nonsense girls' names to be dusted off by the new generation of stylish parents, yet many people will still be surprised to hear that this solid classic is fashionable again. But its straightforward feminine image combined with its royal medieval origins (Eleanor of Aquitaine introduced the name to England in the twelfth century) is striking just the right note for a segment of parents in search of a girls' name that combines substance and style. Some may find further appeal in the name's connection to Eleanor Roosevelt; others may refer to Jane Austen's heroine ELINOR Dashwood (that spelling appeared in the seventeenth century), who represents "sense" in *Sense and Sensibility*. The famous Nell Gwinn's real name was Elinor, as was Dickens's Little Nell. Modern celebrities who have chosen this name are split on its spelling: Diane Lane and Christopher Lambert named their daughter Eleanor Jasmine, while Katie Couric chose the more streamlined Elinor. Obviously, Eleanor is not a name that attracts a whimsical crowd, though some variations have a lighter feel than others. The Italianate ELEANORA or ELEONORA seem fashionable and feminine, thanks to the final *a*. Eleanor also has a raft of appealing nicknames, several of which have become favorites on their own: Ella, Nora, and Nell.

ELECTRA. Perhaps one reason this name is rarely heard is the violence of the myth attached to it: Electra, with the aid of her brother, avenges the murder of her father by killing her mother and her lover—a saga modernized by Eugene O'Neill in his play, *Mourning Becomes Electra*. On the bright side, the name does mean "one who shines brilliantly" (as in electric), and not everyone knows the Greek myths. Isabella Rossellini chose the gentler Italian version, ELETTRA, for her daughter.

ELIZA. Eliza was a highborn favorite of the eighteenth century that had slid way downscale by the era of *My Fair Lady*'s Eliza Doolittle—and it's never quite recovered its upper-class image. But Eliza is a lot livelier than the original Elizabeth, and parents who would like to honor an Elizabethan ancestor but are put off by that name's Top 10 status would do well to consider Eliza. Liza, as in Minnelli, is the less substantial short form. ELISA, with its overwhelming variety of forms from ELISSA to ALYSSA to ALISA ad infinitum, is worlds less distinctive.

ELIZABETH. Elizabeth is, in many ways, the girls' name with the most of everything: the richest history, the broadest appeal, the highest fashion status, the greatest variety of offshoots and nicknames. Elizabeth is the world's premier queen and richest woman as well as its most enduringly sexy movie star; Elizabeth is an Old Testament figure and a Christian saint. The name has been back among the Top 20 girls' names for over a decade now, yet manages to retain a good measure of fashion status. Especially when shortened to LIZZIE, Elizabeth has been one of the quintessentially Yuppie names. The only real strike against Elizabeth as a current baby-naming choice is its very popularity. The big question: Is Elizabeth so classic it transcends any level of trendiness, or has the name reached the cultural saturation point? Our opinion: Lizzie has had its day in the sun. But there are enough other nicknames and so many variations on Elizabeth that if, for whatever reason, you feel it's the right name for your child, you can use one of the stand-ins with confidence. ELISABETH, for one, is the accepted version in many European cultures, that middle *s* serving to soften the name and set it apart. But please don't be aggressive about insisting on some deviant pronunciation, forcing everyone to say, for instance, E-lee-sa-bet. ELIZA is one very good option for parents who love Elizabeth but want a name that's less widespread. But other, more nouveau variations—from ELISA to ELISE to ELISSA to ALYSSA—do not carry the same pedigree or the same interest. ELSPETH, Elizabeth's Scottish cousin, is for the very adventurous. ELSA seems too terminally Teutonic and leonine. Other alternates to consider on your own terms and use at your own risk: LIZETTE, LIZBETH, BETTINA. Of the nicknames, with LIZZIE and LIZ nearing fashion retirement age, Libby and Bess seem the most vital. Betty, BETTE, Beth, Betsy, and even Liza and Lisa are dated, albeit to different eras, while BESSIE and ELSIE are stuck down on the farm. The most fashionable twist on Elizabeth is to Isabel or Isabella; more on that under *I*.

ELLA. Ella is a name that began to spring back to life in the past couple of years, suddenly sounding just right for today's little girls: strong yet soft, spirited but traditionally grounded. Sometimes used as a short form for Eleanor, Ella also has a full life of its own, recorded for centuries as a name unto itself. Some parents today may want to use it to honor jazz great Ella Fitzgerald.

ELLEN. Like Lisa and DEBBIE and Sharon, Ellen is a name that belongs to lots of today's mothers but very few of its babies. An Old English form of Helen, the sensitive but clear-eyed Ellen has swung far in and out of style over the centuries. In *The Age of Innocence*, set at the end of the nineteenth century, one character wonders why the Countess Olenska has not changed her "ugly" given name of Ellen to something prettier, like Elaine—a statement no one would make today. Ellen is far from an ugly name, and not terminally dated, so no one would be shocked if you were to choose it, but neither does it sound very contemporary. There are a few Ellens currently on the scene, namely Ellen Barkin and Ellen DeGeneris. Some feasible foreign variations are ELENA, the Latinate form, and ELENI, the Greek one.

ELOISE. Eloise will always be the imperious little girl who roams the Plaza Hotel; the name also recalls Heloise of Household Hints fame. These are not the worst associations in the world for a name, but pretty airtight ones nonetheless.

ELODIE. Pronounced to rhyme with Melody, this is an attractive French name all but unknown in this country. Only recommended for parents with exotic tastes and a fairly straightforward last name.

ELVIRA. Before there was the campy, vampirish TV Elvira, Mistress of the Dark, the name had quite a different image, first as the long-suffering wife of Don Juan (you can just imagine what that was like!), then as the romantic adolescent heroine of *Elvira Madigan*. In spite of this colorful background, however, Elvira, and the similar ELMIRA and ELVINA, all sound too old ladyish for today's baby.

EMANUELLE. The French Emanuelle has a much sexier image than it deserves, thanks to the erotic heroine of the sensational film of a few years back. Another spelling is EMMANUELLE. Other feminine forms of the boys' name EMANUEL, are EMANUELA and MANUELA.

EMELINE. Emeline is a very old name with its own source and history, distinct from both Emma and Emily. Introduced to Britain by the Normans in the eleventh century, Emeline's most accepted variant is EMMELINE, but some of the many others spawned over the years include EMMALINE, EMELYN, and EMALEEN, reflecting the name's varied pronunciations, with the ending spoken as *-een*, *-in*, or (most appropriately) as in the word line. New Age guru Marianne Williamson's use of the name for her daughter, India Emmeline, may inspire other parents to move beyond Emily and Emma to this quainter version.

EMILY. Everyone loves Emily. Kids love it, mothers and fathers love it, teachers love it. And why not? It has dignity, daintiness, and drive, as well as a legacy of having been borne by such distinguished writers as Emily Brontë and Emily Dickinson, not to mention the Miss Manners of her day, Emily Post. Emily is a clear favorite of upwardly mobile parents: According to research by a Harvard sociology professor, it is the most likely among the Top 50 girls' names to be selected by highly educated mothers. But of course such approbation brings with it mass popularity—Emily has been in the American Top 10 and hovering near number one in Britain for several years now. Emily is everywhere, having reached such widespread use that it may, in keeping with the hundred-year cycle theory, be doomed to repeat its pattern of a century ago, when it rose to popularity in the 1870s and then declined steeply after 1900. Some parents are already searching for alternatives to this lovely but overused name, turning to Emma, EMILIA, Amelia, Emeline, or the French form, EMILIE.

EMMA. As Emily's popularity boomed, many parents have turned to Emma for relief, only to find its own star zooming skyward. It's questionable, however, whether Emma will ever attain Emily's heights on the official popularity charts, which most Emma fans would consider a very good thing. Though a very fashionable name—parents in artistic professions on both coasts will undoubtedly count several young Emmas among their acquaintances—its appeal might be too snobbish for mass consumption. Heroic Emmas of the past—Jane Austen's Emma, for instance, or Flaubert's Madame Bovary or Lady Hamilton or Avenger Emma Peel or socialist leader Emma Goldman—may inspire only the cognoscenti. A very old royal name well used through the centuries, Emma has substance as well as style and a dulcet sound. Still, if you want a name that sets your child far apart from her crowd, keep looking.

ENID. Though no one compiles a record of every name on every birth certificate filed in the United States, we would be surprised if there were even a single baby girl born this year named Enid. And yet, hard as it may be to believe, this Celtic name was once thought of as a lovely and romantic appellation, for in Arthurian legend, the beautiful Enid was the personification of feminine nobility, and the greatest compliment you could pay a woman was to call her "a second Enid." Tastes change.

ERICA. Erica—the Latin botanical word for "heather"—has been among the Top 50 girls' names since the early seventies and still has its fans. The notorious soap opera character Erica Kane, played by queen of daytime Susan Lucci, did much to spread this strong-minded name. The Scandinavian form ERIKA is sometimes used as well, but nickname RICKI and variations belong to a bygone era.

ERIN. Erin and cousins like Shannon and Tara were the successors to older Irish-American favorites like Kathleen and Colleen, but now they too are moving aside to make room for a new wave of more genuine Irish names: girls' names like Maeve, Siobhan, and GRANIA; androgynous choices such as Cassidy, KENNEDY, and Flannery. Parents in search of an Irish name should know, in any case, that ERIN, which is the Gaelic word for Ireland, is not used as a name in Ireland at all.

ERNESTINE. If it hadn't already been dead—and it pretty much was—Lily Tomlin certainly killed off Ernestine as a baby name possibility when she created her eccentric telephone operator character for *Laugh-In*.

ESMÉ. The unique appeal of this distinctive name is as singular and eternal as that of the classic J. D. Salinger story, "For Esmé, With Love and Squalor." Related to the French Aimée, it, too, means "beloved," and was originally a male name exported from France to Scotland via a member of the royal family.

ESTHER. One of the major female figures in the Old Testament, Esther was the captured Jewish wife of the king of Persia (the name means "star" in Persian), who risked her life to save her exiled people from the plots of Haman to annihilate them. It is this story that Jews celebrate on the holiday of Purim, and thus Esther is a name that has traditionally been given to girls born at that time. But since around 1925, the name has hardly been used, even in Jewish families. The variant ESTELLE seems similarly dated, but other names that mean "star"—ESTELLA (which was introduced by Dickens in *Great Expectations*) and especially Stella—are far more usable. STAR itself, however—particularly when it's spelled STARR—seems to be a name in search of a topless-club marquee.

ETHEL. These days it's likely to be confused with the hydrocarbon that's spelled with a *y*, but in the early years of this century, when Ethel Barrymore was the belle of Broadway, her first name was wildly fashionable. In the interim there were the booming Ethel Merman and the prolific Ethel Kennedy and Lucy's friend and neighbor, Ethel Mertz. We think it was the mere sound of the latter that may have killed the name off forever.

EUDORA, et al. Names that begin with the letters *Eu*—the "you" sound—were fashionable around the turn of the twentieth century and for the most part now feel terminally dated. Eudora, however, one of the more euphonious of the group, has something else to recommend it in namesake and writer Eudora Welty. EUNICE, the New Testament mother of Timothy, is most recognizable as the name of one of the Kennedy sisters and the mother of Maria Shriver, who used it as a middle name for her and Arnold Schwarzenegger's oldest daughter. Eunice was not helped, though, by its association with Carol Burnett's unlovable character on *Mama's Family*. EUPHEMIA is an early saint's name often shortened to EFFIE in the nineteenth century, and EUSTACIA is almost more noteworthy now as the name from which Stacy sprang than as the passionate Eustacia Vye in Thomas Hardy's *The Return of the Native*. The Greek EULALIA has no special claim to fame, though it has a pleasant sound and the nickname LALLY is sort of endearing.

EUGENIA. Eugenia—or more precisely its French form EUGENIE— has managed to escape being relegated to fashion limbo along with the rest of the *Eu-* names because Fergie and Andy, the Duke and Duchess of York, chose it for their second daughter. Eugenia/Eugenie is a well-established royal name in Europe, first made famous by Napoleon III's glamorous empress.

EVE, EVA. Not for nothing does a name manage to survive from the beginning of time. Eve's appeal is its simple elegance, its synthesis of sensuality and innocence. The name was popular even before the Reformation (when Old Testament names were rarely used) because of a belief that girls named Eve would have long lives. The form Eva was heard less often until the 1852 publication of *Uncle Tom's Cabin*, the best-selling novel of the nineteenth century, whose tragic figure, Little Eva, made a huge impression on the Victorian reading public. Nowadays, neither version is particular prevalent, although Susan Sarandon and Harry Anderson have both picked up on Eva for their daughters. And although Eve had a bad moment in the film *All About Eve*, we think this pure form is equally appealing, either as a first or middle name. Beware, however, EVITA, as in Peron, dominatrix of Argentina.

EVANGELINE. Evangeline combines an exotic femininity with an offbeat quality that conjures up a poetic image of a young beauty with flowing, waist-length hair. The name, which means "gospel" in Latin, was introduced to the English-speaking world by Longfellow in his

1847 poem of the same name and can also be found in *Uncle Tom's Cabin* (it was Little Eva's full name) and in two novels by Evelyn Waugh. Evangeline would be a delightful name for a fashionable little girl, who can either conform to its image or successfully play against it.

EVELYN. A name so soft it has simply faded away, Evelyn was in the Top 50 from 1900 to 1925. The name has gone through both a spelling and a sex change. It moved from AVELINE to EVELINE to Evelyn, and its most famous bearer was a male writer, Evelyn (with a long *E*) Waugh. Older forms Eveline and especially EVELINA seem once again more appealing.

F

〰〰〰〰〰〰〰〰〰〰〰〰〰〰 ◎ 〰〰〰〰〰〰〰〰〰〰〰〰〰〰

FAITH. Faith is one of the Puritan virtue names that's begun to sound very appealing to modern parents who like the name's straightforward feminine image as well as its meaning. Indeed, it does take faith nowadays to get married and start a family—faith that you'll be a good parent and your child will turn out well. If you don't have that kind of confidence, better opt for Hope. One caveat: Parents of a Faith we know say people often ask if the name symbolizes their religious zeal. If you're less than zealous, think twice. The name's short form, FAY or FAYE, which also relates to an archaic word for "fairy," and which is still used, although not very often, in its own right, sounds a little more dated, yet might make an out-of-the-ordinary middle name (Harry Anderson has a daughter named Eva Fay.) Actress Faye Dunaway (born Dorothy Faye) uses the alternate, somewhat more substantial, form.

FALLON. This was one of several forward-looking boyish last name names to have been spawned by *Dynasty* (a hotbed of creative character naming) in the late eighties. Despite its sleazy origins, we find it to be an attractive Gaelic surname choice, much more suited to a girl than a boy.

FARRAH. For a few seconds there in the late seventies, Farrah Fawcett's name was as frequently cloned as her hairdo. Both are now equally passé.

FATIMA. An Arabic name, Fatima was Mohammed's favorite daughter and one of the four perfect women in the world. The name's problem, if used in our culture: nicknames referring to fat.

FAWN. As retrograde as Bambi, Fawn was most famously the name of Oliver North's loyal secretary-shredder, Fawn Hall. And like other names such as Tawny and Taffy, it just doesn't, in our opinion, give a girl child enough to live up to. FAUNA, besides being the Latin blanket term for the animal kingdom, was the name of one of the three fairies—Flora, Fauna, and Meriwether—who protected Sleeping Beauty.

FELICITY. A stylish, self-contained name that's recently gained a lot of attention—among six-to-thirteen-year-old girls and their parents, at least—as the name of the redhaired Colonial doll in the American Girl series. Realistically, the eighteenth-century form of the name would more probably have been FELICE or FELICIA; Felicity has surpassed those versions in popularity only in the last hundred years. All are forms of Felix, have been around since Roman times, and mean lucky; in fact, the Roman FELICITAS was the goddess of good luck. Other girls' names that mean luck: FAUSTINA, FORTUNA, and FORTUNE. And for what it's worth, there has been a spate of Felicias on soap operas of late: We've counted them on at least three.

FERN. Fern is a name with a terminally barefoot, backwoodsy feel: Among the botanicals, it's never moved into the front parlor along with Rose or Violet or even Daisy. Its most appealing reference is to the young human heroine in E. B. White's classic children's story of a pig and spider, *Charlotte's Web*.

FIFI. Actually a pet name for Josephine, Fifi would be best left for your French poodle.

FIONA. Since the opening of *Brigadoon* in 1954, Fiona has been the best-known of a group of related Gaelic names, which is ironic since it's the only one without genuine traditional roots—it was invented in the late nineteenth century as a feminine pseudonym for a Scottish male writer. Today, Fiona is well used in England, Scotland, Australia, and even Ireland, and is found here occasionally; it's Julia Roberts's middle name. We slightly prefer the more genuinely Irish version, FINOLA, with FIONNUALA the native spelling, and the forbidding FINNGUALA the full kettle of cockles. FINELLA or FENELLA are Scottish variations. Or you might want to go all the way and call your daughter FINN after the greatest hero of Irish mythology and bearer of one of the coolest names ever, Finn Mac Cool.

FLANNERY. One of the few currently en vogue Irish surname names that actually has some history as a first name—and a first name for girls, at that—in the person of writer Flannery O'Connor (born Mary Flannery). It also has a warm (flannelly) feel. But if you find the link to the author too strong to transcend the name's melodic sound in your mind, you might want to consider some related options: FLANN, the name of two Irish queens as well as a custard dessert, FLANAGAN, FINN, FLYNN, or FARRELL, to name a handful.

FLORA. Flora is one of the gently old-fashioned names that, along with other botanical favorites, is due for a comeback. The Roman goddess of flowers and spring, Flora was the name of a saint and has long been a favorite in Scotland, especially in the MacDonald clan, because of the young heroine by that name who helped Bonnie Prince Charlie make his escape to France. FLORIA is a long-dormant variation with modern possibilities. The French FLEUR, which became well known in the English-speaking world when Galsworthy bestowed it on one of the Forsytes in his celebrated saga, is a bit too precious, and FLOWER, the name of the little skunk in *Bambi*, a too literal translation of the name.

FLORENCE. Florence is a quintessential grandma name getting unexpected new life today from the boom in place-names (and the fashion status of the Italian city) as well as the taste for quaint, even stodgy, old favorites. Even if you haven't heard it on your block yet, take it from us—it's already a very stylish name in London and it's headed this way. Florence began life as a male name; its modern use is almost entirely due to the popularity and fame of Florence Nightingale, who had been named for the city of her birth. A recent bearer of note: Florence Griffith Joyner, track star and Olympic gold medal winner. Some nicknames, à la the Bobbsey Twins: FLORRIE and FLOSSIE.

FLORIDA. Florida was one of the first place-names to be heard on television, in the person of Florida Evans on *Good Times*, the understanding African-American mother who had formerly worked as a maid for Maude. Like the state itself, this name does not have the cachet of some of the other more western and more international geographical names.

FRANCES. This was a name that was perceived as far too faded for consideration until very recently, when a few supercool and very visible parents used it for their offspring. Most famously, singer Courtney Love and the doomed Kurt Cobain called their daughter Frances Bean, after doomed forties star Frances Farmer, and Sean Penn and Robin Wright also have a young daughter named Dylan Frances. With that kind of promotion, Frances has leapt the tall building of high fashion in a single bound. Pretty in its formal version, Frances (the real name of both Dinah Shore and Dale Evans) becomes more down to earth with nickname FRANNY and even earthier with FANNY, hip again for the first time in a century, but still perhaps too blatant a name for this era of plainspoken children. As quaint and charming a name as Fanny may be, and as colorful as its literary heritage is (appearing in such novels as *Fanny Hill*, *Little Dorrit*, *Dombey and Son*, *Sense and Sensibility*, *Mansfield Park*, and even Erica Jong's *Fanny*), we do have qualms about her early years at school, and even her later years at school, for that matter. As Fanny may err in one direction, FRANCINE and FRANCOISE and FRANCE move too far the other way, fancifying the name too much for today's unaffected tastes. FRANCESCA is the likable Latin version.

FREDERICA, FRIEDA. Frederica is an interesting possibility for the parent not intimidated by such a formal, old-time appellation. It's got some charm and verve lurking within its nineteenth-century stuffiness. And to us it's more appealing, certainly, than the Germanic FRIEDA, though we do admire painter and potential namesake FRIDA Kahlo. Nickname possibilities include the tomboyish FREDDI and the so-impossible-it's-almost-possible FRITZI.

G

⁓⁓⁓⁓⁓⁓⁓⁓⁓⁓⁓⁓⁓ ◉ ⁓⁓⁓⁓⁓⁓⁓⁓⁓⁓⁓

GABRIELLE. Neither as overused as Danielle nor as au courant as Isabelle, Gabrielle is one of the quintessentially graceful and worldly French names accessible to parents here. Chosen by Debby Boone for one of her twin daughters, it was also the given name of fashion great "Coco" Chanel. Its Italian sister GABRIELLA (also spelled GABRIELA), softened and enlivened by the *a* ending, is borne by the Argentinian tennis star Gabriela Sabatini. As a nickname, GABY provides a different, dizzier image. GAVRIELLA and GAVI are the Israeli versions of this originally Hebrew name.

GAIL. Gail sounded really spiffy when it replaced ABBY as a short form of Abigail in the forties, but that was fifty years ago, and there are very few babies named Gail (or GALE, GAEL, or GAYLE) today. Most modern parents would probably prefer to go back to the most old-fashioned version of all, the original Abigail. Some related names are GAY, which of course, has its own special problems, insurmountable even when it's spelled GAYE, and GALEN, the name of a character on *All My Children*. GALIA is a Hebrew name, also spelled GALYA, that is well used in Israel and seems eminently adaptable to American life.

GELSEY. Thanks to ballet superstar Gelsey Kirkland, this name has taken on a lithe and graceful image. Parents who are finding too many little Kelseys in their neighborhood might want to consider this instead. The initial *G*, by the way, is soft.

GEMMA. In England, Gemma, sometimes found as JEMMA, is a perennially stylish name, long favored by the upper crust. In the United States, it's hardly heard at all, except occasionally in Italian-American families. Stemming from a medieval Italian nickname for a precious jewel, it was used by Dante, and was borne by a nineteenth-century saint, and we think it could make a classy and stylish choice.

GENEVA. Unlike the somewhat cold and formal city it represents, Geneva is a lively and appealing place-name option, beginning to surface more frequently on this continent. Trivia tidbit: Geneva was First Lady Mamie Eisenhower's middle name.

GENEVIEVE. A name that might be of Celtic, Germanic, or French origin, Genevieve also leads a double life in its pronunciation—it may be either Gen-uh-veev or Jhon-vee-ev. And for anyone who likes the Gen/Jen sound and nickname, and is tired of Jennifer, JENNA, Jenny et al., this could make a retrostylish replacement. St. Genevieve is the patron of Paris, credited with saving her city from Attila the Hun and his hordes in the fifth century—she told her compatriots to put their trust in God and be saved, and sure enough, the Huns bypassed the city. GINETTE and GINETTA are French pet forms.

GEORGIA. Georgia is a name so rich, so lush, so gorgeous we wonder how anyone could fail to fall in love with it. After a few decades of languishing, this peach of a name seems poised to scale the heights of fashion—it's already been selected by Mick Jagger and Jerry Hall for their daughter, and it also brings to mind one of America's most renowned female artists, Georgia O'Keeffe. One reason for its resurgence is the current interest in place-names as first names—and this is one that has the advantage of being an established personal name as well as a real geographical locale. Another: Georgia and its variants are among the once-quaint feminizations—like Josephine, Charlotte, Cornelia—that have begun to sound fresh and stylish again. And last but most important: It's a beautiful name, redolent with sweet-scented Southern charm. Also wearing our seal of approval are the Scottish GEORGINA (with echoes of *Upstairs, Downstairs*) and the more patrician GEORGIANA (favored by Dickens and Jane Austen), one of the ten most popular baby names in England and often pronounced there as George-Jane-a although it might just as well be said as George-anna. Unfortunately, the French GEORGETTE, at one time associated with the somewhat vacant wife of Ted Baxter on the old Mary Tyler Moore show, is several degrees downscale.

GERALDINE. Geraldine is one feminized male name that does not seem ready for a fashion comeback. Why? Maybe because Gerald itself, as well as the ambisexual nickname GERRY/JERRY, feel dated while other male stalwarts—Joseph and Henry and Harry and even George—are coming back into fashion in tandem with their female forms. The name was invented in the time of Henry VIII by a noble poet who fell in love with a Lady Elizabeth Fitzgerald. Taking off from her surname, he referred to her as the "Fair Geraldine." The name had its fifteen minutes of fame in this country in the early seventies as Flip Wilson's sassy female alter ego, and, more seriously, as the name of the first woman to be a major party vice presidential candidate in the United States, Geraldine Ferraro.

GERMAINE. Feminist writer Germaine Greer has been almost single-handedly responsible for keeping this French name alive in the English-speaking world. Although it's a perfectly fine name, be aware that using it will, at least for the next few decades, tend to align you with Greer's ideology.

GERTRUDE. Gertrude is a very old name that was at the pinnacle of fashion around 1900 but feels heavy as lead today. It might be tempting to dismiss Gertrude as a name on its way through the door marked OUT FOREVER except that its long and honorable pedigree—it's a saint's name (the gentle and mystical St. Gertrude the Great), was also borne by one of the Norse Valkyries and used by Shakespeare in *Hamlet*—earns it a place on the permanent roster. And who knows? Our own parents considered names like Anna and Sophie and Sam and Max too dowdy and old-fashioned ever to be considered again, and yet today they've reached the heights of chic. Perhaps the parents of today will have grandchildren named Gertrude and GUSTAVE. And we must admit, the nickname GERTIE did sound kind of cute when worn by the young and innocent Drew Barrymore in *E.T.* GERDA, really an unrelated Norse name that is nevertheless sometimes used as a short form of Gertrude, takes its sole charm from the young heroine of Hans Christian Andersen's *The Snow Queen.* A shortened form of Gertrude is TRUDY.

GIGI. Gigi, like Mimi and BEBE, COCO and Fifi, have a lot of spunk but not much substance. In Colette's novel, later made into an exuberant movie musical, it is explained that Gigi is short for GILBERTE.

GILA. Gila and its many variants all have meanings that convey joy in Hebrew. Alternatives include GEELA, GILANA, GILAT, GILIA, GILADA, and GILI.

GILDA. Gilda, like other gilt and golden names GOLDA (as in Meir) and GOLDIE (Hawn), has definitely tarnished. It once shimmered with the seductive image of Rita Hayworth in the torrid film *Gilda*, then was associated with the beloved *Saturday Night Live* star Gilda Radner. In opera it lives on as the name of the daughter of Rigoletto.

GILLIAN. In medieval England, the name Gillian was so common that it was used as a generic term for a girl, just as Jack was used for a boy: hence the nursery rhyme, Jack and J(G)ill, and the expression, "Every Jack has his Jill." But although not unknown over here, GILLIAN—like clotted cream and Yorkshire pudding—has never truly crossed the ocean and remains rooted in the American mind as quintessentially British. This is something we hope will change, and offer up the alternate spelling JILLIAN (the one used by Vanessa Williams for her daughter) to make the pronunciation process easier. Variations include GILIANA, GILLIE, and JILLY—à la the superfamous (there, at least) English pulp novelist Jilly Cooper. James Joyce named a character GILLIA.

GINA. Originally a nickname for GEORGINA or Regina, Gina has been used on its own since the twenties. The hot Italian actress Gina Lollobridgida popularized the name in the 1950s, and Oscar winner Geena Davis provides a modern role model and spelling alternative. But as a nickname name, Gina has never quite grown up and seems, somehow, like only half a name. The unrelated Hebrew name Gina, while identical in spelling and pronunciation, is somewhat a different story. It means "garden," and would be a good name for bridging cultures and ethnic backgrounds.

GISELLE. This French form of the German GISELA (hard *G*), has a fluid, graceful aspect both through its association with the ballet (pronounced Jiz-elle) and similarity to the word gazelle.

GLADYS. Hard to believe, but Gladys was the Ashley of 1900, emerging from nowhere to take the naming world by storm and becoming a favorite among parents for several decades. A Welsh form of Claudia, Gladys was seen, in its heyday, as an exotic and romantic name. Today, it's so far-out we wonder whether even a single child has been given the name in the past decade.

GLENDA. Glenda, along with GLENYS and GLYNIS, all derive from the same Welsh root and seem rooted, themselves, in the thirties and forties. Several British actresses, including Glenda Jackson and South African-born Glynis Johns, have transported their names across the Atlantic (and there's a soap opera Glynnis on *Days of Our Lives*), though American children will undoubtedly be more familiar with the similar but different Good Witch GLINDA from *The Wizard of Oz*. As a group, all these names, plus GLENNA, seem outmoded for a modern American baby, though GLEN or GLENN—the related male name—has some modern feminine punch via actress Glenn Close.

GLORIA. Playwright George Bernard Shaw was the first to use this form of the ancient Latin name GLORIOSA in his play *You Never Can*

Tell. From Shaw's invention in 1898 through the first half of the twentieth century, Gloria was seen as a modish and exotic name; now, however, it feels dated, except maybe if you're watching a Gloria Estefan video. It has also been associated over the years with silent screen star Gloria (*Sunset Boulevard*) Swanson, socialite-designer Gloria Vanderbilt, feminist leader Gloria Steinem, and *All in the Family* daughter, Gloria Bunker Stivik. GLORIANA, the form used by poets for Queen Elizabeth I, has some mild appeal; GLORVINA is a strange Irish invention; and GLORY, if overly ambitious, at least sounds like someone under fifty.

GRACE. One of the simplest, purest, and most luminous of names, Grace existed as GRACIA in the Middle Ages but was not in common use until the Puritans adopted it, along with other Christian-attribute names, in the sixteenth century. Embraced for its virtuous image by Americans of the Victorian era, it was the eleventh most popular name in the country in 1875. Now, after a long latent period, Grace has begun a quiet reascendance with parents looking again for upright, durable classic names, no doubt influenced by the majestic Grace Kelly, Princess of Monaco, who conferred an additional measure of class and beauty on the name. Of late there have been a variety of other images attached to it: the cool Grace Van Owen on *L.A. Law*, the outrageous singers Grace Slick and Grace Jones, and the outspoken protagonist of *Grace Under Fire* on television. Meryl Streep chose the name for her first child. Grace has always been particularly popular in Ireland, where more authentic forms like GRAINNE and its phonetic version GRANIA are also used. One of the great heroines of Irish legend, Grainne/Grania—which means "love"—was engaged to the famous chieftain Finn Mac Cool until she fell in love with his nephew. Grania is certainly worthy of consideration by parents looking for an offbeat, authentic Gaelic name. The nickname GRACIE, used by Rhea Perlman and Danny DeVito for their daughter Grace, comes in handy should your little one be less Grace Kelly and more Gracie ("Say goodnight, Gracie") Allen.

GREER. Actress Greer Garson made this name famous in the forties, it being the family name of her Irish mother. Today, it still has some life because of the popularity of androgynous surname names—Jordan, Morgan, ARDEN—for girls.

GRETA, GRETCHEN. The German pet forms of Margaret—Greta and Gretchen, as well as GRETEL—have all been used by American parents who want a somewhat-but-not-too-ethnic name for their daughters. Of the three, Gretchen is the most Americanized; Greta is still tied too closely to Garbo—although Kevin Kline and wife Phoebe Cates have recently appropriated it for their daughter, Greta Simone; and Gretel still seems to be out strewing crumbs in the forest with brother Hansel.

GUINEVERE. The name of King Arthur's beautiful but unfaithful queen, is used now only by Round Table enthusiasts, having long been supplanted by its modern form, Jennifer. GWENIFER is a Welsh compromise.

GWENDOLEN. Decades ago, Gwendolen, an ancient Welsh name, retired in favor of its more modern sounding short form, GWEN, but now, as it is all across the naming board, the nickname has disappeared and the more distinguished original is being reappraised. Gwendolen means "white circle," probably alluding to an ancient moon goddess, and appears frequently in Welsh as well as in English legend, where one GUENDOLEN [sic] was a fairy with whom King Arthur fell in love, and another was the wife of the wizard Merlin. Later the name appeared as one of the principal characters in Oscar Wilde's 1895 *The Importance of Being Earnest*, and in 1950 GWENDOLYN (probably the more common spelling in this country) Brooks became the first African-American woman to win a Pulitzer prize for poetry.

GWYNETH. Another Welsh name—also used as GWENYTH and GWENETH and abbreviated to GWYNNE (GWYN is primarily a male name)—this mellifluous appellation means "blessed" or "happy," and is definitely becoming more and more appreciated by American parents. Its media appearances have included a character on the soap, *Loving*. Onetime Walton Richard Thomas chose the name for a third of his set of triplets, and actress Blythe Danner picked it for her daughter, actress Gwyneth Paltrow.

H

HADASSAH. This Hebrew form of Esther is well used in Israel but shunned by nonorthodox Jewish parents here, no doubt because its association with the Jewish women's philanthropic organization gives it a hyper-religious feel—something like, if you're a Catholic, naming your daughter Mary Immaculata. Too bad, because removed from that context it's a pleasant, if weighty, name with a significant history.

HALIMA. A Swahili and Muslim name popular in Egypt and Somalia, Halima was the prophet Mohammad's nurse. A pretty and sound choice for the parent who wants an African or Muslim name. Alternate spelling: HALIMAH.

HANNAH. Hannah is one of those hares of a name, zooming from the hind ranks to the forefront of favor in the space of a few years, starting not long after the release of Woody Allen's *Hannah and Her Sisters*. Not that we think Hannah is any nine days' wonder. Hannah is a classic, with Old Testament roots and a stylish background both in Georgian England and the pioneer West. Its appeal may be perceived as traditional or homey, aristocratic or down-to-earth. As Hannah, HANNA, or HANA, it relates to many different cultures, from Hebrew to Arabic, European to Asian. And it provided a new twist to Anna/Annie which had become a bit overused. But now Hannah has become popular to the point of trendiness—inevitable, we fear, when a name leaps from obscurity to the Top 25 in a year or two. Now the third most popular baby name in Britain and number nine in the state of Oregon, it has appealed to such celebrity parents as Jessica Lange and Sam Shepard, Mel Gibson, Tom Selleck, and Elizabeth Perkins. Hannah is also the name of the first *Beverly Hills 90210* baby. So although Hannah is a wonderful name, consider yourself warned.

HARRIET. See Henrietta.

HASSIBA. A Muslim name popular in North Africa and the name of a runner, Hassiba Boulmerka, who won Algeria's first Olympic gold medal. Hassiba sounds similar to another popular North African Muslim girls' name, HABIBA.

HAYLEY, HALEY. This name was born with Hayley Mills, whose mother's middle name became her first. But one of the most interesting things about the boom name Hayley is that its stardom did not coincide with its originator's. Rather, the name didn't truly become popular until the 1980s, when Hayley Mills's contemporaries and childhood fans began having children of their own. Today, like a latter-day Wendy, the name has become so widespread as to have escaped its original connection. In fact, the more direct Haley is now the favored spelling, though variations from the reasonable HAILEY and HALLIE to the outlandish HAYLEE and HAILEIGH abound. And while we liked the original Hayley as much as the next baby boomer, and still can appreciate its breezy, androgynous-but-not-pretentious charm, we find Haley to be a name that's too thoroughly of the moment: a Hazel, perhaps even an Ethel of tomorrow.

HAZEL. Hazel has a double image. It has a kind of pleasantly hazy, brownish green-eyed feel, which is combined with—or contradicted by—an opinionated, gray-haired *Hazel the Maid* cartoon. One of the botanical names that were all the rage around the turn of the twentieth century, Hazel then quickly fell out of favor, and has hardly been heard of since. But though it seems so musty as to be nearly moribund, there's something about the name that could conceivably restore it to favor among parents with a taste for the offbeat. It's got that irreverent Mabel, Mamie, MAE, Daisy kind of tone that reminds us of spring, and renewal.

HEATHER. Where Hazel is hidden beneath thick bushes, damned, perhaps, to permanent obscurity, Heather lies trampled underfoot, the victim of too much attention. The name's chronic popularity was celebrated in the movie *Heathers*, in which every girl (including Shannen Doherty) in its snotty high school in-group was named Heather, while rebel Winona Ryder was a Veronica. Heather has been a very popular name since the seventies. It is a pretty name—all those Scottish moor implications—but, even though Heather Locklear has taken over *Melrose Place*, it's beginning to feel as dusty as a bouquet of dried flowers.

HEDDA, HEDY. As far back as we can remember, Hedda has been the basis of cruel-joke names, like Hedda Hare (yes, there are parents who really do that), as well as a card-carrying member of a category of slightly bohemian, big city names such as NEDDA, CHARNIA, and ANDRA. It does have two strong associations: the heroine of the Ibsen play *Hedda Gabler* and the crazy-hatted Hollywood gossip, Hedda Hopper (born with something close to one of those above-mentioned cruel names: Edda Furry). Hedy, although associated with one of the most exquisite creatures ever to appear on the screen, Hedy Lamarr, is a name that has never appealed much to Americans, but not as little as her full German name, HEDWIG.

HEIDI. Despite decades of American Heidis of every size, shape, coloring, even age, the name somehow seems permanently tethered to that little girl on the Alpine mountaintop whose story was first published in 1881. It's a Swiss nickname for the unmanageable German name of ADELHEIDE.

HELEN, HELENA. Helen has been a name that has connoted female beauty since ancient times, when, in classic mythology, Helen, ravishing daughter of Zeus and Leda and then-wife of the king of Sparta, ignited a ten-year war because Trojan prince Paris just had to have her. She had, as Christopher Marlowe later wrote, "the face that launched a thousand ships." The name's popularity in England was due to the fourth-century St. Helen(a), mother of Constantine the Great, and soon took on a variety of forms, moving from ELENA to Elaine to Ellen. Over more recent centuries, it's gone in and out of favor both in the United States and Britain, often alternating with Ellen. Helen was in during the seventeenth century in England, for instance, while Ellen predominated in the eighteenth and nineteenth. In the first half of the 1900s in the United States, Helen was the winner, then in the fifties

Ellen again captured center stage. Now both are out of favor in America, though Helen is somewhat stylish in Britain. We believe Helen is a name that will come back here, too, and parents confident enough to take on its now-dowdy image will be rewarded, down the road, for their foresight. Helena is more delicate and dainty, a favorite of Shakespeare, who used it in *All's Well That Ends Well* and *A Midsummer Night's Dream*. The porcelain-skinned British star Helena Bonham Carter has done much for the name's image—helping to make it the preferred choice for those who find Helen too colorless. Beware, however, HELENE and HELAINE, which seem fussy and dated. Eastern European variants include JELENA, JELINKA, and ILONA; Lena, originally a pet form, is now used in its own right, as are other offshoots Elaine, Ellen, Leonora, Eleanor, Nell, NELLIE, Eileen, and ELENA.

HELOISE. This somewhat pretentious-sounding French version of Eloise was borne by the beloved of Abelard—considered to be one of the most learned women of the Middle Ages—and, more recently, by a prolific purveyor of household hints.

HENRIETTA, HARRIET. This is one of the few instances where we are of two minds. The member of our team who spent a recent extended sojourn in London sees these names as charmingly offbeat and loves them both unabashedly, while the other of us still sees them as fusty old maiden aunts in black galoshes and clear-plastic rainhats. The bottom line: These are names unlikely to inspire neutrality in *anyone*. If you choose either of them for your child, be prepared for years of double takes or downright disapproval. The two go together because Harriet emerged as a short form of Henrietta, which is a feminization of Harry's proper form, Henry. Henrietta has the advantage—if you see it that way—of being a name with a well-padded royal pedigree, while Harriet is more literary (Harriet Beecher Stowe, author of *Uncle Tom's Cabin*) and historic (Harriet Tubman, the former slave who led more than three hundred others to freedom on the underground railroad, and was called the Moses of her people), also becoming half of that fifties and sixties happy-family icon, *Ozzie and Harriet*. HENRIETTE is the unusual French form of Henrietta: HETTY, ETTA, HENNY, and even HENRY and HANK are nicknames. Harriet variations include HARRIETT, HARRIETTE, HARRIOT, HARRIETTA, HATTY, HATTIE, and HATSY.

HERMIONE. This Greek name of the mythic daughter of Helen of Troy might be completely extinct were it not for Shakespeare (*The Winter's Tale*) and the British actress Hermione Gingold. In any case, it's hardly ever been heard in this country and we doubt it ever will be.

HESTER. A truly unpleasant-sounding name, almost on the level of HEPZIBAH, this variant of Esther was borne by the persecuted heroine of Hawthorne's *The Scarlet Letter*.

HILARY, HILLARY. Since we are now living in a Hillary era, the name having become as single-celebrity linked as Madonna, it is difficult to be objective about it: Most people's opinion of the name will be colored by their opinion of the person. In truth, Hilary might have continued its century-long life as a somewhat-obscure, upper-crusty girls' name had it not been for the emergence of Hillary (she uses the variant spelling) Rodham Clinton, the first First Lady with a really contemporary-sounding name, in sharp contrast to predecessors Nancy and Barbara. Originally a boys' name (though there was a famous female St. HILARIA in the fifth century), Hilary as a name has a lot going for it. It has the rhythmic three-syllable structure so popular at present, it is strong but light, proper yet jaunty, and has an irresistible meaning, deriving from the same root as hilarious. Its biggest problem may be that, with Mme Clinton's fame, it will become too popular too quickly and lose its distinctiveness.

HILDEGARDE, HILDA. Hildegarde is one of those unfortunate names that have become synonymous with a heavy, plodding, cartoon-Teutonic stodginess, as well as an overdressed (never without long white gloves) pianist and singer of the forties. While HILDA (the name of one of the Valkyrie of Teutonic legend) and HILDY may pick up the pace and lighten the feeling a bit, we don't think you would really want to hang any of these iron ID tags on your modern American child.

HOLLY. Holly enjoyed a surge of popularity in the sixties—inspired, perhaps, by the madcap Holly Golightly of Truman Capote's *Breakfast at Tiffany's*, portrayed on screen by Audrey Hepburn. It does continue to be used today, although by no means could you call it trendy, or even fashionable, while in England, for some reason, the name is positively hot at the moment. Always favored for children born around Christmas, and frequently used on soap operas, it was recently in the spotlight when Holly Hunter won her Academy Award. Parents wishing to put an androgynous eighties spin on Holly could consider transforming it into the surname name HOLLIS.

HONOR. This virtue name, heard less often than Faith or Hope, might be a little harder for a child to handle, just because it is not immediately recognized as a name. But it is so strong and true it may be worth the trouble. In ancient Rome, it was originally HONORIA, though that form and the equally interesting Norman version HONORA, have all but died out except in Ireland where they are fairly common. The Irish have also turned the name into ANNORA, before long shortened to Nora. While all these variations have merit, we like the undiluted English version—Honor—the best.

HOPE. Hope is another sublime virtue name, this one popularized beyond its sisters in recent years via the saintly Hope Steadman of *thirtysomething*. But a little media focus is only a positive in this case: Hope (used by the Puritans for both boys and girls) is too high-minded—if we don't have hope, what have we?—to be corrupted, and is such a lovely classic name that it deserves all the attention it gets.

HORTENSE. No!

HUNTER. This name is a real comer for girls—it could well be the Taylor of tomorrow. And once more there has been a soap opera activator, this time a high-profile actress (and model), Hunter Tylo, who plays a character called—you guessed it—Taylor on *The Bold and the Beautiful*. Like Taylor before it, Hunter sounds cool and cutting edge for a girl, but, as with Taylor, this may not be for long.

〰〰〰〰〰〰〰〰〰〰〰 ◉ 〰〰〰〰〰〰〰〰〰〰〰

IANTHE. A romantic Greek name used by the poet Shelley for his daughter. Ethereal and unusual, Ianthe was in Greek myth the daughter of Oceanus, supreme ruler of the sea and of cosmic power.

IDA. A hundred years ago, Ida was considered "sweet as apple cider," and was number ten on the hit parade of girls' names. Its popularity then was prompted by the Gilbert and Sullivan operetta, *Princess Ida*, and perhaps vaguer associations with Mount Ida, where Zeus was supposed to have been raised in Crete, but neither of those means enough today to give the name any chance of returning.

ILANA, ILIANA, ILONA. Ilana (also spelled ELANA) is an Israeli name that means "oak tree," and is therefore sometimes chosen for little girls born on the holiday of Tu b'Shvat, the New Year of the Trees. The more melodious Iliana (or ILEANA) and Ilona are both Hungarian forms of Helen, and mean "bright one."

ILSA. Ilsa is the radiant but tragic heroine of *Casablanca*, portrayed by Ingrid Bergman. But she also was Ilsa, she-wolf of the S.S.

IMAN. A Somali and Muslim name that means "faith," Iman is one of the best-known African names in this country because of the famous Somalian model and wife of David Bowie. A similar-sounding African name, IMANA, is the name of the supreme god of the Batutsi of Rwanda and Burundi.

IMARA. This Kiswahili word meaning "firm" could make a hauntingly evocative first name. As an ethnic name for an American child, it strikes the perfect balance of the exotic and the familiar.

IMOGEN. This name, which originated as a Shakespearean misprint for INNOGEN, is one of the sizable group that is highly fashionable in Britain but rarely used here. Perhaps that's because we associate it with the daffy comedian Imogene (pronounced Imo-jean) Coca. More correctly the name is pronounced Imo-jen, and is a choice that's as pretty and classy as it is unusual. It was used by Shakespeare for a charming and impetuous character in one of his last plays, *Cymbeline*, was the name of one of our most noted female photographers, Imogen Cunningham, and was chosen for his daughter by mega-musical-hit-producer Andrew Lloyd Webber.

INDIA. India has decades more history as a name than most of the atlas-full of place-names that are all the rage today. The British aristocracy used it during the years of the Raj, and Americans adopted it after the character India Wilkes in *Gone with the Wind*, which was a catalyst for almost every name it contained. As a name, India is both exotic and euphonious, fashionable but with more depth than the blow-away INDIANAS and MONTANAS newer to the map. It was used for the protagonist of the novel *Mrs. Bridge*, and chosen for their daughters by such diverse celebrities as actors Catherine Oxenberg and Phillip Michael Thomas, as well as successful guru Marianne Williamson.

INDRA. Indra is the name of the chief god of the early Hindu religion, also the god of rain and thunder, while INDRE, pronounced the same way, is a river in France. Occasionally heard as a name for girls in England, Indra might be worth considering if you have a strong taste for the exotic.

INGRID. Ingrid Bergman's allure was strong enough to lend universal appeal to this classic Scandinavian name, and parents with Nordic roots may want to consider it. It's a usable feminine form of the name of the god Ing—ruler of fertility and crops, peace and prosperity. But other variations—INGA, INGER, INGEBORG—remain permanently tied to the Old Country despite brief visits here.

IOLA, IOLE. Iole was the name of a princess with whom Hercules fell in love in Greek mythology. Iola was an obnoxious character on *Mama's Family*. No question which of the two has more potential.

IONA, IONE. Another pair of similar but different names, both of which are being used with increasing stylishness as first names in Britain. Iona is a tiny Scottish island in the Hebrides, while Ione, a Greek flower name for violet, has gained attention because of the young actress Ione Skye, daughter of the "Mellow Yellow" pop singer Donovan.

IRENE. There is a tendency for Irene to be lumped in with the jumble of *-een/ene* names so popular from the twenties through the fifties, Maureen, Arlene, et al., but it has a more classic pedigree. One of the most popular names of the Roman Empire and the name of an ancient saint, this originally Greek name (representing the Greek goddess of peace) has spawned variations throughout the cultures of Europe, where it usually has a three-syllable pronunciation. A lot of its British usage derived from the character of Irene (pronounced with three syllables) in Galsworthy's *The Forsyte Saga*, while Americans identified it with the sparkling Irene Dunne of Hollywood's golden age. But although it was found among the United States Top 50 in 1900, Irene definitely seems faded and flimsy today. Eastern European versions such as IRINA (one of Chekhov's *Three Sisters*) and IRENA sound a bit fresher.

IRIS. Around the turn of the last century, Iris was lucky enough to be caught in the updraft caused by two simultaneous fads—those for flower names and for classical names ending in an *s* sound. But although many of the flower names are returning, Iris seems terminally wilted. And it has such a colorful history, too. In Greek mythology, Iris was the goddess of the rainbow, a messenger for Zeus and Hera who rode the rainbow as a multicolored bridge from heaven to earth, which makes it a logical name for both the brightly hued flower and the colored part of the eye.

IRMA. There was an old show called *My Friend Irma*, but unfortunately, most of Irma's friends by now have senior-citizen passes to the movies, and have retired along with the name.

ISABEL, ISABELLE, ISABELLA. Eavesdrop at a play group in SoHo or Santa Monica tomorrow and we'll lay odds that you'll hear at least one version of this so-hot-it's-afire name. A venerable Spanish and Portuguese variation of Elizabeth (it went from Elizabeth to ILSABETH to ISABEAU to Isabelle), Isabella is known to every school child as the name of the Queen of Castile who helped finance Christopher Columbus's expedition to the New World. And since then it has had an incredibly rich history as a royal name, a literary name (Shakespeare's *Measure for Measure* and *Henry V*, a narrative poem by Keats, novels by Jane Austen and Henry James), even a soap opera (*Loving*), and star-baby (chosen by Tom Cruise and Nicole Kidman, Geraldo Rivera, and Jeff Bridges) name. But despite its burgeoning popularity, we still can't restrain ourselves from recommending it, because it is simply one of the most enduringly beautiful names we know. It's got some pretty terrific nicknames and foreign variations too: IZZY, IBBY, BELLE, and BELLA; the Gaelic ISHBEL and the Scottish ISOBEL, and the Old French ISABEAU (the name of Michelle Pfeiffer's character in *Ladyhawke*).

ISADORA. Most people still relate this name to Isadora Duncan, the arty early modern dancer who was done in by her long flowing scarf, which gives it a slightly absurdist image. But putting that aside, the name has quite a lot going for it, namely a pleasant sound and its relation to ISIS, the mythological goddess of fertility and birth who guarded the Nile River. According to ancient Egyptian texts, Isis was a Black woman, which may make this name appealing to African-American parents. Isadora Wing was the heroine of Erica Jong's *Fear of Flying*. Variations include ISIDORA and IDORA.

ISOLDE. Isolde was a beautiful Irish princess of medieval legend and the tragic lover of Tristram in Arthurian romance—and immortalized in a Wagner opera. Unfortunately, the image of the mythical ISEULT, is a lot more attractive than the name itself, which is also found as ISOLDA, YSOLDE, and YSEULT.

IVORY. A name that, along with its converse, Ebony, is currently very strong with African-American parents—sometimes because of its relation to the Ivory Coast, sometimes because of its association to the African precious material, and sometimes simply because it's a pleasing and fashionable name. Ivory has been used as a girls' name for about a century, but in the last couple of years has really taken off, sometimes reaching the Top 10 on lists of Black names, and being featured on the soap opera, *Days of Our Lives*.

IVY. Many might consider Ivy to be prohibitively old-fashioned, but we prefer to see it as offbeat, kinetic, energetic, and perfectly adaptable to the modern world. Possible drawback? Lots of Poison Ivy jokes.

J

〰〰〰〰〰〰〰〰〰〰〰〰 ◉ 〰〰〰〰〰〰〰〰〰〰〰〰

JACQUELINE. Although this is a centuries-old French name, to most Americans it represents the Kennedy era, the years of a cultural Camelot. The name was imported into England by a French sister-in-law of Henry V (she was known as Dame Jack) and was well used in this country by the twenties. By now, the name has lost most of its glamorous image, and even its Gallic gloss. Parents looking for a fresher French image might consider such names as AMALIE, FABIENNE, or ELODIE. This is one of those names with more spellings than you can shake a pillbox hat at, but JACQUELYN is the only acceptable alternative.

JADE. This is the most modern of all the jewel names, projecting a contemporary polish lacking in all the others. Of course its glamorous image was only enhanced by the fact that it was chosen by Mick and Bianca Jagger for their daughter, now with a trend-setting little daughter of her own: ASSISI. Jade is also currently appearing on two different soap operas, on one of them as the name of an Asian character.

JAEL. Pronounced Yah-el, this attractive Old Testament name is often heard in Israel. YAEL is an alternate version.

JALEESA, JALISA. Currently on the list of Top 50 names chosen by African-Americans, this name, like several others—Kadeem, Jasmine, WHITLEY—was given a substantial boost by the names of cast and characters on the television show *A Different World*.

JAMIE. Jamie is one of the prototypical ambisexual nickname names that were the epitome of cool in the sixties, after decades of Jeans, Joans, Joannes, and Janets. The Scottish diminutive for James, Jamie is one of the few names that managed to become popular for girls while remaining well used for boys. JAIME is a common alternative (and the one used, for some reason, as the name of *The Bionic Woman*), though Spanish students know that's correctly pronounced Hy-mee. On current TV, Jamie is visible as the lead character on *Mad About You*—whose nickname is James. The traditional feminine form of James, JAMESINA, sounds better these days now that more formal and elaborate feminizations—Josephine, Augusta, Cornelia—have become fashionable, but we prefer the more substantial JAMESON. Another new direction: adopting the conventional masculine name itself. A girl named JAMES? Sounds good to us.

JANE. We don't think Jane is plain. In fact, for a venerable and brief one-syllable name, we think it packs a surprising amount of punch, as compared to others like Jean and Joan. A very old name, Jane has been around since Tudor times: Just as in our day Jessica replaced Jennifer, so did Jane come in to replace Joan. In this country it has moved in and out of fashion and now seems to be making a comeback. It's got that unpretentious brand of honesty so prized these days— think of other stylish and direct names like Anna, Ben, Sam—plus a strong grounding in history. And there are all those great Janes of the past: Eyre, Austen, Grey—even JAYNE Mansfield (born Vera) contributed something to popular culture when she came up with a new spelling of the name.

JANET. It started as a pet form of Jane, but Janet has long been a name in its own right. Five hundred years ago Janet was a royal favorite in Scotland, where it remains a popular name. Here, however, Janet's been on a downhill slide since the sixties, and we see no signs of a turnaround, its general image at present matched more to Janet Reno's than Janet Jackson's. Also deep in fashion limbo are most other Janet and Jane variations: JAN, JANICE, JANIS, JANETTE, JANA, JANNA, and JANINE (despite the very modern magnetism of *Northern Exposure* star Janine Turner). If you are interested in translating Janet into your ethnic heritage, you could consider Sheena (Scottish) or Sinead (Irish).

JASMINE. The aromatic Jasmine, evocative of the delicate and fragrant bloom, was first used here as a girls' name around 1900, during the blossoming of floral-name fashion, and then was rarely spotted until a few years ago, when two powerful forces combined to bring it back. The first was the popularity of the attractive Black actress Jasmine Guy, in television and then film, after which Disney's Princess Jasmine exploded onto the scene in the movie *Aladdin*. While names popularized by film characters—cartoon ones, no less—are usually flimsy and faddish, we believe Jasmine is one of the rare exceptions. The French version of the Arabic YASMIN, it's a lush and exotic beauty, already appearing on some popularity lists. In both California and Pennsylvania, Jasmine was the top name for African-American girls born in 1993 and it has just broken into the national Top 20. Basketball great Julius Irving was ahead of the pack when he gave the name to his daughter, spelling it JAZMIN; JAZMINE is another common spelling variation. If you feel that Jasmine's associations are too loaded, you might want to go with Yasmine or YASMINA. Or, perhaps even more appealing, consider early versions of the name now used independently in Britain but rarely heard here: JESSAMINE, JESSAMYN, JESSAMY.

JAY. One of the boys' names newly appropriate for girls, Jay—or JAYE, as spelled by androgynous star Davidson—may be used on its own or as a nickname for any *J* name or as a distinctive middle name.

JEAN. Like sisters Janet and Joan, Jean has been falling from grace for nearly half a century now: There are many grandmas and even mothers carrying the name, but almost no babies. Not that lots of men haven't dreamed of JEANNIE—first there was the Stephen Foster song of that name, then the TV series, and somewhere in-between there was the ultimate symbol of Hollywood glamour, Jean (born Harlean) Harlow. Originally a feminine of John, Jean was popular in Scotland long before it found favor in the world at large. The French form is JEANNE; variations JEANETTE, JEANNETTE, JEANINE, and JEANIE have all followed Jean down the slide and out of sight.

JEMIMA. Jemima is a name we'd love to liberate. Chained in this country to the stereotypical smiling Aunt of pancake fame, in England Jemima is the most chic of aristocratic favorites, bestowed fashionably upon young ladies who are brought up to read Beatrix Potter's *Jemima Puddleduck* and later go on to marry St. Johns and Sebastians. It's time we, too, focused on Jemima's illustrious classic roots. In the Old Testament, Jemima was one of the three daughters of Job, a trio so strong and beautiful that Job treated them as sons in his will. JEMIMAH is a variation; JEM, JEMMY, and even JEMMA can be used as nicknames.

JENNIFER. When we called our earlier book *Beyond Jennifer & Jason*, it was because Jennifer had already become, in the late eighties, the embodiment of the overly trendy name. It was an overnight success in the early seventies, and it's still easy to see why Jennifer was able to hold on as the most popular girls' name for more than a decade: It was one of the first names with the sentimentally feminine Victorian flavor that would dominate the eighties, and it came with the ready-made ideal nickname for everyday use. It was replaced by the similar-sounding Jessica, but at this point most parents are tired of the pair, eschewing them in favor of fresher alternatives. One of these is JENNA, a modern variation on the name that is, at least, a bit newer and not such a cliché. The most intrepid of parents could also consider the name's Welsh original: Guinevere.

JENNY. Jenny has become a perennial favorite. Like Molly and Maggie, it's both a long-popular nickname and an established independent name in its own right. Long before Jennifer became the nom de l'age, Jenny was a fashionable nickname for Jane and Janet and even Jean, and, spelled JENNIE, was in the Top 20 names of 1875. Despite its origins as a diminutive, Jenny has more character, in many ways, than Jennifer.

JERSEY. An established feminine place-name that carries a lot more class when you attach it to the British island than to the overpopulated Garden State.

JESSICA. Jessica was Jennifer's somewhat unlikely successor at the top of the popularity lists. True, it began with the letter *J*, had three syllables and an old-time feel. But Jessica is a more classic name than Jennifer and, more important, one that's long been associated with Judaism, first in the Old Testament and later as the name of Shylock's daughter in Shakespeare's *The Merchant of Venice*. Still, in the mid to late eighties, lots of parents of all ethnic backgrounds flocked to the name Jessica. As we write, it is still the second-most popular girls' name in America, but names like Kayla and Kelsey and Chelsea are coming up fast behind, ready to dethrone it. Nicknames JESS and JESSIE have held mass appeal in tandem with Jessica, sometimes on their own. Parents whose sole interest is in arriving at the nickname Jessie should know it was first used as a Scottish diminutive of Janet in the eighteenth century and has also been used over the years as the short form for names ranging from Josephine to Jocelyn. The abbreviation JESSA, or the British JESSAMINE, or JESSAMYN, or JESSAMY—variants of Jasmine—would make fresher substitutes for Jessica.

JEZEBEL. Like Desirée, this name gets an *R* rating: not suitable for children.

JILL. Perhaps it's because of its nursery-rhyme associations (check also under Gillian), but Jill has the air of a perpetual, rosy-cheeked child. In fact, Jill is one of the oldest names going, a medieval Anglo-Saxon variation on the Roman Julia. Knowing that bestows on the name a patina of depth and character, even elegance in its simplicity; otherwise it would feel like a cute but shallow mid-twentieth century invention. It is now most prominent as the real female character on the top-rated *Home Improvement*.

JOAN. Joan has become a middle-aged name, not surprising since it hasn't been used much since the forties. Its first English bearer seems to have been Henry II's daughter, JHONE, but the modern spelling was soon established, which is why St. Jeanne d'Arc was translated as Joan, making her the most famous bearer of the name. By Shakespeare's time, Joan had become so overused that it was ripe for replacement by the newly coined Jane, the reverse of what happened in twentieth-century America. There were lots of JOANIES still around in the fifties and sixties, but we can't imagine anyone giving the name to a baby of today.

JOANNA, JOANNE. Like Diana, Joanna is a clear example of a name that is perfectly fashionable, in an unobtrusive way, right now, but quite unfashionable in its fifties version, Joanne, which took over from Joan and managed to reach fifteenth place on the popularity polls of the day. Joanna is found in the New Testament as one of Jesus' early followers. JO is its sprightly nickname, JOJO even sprightlier. JO-HANNA, we feel, may be a bit affected with its old country *h*. Other "Jo" names that sprang to life in the forties, with the popularity of Joanne: JOELLE, JOLENE, and JOELY, the name of Vanessa Redgrave's daughter, actress Joely Richardson, and of actress Joely Fisher, daughter of Eddie, sister of Carrie.

JOCASTA. A mythological name fashionably used among high-class Brits but mostly ignored here, Jocasta was the mother of Oedipus whom he (oops!) married. Any parent in search of a *J* name that's neither overused nor terminally dated should stop for consideration here.

JOCELYN. Jocelyn never really caught on in this country the way its cousin Joyce (both were originally boys' names) did—a shame, we think, because we find it a much prettier, softer name. The parents of the first female United States Surgeon General managed to combine both names to arrive at Joycelyn Elders. Jocelyn was chosen by director Ron Howard as the name for his daughter, twin sister of Paige.

JODY. Jody, like Jamie, is one of the cute bouncy nickname names so popular in the sixties and seventies, but today as out-of-date as turquoise plastic beanbag chairs. Jodie Foster (born Alicia) has brought some distinction to the alternate spelling, though even the star's strong, intelligent persona has not bolstered that of her name.

JORDAN. As far back as 1925, there was a female character named Jordan Baker in F. Scott Fitzgerald's *The Great Gatsby*. But that was an aberration. It wasn't until sixty years later that the name would take off and become among the most popular and familiar of the ambisexual surname names to rise to prominence in the eighties. At first used almost exclusively for boys, then in equal measure for both sexes, Jordan—like other names of this ilk—is now heavily female-dominated. So while we consider Jordan to be an extremely attractive name, it is certainly too overexposed at this point to offer the distinctiveness most parents are seeking when they investigate androgynous names for their daughters.

JOSEPHINE. Some may find the name Josephine, which harks back to the days of flying machines and Stanley Steamers, too clunky and dated to hold any modern appeal. But while the name is not, admittedly, conventionally pretty, it has tons of class and character and a gently offbeat quality that can count for style. And there are many wonderful and provocative Josephines in the past to look to: Josephine Bonaparte (born Marie Joseph); Jo, the driving force of *Little Women*, and singer-dancer Josephine Baker (born Freda), to name a few. The name has more than its share of vivacious nicknames: JOSIE, the best of the lot, was chosen by actress Brooke Adams for her daughter; others include JO, JOJO, POSEY, FEENY, and FIFI. JOSETTE, a French form, is both less interesting and more downmarket than the original, even in France.

JOY. Joy is a high-pressure name, like BLISS and GLORY and MERRY and others of that ilk, and we personally are not in favor of placing this kind of personality-control name intimidation on a child. Hope would be a safer bet.

JOYCE. A seminal grade-school experience is learning that poet Joyce Kilmer was a boy. A boy named Joyce! The fact is that all Joyces used to be male—until the fourteenth century, at least. Today, of course, Kilmer excepted, there are no boys named Joyce. But there are no girls being named Joyce anymore either.

JUANITA. Juanita is one of the most familiar of the Spanish women's names but has never become assimilated. It's difficult to imagine that anyone would want to use it or JUANA for other than family or cultural reasons.

JUDITH. When this name was at its peak (it was the fourth most popular name of 1940), most JUDYs would have died rather than be called Judith. Perhaps this is why Judith does not seem as outworn as some of its fellow top-rated names of the period—such as Nancy, Carol, and Sharon. And unlike most of those, Judith has a solid biblical background—Judith of Bethulia was the singularly beautiful wife of Esau who delivered her people from the invading Assyrians. The upshot: Judith (but not Judy) just might be ready for a comeback. After all, it was the name of one of the great namers in literary history, William Shakespeare, chose for one of his daughters.

JULIA, JULIE. Julia (especially when given its full three-syllable pronunciation) is one of the loveliest of classic names—elegant and delicate as well as strong. And after having been pushed aside by the more modern sounding, squeaky clean Julie for several decades, Julia is now definitely the preferred choice again, thanks in part to the high-profile Julia Roberts. An Imperial Roman name given to women in the household of a Julius (as in Caesar), and also the name of several early saints, Julia was last well used in America around the turn of the century. Now, just about every form of this name—except Julie— has contemporary appeal: from the Dutch royal JULIANA (what Shelley Long called her daughter) to JULIAN (the boys' name occasionally used for girls) to the lovely Juliet, which is rapidly gaining a vibrant life independent from Romeo.

JULIET. One of the freshest-sounding versions of Julia, Juliet is being rediscovered today as a formal name in its own right—not, as it was a few decades ago, shorted to Julie. Attractive and quirky young actress Juliette Lewis (JULIETTE is the French spelling) is giving the name a new spin. Another version: JULIETTA.

JUNE, JUNO. Of the three spring month names, none has cooled down more than June, seeming to hark back to the days of the supermom of the Cleaver clan, to one of the actresses who played the supermom of the Lassie family clan, and to perky June Allyson (born Ella), who smiled her way through many old MGM musicals. We have a fresh idea to replace it: Juno. This Roman mythological name (Juno was the wife of Jove and queen of heaven) has a lot more bounce due to its jovial O ending, and is familiar because of the Sean O'Casey play, *Juno and the Paycock*.

JUSTINE, JUSTINA. The French name Justine came to the attention of the book-reading public in the late fifties with the publication of the first of Lawrence Durrell's *Alexandria Quartet*, the novel *Justine*. The name continued to be used by creative-type parents for about twenty years, but, with all those Justines now well out of college, it just doesn't seem like a baby name anymore. Justina is a less usual and more interesting twin sister.

K

∿∿∿∿∿∿∿∿∿∿∿∿∿∿∿∿ ◉ ∿∿∿∿∿∿∿∿∿∿∿∿∿∿∿∿

KAI. Kai (rhymes with eye) is most famous as the name of the little boy in the fairy tale "The Snow Queen," but it feels like a name ripe for feminine takeover. Kai is also a Hawaiian place-name (and sometime name-name) meaning "sea."

KAITLYN, KATELYN. See Caitlin.

KALINDI, KALINDA. Of these two exotic Hindu nature names, Kalindi is the original appellation of the Jumna, one of India's seven sacred rivers, and Kalinda—which can be translated as "the sun"—refers to a mythical mountain range.

KAREN. Karen, a sweet, good-girl Danish import, was so popular during the baby boom—Number 10 in 1950, up to third place ten years later—that it's locked firmly into fashion limbo today. Is there any way it can be seen as a fixer-upper? Well, as with many girls' names today, adding an *a* gives a big boost to this name's style quotient. **KARENA** or **KARINA** (another variant might be **CARINA**) sound more au courant than Karen: Karina ranks among the Top 20 Hispanic girls' names in California. Fresher sounding still is **KARENZA**, which is a Karenization of the romantic Cornish name **KERENSA** or **KERENZA**—the best of the lot. **KEREN**—short for the jawbreaker **KERENHAPPUCH**, one of the three daughters of the Old Testament Job—provides another twist, though many people would consider it either an invented name or a mispronunciation of Karen. **KARIN** is the Swedish diminutive of **KATARINA**.

KATE. There is something almost invincible about Kate. It has a strong, no-frills pioneer feel that seems to be impervious to the vicissitudes of naming trends. Not that it hasn't been tested. In fact, counting baby girls whose full given name is Kate or **KATIE** as well as Katherines and KATELYNS—often shortened to Kate—there are *twice* as many girls with that name as with any other in some states! It's easy to understand why Kate enjoys such widespread appeal. Like one of its most famous bearers, Katharine Hepburn, the name Kate is an aristocratic, gutsy, independent, smart, energetic beauty, the kind earlier epitomized by the heroine of *The Taming of the Shrew/Kiss Me Kate*. Kate also straddles the line between two very popular groups of names: the folksy old-fashioned nickname names like Annie and LIZZIE and such Waspy Yuppie favorites as Caroline and Alexandra. While a classic like Kate will never truly be out, parents would be wise to back off from the name because of the sheer volume of little Kates. KADY is an unfortunate variation.

KATHERINE, KATHARINE, KATHRYN. The classic Katherine and Catherine have been playing popularity-leapfrog for centuries, but the two, in terms of image, are not absolutely interchangeable, the *K* version seeming more modern, more forceful, and certainly more stylish in America these days. It is Catherine that has been the saint (for more on this, see Catherine) and saintly heroine, like Catherine Earnshaw in *Wuthering Heights*; Katherine has played the more spirited roles, such as the determined heroine in Shakespeare's *The Taming of the Shrew*. And, while both share the cute CATHY/KATHY nickname, the *K* variations have exclusive rights to the more desirable Kate and Kitty. After Catherine had been far in the lead until the sixties, Katherine pulled out in front, where it remains: *K*s generally outnumber *C*s four to one. But knowing the history of naming, we think the pendulum might just start swinging back in the near future: Catherine is already the preferred version in England. Some celebrity parents have used the Katherine spelling (Maria Shriver and Arnold Schwarzenegger, Martin Short), while Jane Seymour spelled it Katharine as in Hepburn. KATHRYN is a more relaxed spelling popularized by actress Kathryn Grayson (born Zelma) in the forties—not fashionable, but number two.

KATHLEEN. There must be fifty baby girls named Caitlin for every one called Kathleen these days, but in a sense they are really the same name, Kathleen being the anglicized phonetic spelling of the Irish Gaelic Caitlin and the most usual form of the name in Ireland itself.

Surprising as this may sound, we, at this point, slightly prefer the discarded Kathleen to its supertrendy sister, and think that using the name in its full formal version gives it a freshness it long ago outlived when almost universally abbreviated to KATHY. CATHLEEN is an acceptable spelling variant. Be warned, however: You can get away with alternative KATHLYN only if you're Warren Beatty and your mother's name was spelled that way.

KATRINA. With its distinctly exotic feel, Katrina is the generic form of many European variations of Katherine, from the Gaelic CATRIONA to the German KATARINA (familiar via ice-skating champion Witt), to the Italian CATERINA. Popular all over Europe as well as among African-Americans, the name can also be spelled CATRINA, changed to KATRINE, or shortened to TRINA or KAT. A more decorative, perhaps too tinkly version, is KATINKA.

KAY. Kay seems rooted in the 1930s: It's a name that wears bias-cut satin evening gowns and fox jackets and goes to nightclubs where there are miniature lamps on each table and everybody smokes. Parents in search of a fresh, more cosmopolitan alternative to Kate might do well to begin looking here.

KAYLA. Kayla is the archetypal dark horse name that galloped from nowhere—it isn't even mentioned in one of the most authoritative name dictionaries, published in 1983—to assume a place among the Top 10 names for girls today. How does a name get so popular so fast? In Kayla's case, a starring role on the soap opera *Days of Our Lives* starting in 1982 gave it widespread attention among a largely female audience, who were attracted to the gentle quality of the Kayla character. By the late eighties, thousands of parents were flocking to the name because it seemed to be fresh, unusual, and distinctive—which it was, for about two minutes. At this point Kayla is, obviously, a must to avoid for any parent who wants to make a truly individual choice. But if, on the other hand, it's a name that you love so much you simply must have it, rest assured that children like having popular names and that Kayla, despite its widespread use, still has a creative and charming flavor. KAILA is also a Yiddish name.

KELLY. It seems as though every beautiful blonde teenager on television is named Kelly, on every show from *Beverly Hills 90210* to *Married . . . with Children*—which is hardly anything new. There was a Kelly way back on *Bachelor Father* (1957) and a *Charlie's Angels* Kelly in 1976. So, obviously, Kelly can't be anyone's idea of a fashionable name anymore, but it will go down in baby name history as one of the seminal Irish surname names so popular today. Parents attracted to the sound and feel of Kelly but who want something more modern and distinctive should bypass Kelsey—already the Kelly of this era—and consider KILLIAN, KENNEDY, CALLAHAN, CLANCY, CONNELLY, or QUINLAN. Another is KIRBY, one of the more inventive names introduced on *Dynasty*.

KELSEY. The first time we heard the girls' name Kelsey was when *L.A. Law*'s fictional attorney Ann Kelsey followed the practice of many mid-eighties feminist working mothers and used her maiden name as a first name for her baby daughter. In a heart-wrenching episode, the character had to return the adopted Kelsey to her birth mother, but the name stuck around. Reinforced by additional attention on the requisite soap opera (this time *Another World*), Kelsey is now in the national number twenty and rising, satisfying the baby namers' appetite for ambisexual names, as well as for cuteness. But fresh and new? Not, alas, anymore.

KENDALL. We think Kendall may be next in the line of names to be propelled by TV onto the charts, following in the fresh footsteps of Kayla and Kelsey. Kendall, the name of a young character on *All My Children*, is a quieter and more composed name than the others, with a more nineties feel. Another name in the same family, KENDRA, has begun to appear on Black popularity charts, as has the geographical favorite, KENYA, which was used by Nastassja Kinski and Quincy Jones. And in this same general family of unconventional *K* names on the brink of stardom, there is a new contender, KINSEY, the name of the protagonist of the Sue Grafton alphabet mystery books.

KERRY. Kerry was one of the cool names of the sixties and seventies (although often confused by hearers of the name with Carrie) that's managed to hang onto a measure of energy and appeal. The name of one of the most beautiful and lush counties in Ireland, Kerry may get a breath of new life now as a place-name. Any of the variant spellings—KERI, KERRI, KERRIE, et al.—destroys whatever character the name has.

KETURAH. Keturah may have replaced Sarah as Abraham's second wife in the Old Testament, but her name certainly won't ever replace Sarah's in popularity as a baby name. This is good news for anyone looking for a truly unique and interesting biblical girls' name. The bad news is that most people would consider it a weird choice.

KEZIAH. An eighteenth-century favorite and one of ours, too, Keziah is a nearly undiscovered jewel these days, little used since its long servitude as a slave name. Its popularity on the plantation inspired many offshoots popular among African-Americans, from the KIZZY of *Roots* to the phonetic rendering KEISHA to KESHIA (Keshia Knight-Pulliam drew attention to this version when she played Rudy, the youngest Cosby kid) and LaKEISHA. It's time now to resurrect the original version of this beautiful Old Testament name. If you think it needs updating, you can spell it KEZIA.

KIMBERLY. Kimberly was the Ashley of its day, but the sun set on this name a couple of decades ago. It would seem to be stretching it to spell the name KIMBERLEY and claim it as a hot new place-name, but both spellings were indeed probably inspired by the South African diamond town. Kimberly has been big in movies and television at least as far back as the seventies, when Jane Fonda played Kimberly Wells, TV reporter, in *The China Syndrome*, and the name was attached to a prominent character on *Diff'rent Strokes*. As the years have gone by, the Kimberly characters have grown more bimboesque. The shortened form KIM had its run of popularity earlier, epitomized by Kim Novak (born Marilyn) in the fifties, and although Kim (born Kimila) Basinger is holding the fort, the name is rarely given to babies today. Alternative KIMBA seemed like an interesting possibility for about as long as Judge Kimba Wood was under consideration for Attorney General.

KIRSTEN, KRISTIN. One problem with naming a daughter Kirsten is that no one will ever remember whether her name is the Norwegian/Danish form of Christine KIRSTEN, the Swedish KERSTIN or KRISTIN, or maybe even the hybrid KRISTEN. Not to mention, of course, the Scottish KIRSTIE, nickname KRISTY, or any of the scores of variations of KRISTINE and KRISTINA. Life will be, in other words, confusing. Pity, too, because Kirsten, Kristin, and cousins are some of the prettiest, most delicate, and crystalline-sounding names around: surely the source of their broad popularity. But there have been so many Kirstens of such variety for so many years now that yours would almost surely have trouble standing out from the crowd. And that's the other main problem: Parents choosing one of these names may be shocked to find how big the crowd is. Undercounted because of its myriad variations, Kirsten/Kristin is in fact among the Top 20 in some states. If you simply must go with this name, you might try to find a distinctive variation (no, that doesn't mean a weird spelling): KRISTA, maybe, or KRISTIANA. For other ideas, check the listing for CHRISTINE.

KITTY. Kitty brings up images of spit curls and shiny period costumes with deep décolletage, saucy chambermaids and crafty courtesans. In this age of Katherines and Kates, Kitty has all but disappeared along with that view of exaggerated femininity. But if those images can be pushed aside, Kitty may yet come back as a lively, spirited name on its own, not as still another nickname for Katherine.

KYLE. Kyle is still primarily a boys' name—and a very popular one, at that, currently in the national Top 20—but it can be used for girls, too. We think, in fact, that Kyle may be better suited to girls than boys, and in the future can see it becoming as thoroughly feminine—and popular—as other K-initial ambisexual names: Kelly, Kerry, and Kelsey, to name three conspicuous examples. KYLA is a feminization that has gotten some individual attention, perhaps because of its similarity to the ultra popular Kayla. And KYLIE, an unrelated name with Aboriginal roots, is one of the top names in Australia spread to Britain via their native pop star Kylie Minogue, but not yet (though we smell a hit of the future) well-known here.

KYRA. We're really surprised that Kyra is not more popular already. It's got all the elements of name stardom: the strong and trendy initial *K*, a basic simplicity, the hint of exotic flavor without being too foreign or weird. It may be, in the end, that Kyra, seen on movie marquees for films starring Kyra Sedgwick, is one of those names that is perceived as trendy without ever truly becoming widely used—which, depending on your viewpoint, can be the best or worst of all possible worlds. **KIERA** is a variant that takes off from the Irish male name **KIERAN**; **KIARA** harkens to the Italian **CHIARA**. Parents who amuse themselves by spelling names in strange ways can have a lot of fun with this one.

L

〰〰〰〰〰〰〰〰〰〰〰〰〰 ◉ 〰〰〰〰〰〰〰〰〰〰〰〰〰

LACEY. Lacey is one of the few names that combines a surname feeling—as in *Cagney & Lacey*, the early eighties female cop team—with real femininity: for some parents, an ideal and hard-to-find mix.

LAILA. See **LEILA**

LANA, LANE. Bombshell Lana Turner made this one of the sultriest names of the forties and fifties, but it doesn't retain much power to attract today, although it still can be found on soap operas. A stronger and more solid choice for a nineties girl would be **LANE**.

LARA, LARISSA. Many of the girls who swooned over the sixties film *Dr. Zhivago* and daydreamed to its sentimental "Lara's Theme" grew up to use the romantic-sounding name for their daughters, who are themselves now roughly the age of actress Lara Flynn Boyle. Comic actor Bob Saget has a young daughter named Lara, but in general the name's fashion status has sagged. Contemporary parents attracted to Lara might instead opt for the more traditionally grounded **LARISSA**, from which the Russians spun off Lara. A pretty, underused feminissima name, Larissa comes from the Greek meaning "playful" and "jolly," and was, in classical mythology, the name of a Nymph who was loved by Mercury.

LATOYA. Thanks to Ms. Jackson, this is one of the most popular of the names beginning with the syllable *La*. Others that rank among the current Top 50 Black girls' names are LATASHA and LAKEISHA. Rap artist Queen LATIFA (born Dana) adopted an Arabic name that connotes gentle kindness.

LAURA. One of the most fashionable classics, Laura projects a quietly haunting feminine image. In the Top 25 in 1875, Laura was still there a century later (strongly boosted by the sympathetic second daughter from *Little House on the Prairie*), and continues to be popular today, with parents turning to it as an alternative to other more overused traditional names like Elizabeth and Emily. The name has given birth to many other forms over the years, but we say forget them all—forget LAURENTIA and LORENA (the names of two of the most notorious female lawbreakers, Laurentia "Bambi" Benbenek and Lorena Bobbitt, of our time), forget LORETTA and LAURETTA (too out of style, too back-country), forget LAURIE and LORI (nickname names of the sixties that are stuck back there)—forget them all because Laura is an eternally lovely name that needs no embellishment, enhancement, abbreviation, or transformation. The only possible exceptions: LAUREL, a distinctive and pretty botanical name, and the original male form Laurence, used in France—and now here occasionally—for girls as well.

LAUREN. The LORI of the nineties, Lauren is seriously trendy (it was in the Top 20 from 1983 to 1993), but manages to hang on to some measure of sophistication and strength. According to a Harvard sociologist's study, it's among the most preferred names of mothers with high educations—or it was in the 1980s. The upscale image of Ralph Lauren has taken off where actress Lauren Bacall (born Betty) and model Lauren Hutton (born Mary) left off. LOREN, the usual male spelling of the name, is sometimes used for girls as well.

LAVERNE. Laverne is a gum-chewing, wisegal kind of name, with either a Bronx/Milwaukee accent (as in *Laverne & Shirley*) or a deep Southern one (the nurse on *Empty Nest*). A name better left where it is, embroidered on an old poodle skirt.

LAVINIA. A prim and proper Victorian-sounding name, Lavinia actually dates back to ancient times, when it was the name of the wife of the Trojan hero Aeneas, who was considered the mother of the Roman people. Used by Shakespeare, Dickens, and Shaw, Lavinia just may have a shot at revival along with other old-fashioned favorites of its period, like Amelia, Winifred, and Maude.

LEAH. In the past couple of years, this gentle biblical name—in the Old Testament Leah was the sister of Rachel, first wife of Jacob and considered one of the four matriarchs of Judaism—has gained a real following, particularly among Jewish families looking for a traditional name not quite as well used as Rachel or Rebecca. Some foreign versions that share the same sweetness: the French LEA and the Italian LIA.

LEE. Lee sounds as if it had been created for middle-naming purposes, but since parents now favor names with real meaning in all positions, it is losing ground even there. The embroidered spelling LEIGH gives it a little more Vivien-Leighish substance, but with so many more interesting ambigender names available as options these days, we wouldn't expect to find Lee very high on anyone's list.

LEILA, LILA. There is a whole lush garden full of similarly pronounced, differently spelled exotic names clustered around Leila, which includes LAYLA, LAILA, and LELIA. Leila itself is a Persian name meaning "dark-haired," which was popularized by the poet Lord Byron in the nineteenth century when he used it for a Muslim child in a poem with a rich Eastern setting; in contemporary times it has been promoted by a popular Eric Clapton song of that name. LELIA is a Latin name used in Roman times and pronounced leh-lee-a; LILIA is a variant. The more commonly used LILA, which rolls off the tongue with rhythmic force (and is also an offshoot of the rare flower name

LILAC), has been a soap opera mainstay, as in the long-running character of *General Hospital* matriarch, Lila Quartermaine. Remotely related also are LEIA, heroine of the *Star Wars* trilogy, and LEILANI, a lovely Hawaiian name meaning "heavenly flower." LEILAN is a South Pacific variation with possibilities.

LENA. A pet form of Helen that became a name in its own right, Lena is famous as coupled with Horne and, more recently, Olin. The grandparent generation might remember with horror the old Al Capp cartoon character Lena the Hyena.

LEONORA, LENORE, LEONA. This group of names started life as European offsprings of ELEONORA, and have pretty much fallen out of fashion, except for Leonora, whose mellifluous sound makes it a revival possibility. It also has the distinction of being the name of three major opera characters, including the heroine of Beethoven's *Fidelio*. Lenore is a "modernization" no longer very modern, and Leona did not gain much from its association with the Queen of the Helmsley hotels.

LESLIE, LESLEY. A Scottish place-name and surname that was once androgynous, Leslie now is almost exclusively female. Last stylish in the sixties, it still has a pleasant, heathery feel, but today's would-be Leslies are much more likely to be Lindsays.

LETITIA. A prim and proper name whose buttoned-up image is only made more pronounced by its most famous bearer, the etiquette expert Letitia Baldridge, Letitia just might appeal to parents trying to strike a note of old-fashioned order in a chaotic world. The older form of the name, LETTICE, had all but died out when it was revived by the popular play, *Lettice and Lovage*. But since it has never gained a foothold in this country, we're afraid it would provoke a veritable salad of teasing for any American child who bore it. LETTY and LETTIE are sweet, gold-locket pet forms.

LEXIE. A pert, pixieish offshoot of the Alex family—from ALEXA to ALEXANDRIA. Use it as a nickname by all means, but we urge one of the more formal forms for the birth certificate.

LIBBY. This is one of the Elizabeth nicknames that has been neglected for years in favor of the Beths and Betsys, LIZ and LIZZIES, and suddenly starts to sound more modern than those others. It was used for the Mom figure played by Patti LuPone on the series *Life Goes On*.

LILITH. This name has been more shunned than neglected over the years because of the negative associations it bore from semitic mythology, which portrayed Lilith as Adam's rejected wife (pre-Eve) who, for refusing to obey her husband, was turned into an evil, ugly demon that haunted the wilderness on stormy nights, and was especially threatening to little children. But then along came Dr. Lilith Sternin, who married Frasier Crane on *Cheers*—icy, perhaps, but not really a demon—to neutralize and humanize the name and make it a possibility for the fearless baby namer.

LILY, LILIAN. One of the delicate century-old flower names making a comeback, Lily has both a cool elegance (it is after all, the symbol of purity) and a slightly offbeat charm—a winning combination. Though it has been used (sometimes with the LILLIE spelling) by several high-profile parents in the last few years—including Kevin Costner, Phil Collins, Jill Clayburgh and David Rabe, Mary Steenburgen and Malcolm McDowell, Amy Madigan and Ed Harris, Kirstie Alley and Parker Stevenson, and Meredith Viera—Lily has managed to stay on the right side of the style street, remaining a contemporary but not overused choice. Lilian, very popular around 1900, still wears a stiff, high-necked collar, but LILIANA (also spelled LILIANNA), the Latinate variant, has panache, as does LILO, a Hawaiian name meaning "generous."

LINDA. Linda will live forever in the annals of nomenclature history as the name that toppled Mary from its four-hundred-year reign as number one. Queen of the mountain in 1950, Linda has fallen even further than Mary from grace today, as rare for babies as it is common for moms. Linda originated as a short form of older German-based serpentlike names Belinda and Melinda, and also ties in with the Spanish word for "pretty." LBJ's daughter LYNDA popularized this variant spelling during the name's last days in the sun.

LINDSAY, LINDSEY. Bionic Woman Lindsay Wagner helped legit-
imize this occasionally used male name as a fitting one for girls; in the
early eighties, riding in tandem with Courtney, it approached the Top
10. Along with thousands of other parents, broadcast journalist Joan
Lunden and comedian Billy Crystal chose it for their daughters. But
while Lindsay deserves recognition as a style pioneer in the now-boom-
ing category of ambisexual-last-names-first, its own currency has faded.

LISA, LIZA. As recently as the 1950s, Lisa was just one of a dozen
or more nicknames for Elizabeth. And then something happened. Did
people become captivated by the second half of the Nat Cole hit song
"Mona Lisa"? Were they influenced by The King's naming his daughter
Lisa Marie Presley? By 1970, Lisa had become the fourth most popular
girls' name in America—and was still number twelve a decade later,
though not many parents would mistake it for a happening name these
days. Then came Liza with a z (à la Minnelli, whom Mama Judy
Garland named after a Gershwin song) that never became as widespread
as Lisa, and so doesn't sound quite so dated. But at this time, one of
the other Elizabeth offshoots, from Eliza to Libby to Bess, would seem
more distinctive and fresh. Leeza Gibbons added a new spelling.

LIVIA. It sounds like it must be a chopped-off version of Olivia, but
the distinctively attractive Livia has been an independent name since
the days of the ancient Romans, when it belonged to the wife of the
Emperor Augustus.

LIZA. See LISA.

LOIS. Lois may live on as the name of the eternal fiancée of Superman,
but ever since it peaked in 1925, it has sounded more and more like
the sweet, gray-haired woman down the street whom everyone in the
neighborhood entrusts with their spare keys. Quite fittingly, Lois
means "good" in Greek, and was the name of the grandmother of
Timothy in the New Testament.

LOLA. Unlike names such as Desirée and Salomé, Lola manages to
be sexy without going over the top, even though in the past it has

been associated with such femmes fatales as the nineteenth-century courtesan Lola Montez (who was actually Irish and born Marie Dolores), the Marlene Dietrich character in *The Blue Angel* and Jean Harlow's in *Bombshell*, the sexpot in *Damn Yankees* ("Whatever Lola Wants, Lola Gets") and, in pet name form, the notorious LOLITA. Despite all that, this onetime diminutive of Dolores remains a charming, offbeat name with a good deal of style for those who defy convention: It was chosen for their daughters by such tastemakers as the Eurythmics' Annie Lennox and artist Julian Schnabel.

LORELEI. Lorelei will be probably forever stuck with its siren image— it was, after all, the name of the beautiful Rhine River seductress whose haunting voice led sailors to hazardous rocks that would cause them to be shipwrecked. Lorelei Lee was the not-so-dumb-blonde siren heroine of *Gentlemen Prefer Blondes*, portrayed on screen by Marilyn Monroe.

LORETTA. See LAURA.

LORNA. One of those names, like Pamela, Vanessa, and Wendy, that was tailored by a novelist to fit the personality of a particular character, in this case the forlorn Lorna Doone. Judy Garland chose the name for her younger daughter, but not that many other mothers have favored it.

LORRAINE. Sweet Lorraine: This French place-name has moved in and out of fashion in the few hundred years it's been used as a girls' first name, somewhat influenced by the alternate name of Joan of Arc— St. Joan of Lorraine. It was quite popular in this country from the twenties to the forties, and very rarely used since. But if it's as firmly fixed in fashion limbo as most people think, how come Jack Nicholson used it for his baby daughter? The alternate spelling LARAINE was popularized by forties star Laraine Day.

LOTTIE. A nostalgic great-grandma name—once short for Char-lotte—that conjures up petit point pillows and lace doilies. It's one of a whole sorority of such names, including NELLIE, LETTY, JOSIE,

HATTIE, MILLY, and Tillie, that some modern parents are beginning to reassess. Really.

LOUISA, LOUISE. In most cases, feminine names are more fashionable with an *a* ending (Diana, SUSANNA, Julia), but in this instance (as with Isabel/Isabella), both Louise and Louisa are making their way back. Louise is seen as a competent, no-nonsense, efficient name for the nineties, whereas Louisa (chosen by Meryl Streep for one of her three daughters) is a bit more feminine and quaint. Very popular in the eighteenth century, Louisa was finally toppled by the French form Louise at the end of the nineteenth, which rose to and remained in the Top 35 girls' names in America during the whole first quarter of the twentieth century. One of Louisa's attractive namesakes is *Little Women* author Louisa May Alcott, and Louisa Swenson is a contemporary character on *General Hospital*; Louise was the character played by Susan Sarandon in the feminist road movie, *Thelma and Louise*. The appealing Spanish form is LUISA; nicknames include the impudent LULU (what designer Betsey Johnson named her daughter), the hard-driving LOU, and OUISA, as in *Six Degrees of Separation*.

LUCILLE. Unlike Lucy, Lucille did get permanently saddled with the Lucille Ball linkage, so that its image has tangerine-colored hair, exaggeratedly round eyes, and a tendency to dress in clown outfits and stage daffy and desperate efforts to perform with her husband's band. Variation LUCILLA may have a shot at escape.

LUCY. Lucy is both saucy and solid, making it an attractive choice on several levels. The English form of the equally appealing Roman LUCIA, which derives from the Latin word "lux," meaning "light," Lucy/Lucia was at one time given to girls born at dawn. An early saint's name later used for characters by Fielding and Dickens, Lucy has managed to survive associations with the bossy little girl in *Peanuts*, with the possible psychedelic implications of "Lucy in the Sky with Diamonds," and with *I Love Lucy* (see Lucille, above). More positive (if more obscure) is the name's heroic attachment to nineteenth-century feminist Lucy Stone. Danny DeVito and Rhea Perlman used the French spelling for their little LUCIE. From the same Latin source comes

LUCINDA, an engaging seventeenth-and eighteenth-century variant first used in *Don Quixote* that might appeal to the modern parent looking for an out-of-the-ordinary, old-fashioned name. LUCIA (pronounced either LOO-sha or Loo-CHEE-a), LUCIANA, and LUCIENNE are further foreign possibilities.

LUNA. Familiar to soap opera watchers via the character of Luna Moody on *One Life to Live*, this moonstruck name would make a daring, evocative choice.

LYDIA. Groucho Marx used to sing a song called "Lydia, the Tattooed Lady," which these days tends to make it sound more hip than it was meant to sound then. A very early place-name, Lydia was an area of Asia Minor whose inhabitants are credited with the invention of coinage and great musical talent. Although mentioned as a first name in the New Testament (Lydia was the first European convert of St. Paul), it did not really emerge as a Christian name until the seventeenth century, gaining notoriety through the character Lydia Languish in Sheridan's 1775 play, *The Rivals*, and the youngest of the Bennet girls in *Pride and Prejudice*. Today, Lydia is quietly fashionable with an offbeat sort of appeal, a kindred spirit to names like Natalie, Olivia, Madeleine, Louisa. Heiress and ex-fugitive Patty Hearst used it for one of her daughters, as did the fictional Mrs. Doubtfire. Also on the scene is New Wave singer Lydia Lunch.

LYNN. Lynn came to life in the forties as a spin-off from the wildly popular Linda, and enjoyed some independent notoriety as one of the most common of mid-century middle names—along with Ann, Marie, and Lee. With the fad for that kind of follow-the-dots middle name now long gone, Lynn is left with nowhere to go. LYNETTE, which enjoyed some low-level long-ago popularity as a Lynn/Linda adjunct, is actually an unrelated variation on a Welsh name.

M

〰〰〰〰〰〰〰〰〰〰〰〰〰〰 ◉ 〰〰〰〰〰〰〰〰〰〰〰〰〰〰

MABEL. A few years ago, when British comic actress Tracey Ullman used this name for her little girl, it seemed like the most outrageously campy choice imaginable. But now—is it just us?—we can really recognize its cheeky charm, that of a whole group of old-fashioned British barmaid, wise-cracking waitress names. Mabel originated as a shortened version of Amabel, which is French for "loveable," losing the initial *A* somewhere along the way and becoming a Victorian favorite, especially popular in this country from around 1870 to 1900. *Queen Mab* is a poem by Shelley about the fairy who carries dreams to sleeping men.

MACY. A cute and upbeat surname beginning to be heard in playgrounds, perhaps inspired by the soap opera character on *The Bold and the Beautiful*. A modern-sounding replacement for such tired old favorites as Stacy and Tracy.

MACKENZIE, MCKENZIE. So far, this is one of the "Mac" names most often used for girls, already in the Top 25 in some states, following the lead of actress MacKenzie (born Laura Mackenzie) Phillips. Other possibilities might be MACALLISTER and MACKINLEY.

MADELINE, MADELEINE. This lovely French name with a soft and delicate image is, unfortunately, verging on the ultratrendy, having been rediscovered by many modern mothers, including actresses Lea Thompson and Mel Harris. The Gallic version of the rarely used MAG-DALENE, Madeline has been found frequently in literature, from the poems of Keats and Tennyson to the charming children's books of Ludwig Bemelmans. The ex-model detective character of Maddy Hayes played by Cybill Shepherd in *Moonlighting* a few seasons back may have returned the name to the public consciousness, and actress Madeleine Stowe is helping to keep it there.

MADISON. It's ambigender, it's a place-name, and it's presidential. So how could Madison miss? It has already shown great strength among fashion arbiters and is rapidly finding favor with other parents looking for a confident, hip-sounding girl's name. Madison has a secure place in name history as the first modern place-name—we don't count Brittany and Chelsea—to break into the girls' Top 50. Actress Sissy Spacek named her younger daughter Madison.

MADONNA. To state the obvious, Madonna Louise Ciccone took her reverent Christian name and turned its image inside out. This Italian title for the Virgin Mary, literally meaning "my lady," has been used as a given name only fairly recently, especially among Americans of Italian descent. Madonna herself has said, "I feel I was given a special name for a reason. In a way, maybe I wanted to live up to my name."

MAEVE. Short but strong, this name of a legendary Queen of Connacht would make a distinctive choice, particularly for a child with Irish roots. It's already been attached to the Kennedy family tree via a young granddaughter of Robert and Ethel.

MAGGIE. Long emancipated from its mother name of Margaret, Maggie has a strong and vigorous, tousled, fun-loving air. It was popular at the turn of the century, was revived in the freewheeling sixties and is still a favorite—though growing somewhat tired, à la Annie and LIZZIE—choice. Through the years, it has been well used by writers—there was Maggie Tulliver, the heroine of George Eliot's *The Mill on the Floss*, Stephen Crane's unfortunate *Maggie: A Girl of the Streets*, Maggie the Cat in Tennessee Williams's *Cat on a Hot Tin Roof*, portrayed in the movies by Elizabeth Taylor—and has also been immortalized in songs like "When You and I Were Young, Maggie" and Rod Stewart's "Maggie May."

MAGNOLIA. An over-the-top flower name, as showy as the large pink, heavily perfumed blossom itself, recommended for the adventurous name giver only. It has gone down in musical theater history via the heroine of *Show Boat*, adapted from the Edna Ferber novel.

MAHALA, MAHALIA. The former is an almost unknown but pleas-ant-sounding Hebrew name meaning "tenderness" and also a Native American name for "woman." Mahalia is firmly connected to perhaps the greatest of all gospel singers, Mahalia Jackson.

MAIDA. An Old English name as outmoded now as the use of the word *maid* for a young woman.

MAISIE. This spirited yet sentimental Scottish pet form of Margaret and Marjorie is a vintage gem, ready to be recycled. Popular in the twenties and thirties, it was the eponymous title of a radio show and series of breezy B movies about an ex-chorus girl in the forties. Henry James wrote a novel, set in England, called *What Maisie Knew*. MAIZIE is another spelling.

MALLORY. This onetime strictly masculine surname name suddenly became a strong girl's choice in the early eighties, no doubt influenced by the character played by Justine Bateman on the popular sitcom, *Family Ties*. It blended in well with the other three-syllable names in fashion at the time, like Brittany and Kimberly, while retaining a firmer, less fluffy image, and is still a viable possibility—unless you think of the homicidal heroine played by Juliette Lewis in *Natural Born Killers*.

MALU. This charming Hawaiian name meaning "peace" was chosen by ex-Talking Head, David Byrne, for his daughter, Malu Valentine.

MALVA, MALVINA, MELVA, MELVINA. Malvina was coined by an eighteenth century poet named James Macpherson and became quite popular in Scandinavia. But neither it nor any of its offshoots sound much more appealing today than their male counterpart, Melvin.

MAMIE. Yet another short form of Mary and Margaret (there are dozens), Mamie had a short pageboy and curled-under bangs all through the Eisenhower years, but now, like Maisie, could be ready for a new life. Meryl Streep's daughter Mary Willa is called Mamie, a good example of how the name can be stylishly put to service as a short form for a more formal *M* name—Mary or Margaret or MARGUERITE or Miriam—used to honor an ancestor. Earlier it had definite Irish associations, as reflected in the song, "The Sidewalks of New York" ("Boys and girls together, me and Mamie O'Rourke"). The shortened form MAME has a dotty, antic feel because of the best-selling *Auntie Mame*, which led to a successful play, movie, and musical. But then again, there was the definitively sensuous Rita Hayworth song from the classic, *Gilda*, "Put the Blame on Mame, Boys."

MANDY and **MINDY.** These nickname names of the sixties just don't cut it in today's more sophisticated times.

MARA. Exotic and evocative, Mara is a biblical name that means "bitter": In the Book of Ruth, Naomi, devastated after the deaths of her husband and two sons, says, "Call me not Naomi, call me Mara." Multicultural, Mara is also a Kiswahili word meaning "a time" and could be conceived as an African geographical name, being a river flowing through Kenya and Tanzania.

MARCELLA, MARCELLINE. Two archaic names that bring to mind overly plucked eyebrows and rigidly marcelled hair, despite the fact that a Marcella was depicted as the world's most beautiful woman in *Don Quixote*.

MARCIA, MARSHA. A name in which both spellings are used almost equally, this short form of Marcella had a short run of popularity in the forties and fifties, when MARCY replaced it, fitting the more casual tempo of those times—but not of these.

maggy, molly, maya

MARGARET. After several decades in storage, buttoned securely within its starchy image, Margaret is being aired out by parents attracted to the name's strong sound and classic status. Margaret is also an important family name for many people, having ranked in the Top 10 through the first half of the 1900s. Following the lead of other Stylish Conservatives such as Elizabeth and Katherine, Margaret even has its own trendy LIZZIE/Kate equivalent nickname: Maggie. But long-dormant Margaret short forms Maisie or Daisy seem fresher, and in keeping with the overall trend many parents simply stick with the full version. An extremely well used name since medieval times and still considered "the Scottish national name," Margaret derives both from the Greek meaning "pearl" and the Persian meaning "child of light." In Persian mythology, oysters would rise to the water's surface at night to worship the moon and catch a single drop of congealed dew in their shells, which the moonbeam would then transform into a pearl. In various eras and cultures, Margaret has been one of the most Christian and royal of female names—attached to the patron saint of women in childbirth and to various queens and princesses in England, Scandinavia, Austria, and the Netherlands, and in modern times to the first female prime minister of Great Britain, Margaret Thatcher. In the fifties, it was seen as the quintessential Mom name, as in *Father Knows Best* and *Make Room for Daddy*. Many of its offspring in addition to Maggie have become independently used names, including MADGE, MEG, Marjorie, Megan, Molly, Peggy, and Rita. Foreign versions also found in this country are Margo and MARGUERITE (French), MARGARITA (Spanish), and Gretchen and Greta (German).

MARGO, MARGOT. This French pet form of MARGUERITE has a lot of elements going for it: Its unusual (especially for a girls' name) *o* ending makes it more dynamic and dramatic than Margaret, though it still shares in the original's classic feel. Movie buffs will remember Bette Davis's archetypal role as Margo Channing in *All About Eve*, and perhaps that Grace Kelly, too, played a Margot in *Dial M For Murder*, while balletomanes will associate the name with the great English dancer, Margot Fonteyn. Margo also appears to be a favorite on soap operas—it has recently been heard on both *All My Children* and *The Bold and the Beautiful*. But the MARGAUX spelling, as in champagne and Hemingway, is too pretentious even for the soaps.

MARIA. The most common girls' name in all Spanish-speaking countries and the favorite form of Mary from Italy to Austria to Eastern Europe, Maria has also been a quietly but consistently used name in upper-class Anglo families. Maria Shriver, daughter of a Kennedy mother and a high-Wasp father, is a prime example of this arcane but intriguing practice. Parents bold (or maybe sophisticated) enough to appreciate Maria's graces will see it as a timeless choice perfect for a child of tomorrow's global village. For further information on all that's right about the name Maria, listen to the classic song from the musical *West Side Story*. St. Maria Goretti, a twelfth-century martyr, is considered the patron saint of teenage girls.

MARIAH. Superstar Mariah Carey has undoubtedly been the prime influence on the growing popularity of this nineteenth-century variation of Maria. Most parents are aware these days that the name is pronounced Mar-eye-a, which is denoted by the final *h*. The *-ah* ending relates to other girls' favorites of the day: Sarah, for instance, and Hannah. The song "They Call the Wind Mariah" has also been an influence.

MARIAN, MARION. Yet another offshoot of Marie, this one a medieval French version, Marian had a respectable run of popularity in this country. It was in the Top 10 at the turn of the century, was still in the Top 20 in the twenties, a Mom name of the fifties (as replayed in the sitcom *Happy Days*) and is one of the very serious great-aunt names that are up for reconsideration today. Robin Hood's Maid Marion provides a timeless romantic image for the name.

The extended edition of the name, MARIANNE is so endemic in France that it has become the personification of the Republic, analagous to our Uncle Sam. More sophisticated than the similarly pronounced MARY ANN, it has been associated with poet Marianne Moore, singer Marianne Faithfull, and the mournful song of that name by Canadian cult singer Leonard Cohen. MARIANNA, with that all-important final *a*, may be the most obviously stylish version of all.

MARIE. Marie, the French form of Mary, tends to sound more dated than either Mary or Maria at this point, although at one time it rivaled both, actually reaching the number two spot in America at the end of the twenties. Marie, right now, is a stenographer who's never become computer literate. The most visible contemporary bearer of the name, Marie Osmond, was born Olive. MARIEL, as in Hemingway, is the Dutch and French diminutive and certainly more inspirational for modern parents. Other versions are MARIELLE, MARIETTE, and MARIETTA.

MARIGOLD. Occasionally used in England, especially in the novels of authors like Barbara Pym, Marigold would definitely be seen as a wildly exotic flower name in the United States, but it does have a sunny, golden feel to it.

MARILYN. We've all known many Marilyns, contemporaries of the Barbaras and Lindas and Carols born at the peak of their names' popularity, from the twenties to the fifties. Yet strangely enough, although Marilyn Monroe (born Norma Jean and renamed in tribute to earlier star Marilyn Miller) was the ultimate sex symbol of her generation, no stardust adhered to the name. Now, in particular, Marilyn has virtually none of the freshness or sparkle that would inspire a parent to use it for a nineties child.

MARINA. This pretty sea-born name was used to dramatic effect by Shakespeare in his play *Pericles* for the virtuous princess who says she is "Call'd Marina, for I was born at sea." The name, which rose in popularity in England when Prince George married Princess Marina of Greece, is also associated with the Russian widow of Lee Harvey Oswald.

MARIS, MARISA, MARISSA. Maris is a name that was hardly heard of until it didn't appear as the unseen sister-in-law in *Frasier*. Unusual and appealing, it comes from the phrase Stella Maris, which means "star of the sea," one of many epithets for the Virgin Mary. Much more familiar is Marisa/Marissa, which never reached the saturation point of its cousin Melissa, and is therefore still a feasible choice. It has been publicized in recent years by Academy Award–winning actress Marisa Tomei, as well as the soap opera character Marissa Perkins on *Santa Barbara*. MARISOL is the dramatic Latina version.

MARJORIE, MARGERY. In case you've always wondered, Marjorie is a Scottish and Margery an English vernacular form of Margaret, both of which were seen as more lively versions of the old standard in the first few decades of this century, familiar to even the youngest child through the nursery rhyme starting, "See-saw, Margery Daw." In the fifties and sixties, MARGIE was seen as a prime pert-teenager name in such TV shows and movies as *Margie* and *My Little Margie*. One name expert thinks that all these names faded with the advent of the word *margarine*.

MARLENE, MARLENA, MARLA. Marlene, originally pronounced as we now pronounce Marlena, was not heard of in this country until the importation of German screen star Marlene Dietrich, who had compressed the beginning and ending syllables of her real first names, Maria Magdalene into the more glamorous new version, which was also heard in the World War II German song, "Lili Marlene." Americans were quick to change the pronunciation to Marleen, consonant with other names popular at the time like Arlene and Maxine. Marlene is virtually unheard of now, but some related (though not much more appealing for today's babies) names have taken its place: MARLENA has had a leading role on the soap opera *Days of Our Lives*; MARLA has been making headlines first as Maples, then as Trump; MARLO seems to have been invented by Marlo Thomas, who was born Margaret. A pair of more contemporary spellings and spins are MARLOW and MARLEY.

MARNIE. This outdated nickname name of the sixties was up in lights via the 1964 Hitchcock thriller of that title, but now seems indistinguishable from Mandy, Mindy, and the rest.

MARTHA. The name borne by our first First Lady still has a prim and proper DAR image, academic and efficient. That quiet traditional tasteful gestalt is exactly what makes Martha appealing to some parents today: Martha's the dark waxed wood floor, the muted Oriental rug of names. The New Testament Martha, sister of Lazarus and Mary of Bethany, was a solicitous housekeeper who looked after the material welfare of Jesus when he was a guest in their home. For this reason Martha has since been identified with domestic labor and hospitality and is the patron saint of housewives, waiters, and cooks. Giving the name a more contemporary spirit are MTV veejay, Martha Quinn and actress Martha Plimpton. Livelier foreign forms that have been used in this country are MARTA, MARTHE, MARTINE, and MARTINA, the latter associated with Czech-born tennis champ Martina Navratilova.

MARY. Someone said recently that if you want to give your daughter a really unusual name nowadays, pick Mary. A true irony for the name that for centuries had been by far the most popular and enduring female Christian name in the English-speaking world (as were Maria and Marie in the Spanish and French)—at least until the 1950s. That was when Mary was finally dethroned by such trendy upstarts as Linda and Karen. The Greek and New Testament form of the Hebrew Miriam—via the Latin Maria—because in earliest times Mary was considered too sacred to be used by ordinary mortals, associated as it was with the cult figure of the Virgin Mary, Mother of Jesus. It finally began to be used in England in the twelfth century, and by the sixteenth had blanketed the female population, to the point where dozens of pet forms had to be contrived for the simple sake of distinguishing one Mary in the family from the others. There was a hiatus due to the odious religious persecutions of Mary Tudor ("Bloody Mary"), but then the name was back, bigger than ever, classless and ubiquitous. In this country, Mary has always been a scrubbed-faced good-girl name (to the tune of "Oh what a pal was Mary"), even in the forties and fifties when an infusion of energy was attempted with any number of middle name add-ons— from MARY LOU and MARY JO to MARY JANE and MARY BETH. Mary was unstoppably pure, as reflected still in those sixties and seventies icons of propriety and wholesomeness, Mary Poppins and Mary Tyler Moore. Numerous future celebrities in fact dropped their birth names of Mary for something that seemed more glitzy, among them Bo Derek, Debbie Reynolds, Sissy Spacek, Lauren Hutton, Meryl Streep, and Lily Tomlin, while others have returned to it for their daughters in an effort, perhaps, to reclaim its moral imperative, including Paul McCartney and the same Meryl Streep who had dropped it for herself. Today, Mary remains fashionable only among upmarket Southerners and Catholics, who use Mary as a silent first name to impart traditionalism and saintliness to an offbeat middle name like WALKER or Courtney.

Virtually every culture in the Western world has a variant of Mary. Among the prettiest are MAIR (Welsh), MAIRE or MARE (Gaelic),

MARO (Armenian), MAREN (Norway), and MAJA and MARJA (Sweden). Mary nicknames, many of which have long been well used in their own right, include Molly, Mitzi, Mamie, Minnie, Polly, and May.

MATILDA, MATHILDA. A sweet, slightly fussy, onetime German name that now has an Australian accent (thanks largely to the song "Waltzing Matilda" and an old movie about a boxing kangaroo), Matilda seems to be making a bit of a comeback. Not surprising that Australian actor Bryan Brown and wife Rachel Ward would choose it, but American Elizabeth Perkins did so as well. Usable nickname offshoots include TILDA and Tillie or, for those looking to steer back toward the mainstream, MATTY. Matilda was introduced to England by William the Conqueror's wife and also his granddaughter, who was known as Maud.

MAUD, MAUDE. Maud or Maude is a lacy, mauve-colored name that was popular a hundred years ago, partly influenced by the Tennyson poem that included the oft-quoted line "Come into the garden, Maud." In the seventies, the vociferous and opinionated TV character Maude Finlay put a very different spin on the name, but now that seems like an aberration, and the name has settled back to the Victorian version. It seems particularly ripe for use as a softening middle name, as Glenn Close employed it for her daughter, Annie Maude.

MAURA, MAUREEN, MOIRA. Of all these Gaelic forms of Mary popular in Ireland and Scotland, Maura is probably the most fashionable form today, easier to fathom (and pronounce) than the more authentic Moira. The diminutive Maureen was almost as popular in the fifties and sixties among the Irish in Boston as among their relatives still over in Bray, but is not used very much anymore.

MAVIS. There are plenty of flower names, but not too many bird names. Mavis, a British World War II period name with friends like Beryl and AVRIL, is another word for the song thrush. It was introduced as a proper name in an 1895 novel called *The Sorrows of Satan*.

One lovely Mavis we know cut her name to make it more fashionable, and is now MAVE.

MAXINE. A Frenchified feminization of Max that popped up in the thirties and now seems condemned to permanent limbo, despite the fashion status of its male counterpart.

MAY, MAE. Definitely sounding fresh and springlike again after more than a century in mothballs, May started as one of the innumerable pet forms of Mary and Margaret, as well as a vernal month name along with April and June. It was recently given a boost by Winona Ryder's Oscar-nominated performance as May Welland in Edith Wharton's *The Age of Innocence*. May is well suited to use as a middle name—Mick Jagger and Jerry Hall called their daughter Georgia May. The Mae spelling, long associated with voluptuous Mae West, is more sexy than sentimental.

MAYA, MAIA. In whichever version (both are pronounced my-ah) these names appeal to parents seeking an exotic, perhaps even mystical, image for their daughter. Maya resonates with the primitive power of the Mayan Indians of Mexico, and is also a Hindu term for God's creative power. As for the most famous bearer of the name, acclaimed poet and playwright Maya Angelou, she was born Marguerite, and, the story goes, was given her new name by a younger brother referring to her as "maya sister." Maia is a light, ethereal name with similarly mystical overtones. In Greek legend, she was the fair-haired daughter of Atlas who mothered Zeus's favorite illegitimate son, Hermes. To the Romans, Maia was the incarnation of the Earth mother and the goddess of spring, after which they named the month of May.

MEGAN. Surely one of the most popular Welsh names to come to these shores in recent years (if we don't count Jennifer), Megan caught on like wildfire in the early eighties with parents who liked its "Irish" sound and spirit. And although it has been so widely used—it's still in the Top 20—Megan retains some degree of spunk. The short form MEG is more closely tied to the original Margaret, and carries with it the charm of all the *Little Women* characters. Keeping it in the contemporary spotlight is actress Meg Ryan. For some reason parents are often tempted to vary Megan with "creative" spellings, but we warn against deviating so much that people aren't sure whether the name is mee-gan or mayg-han or what, exactly. The best, clearest, easiest-to-understand spelling is the original one: Megan.

MELANIE. Melanie is one of several names that got their initial impetus from a *Gone with the Wind* character, in this case Melanie Hamilton Wilkes, played by Olivia de Havilland. The spread of this Greek name (meaning "dark") has been slow but sure; since it was never popular enough to be considered trendy, it is still a viable possibility. An elaborate—and more distinctive—version is MELAN-THA. Trivia tidbit: Melanie Griffith was named after the character her mother, Tippi Hedren, played in Alfred Hitchcock's *The Birds*.

MELBA. This name can be traced back to the influence of Australian opera star Nellie Melba, whose stage name was taken from that of her native Melbourne. Now relegated to style limbo along with MELVA, BELVA et al., the only contemporary noteworthy example is singer Melba Moore, who, in fact, was born Beatrice.

MELIA. This charming name is sometimes used as a pet form of Amelia and Cornelia, but is also, in classical mythology, the nymph daughter of Oceanus, the Titan god of the outer seas.

MELINDA. _Lindy_ In the seventeenth and eighteenth centuries there was a poetic fad for names with the *inda* sound, and Melinda was one of those created at that time. But although it doesn't sound as dated as Linda itself, or as tired as Melissa, Melinda is still not a favorite among nineties baby namers.

MELISSA. _Lissa, Missy_ The fact that the two leading child actresses on the big-time seventies series *Little House on the Prairie* were both named Melissa gives some indication of how popular that name was, and would remain, for the next two decades, chosen by parents for its beribboned and beruffled femininity. Parents are still using the name, though less fashionably, today: It hangs onto the most popular list at number twenty-five. From the Greek for "bee," suggesting the sweetness of honey, the mythical Melissa was nursemaid to the infant god Zeus. It was used as a given name by the early Greeks, as well as for fairies by Italian Renaissance poets.

MELODY. A lilting but lightweight name favored by parents who would probably name their next daughter HARMONY or LYRIC.

MERCEDES. This is one of the few names attached to luxury living (as opposed to, say, Tiffany or Sterling) that we can wholeheartedly recommend, it being a legitimate Spanish appellation stemming from one of the epithets given to the Virgin Mary—Our Lady of the Mercies. The car, by the way, was named after the eleven-year-old daughter of the Daimler company's French distributor in 1901.

MERCY. This Puritan virtue name, quite popular with the early settlers of this country, makes an infinitely more interesting and meaningful choice than the similar-sounding but vacuous MARCY. MERRY is a cheerful shortened form that also lacks substance. In the Dickens novel, *Martin Chuzzlewit*, the two sisters named Mercy and Charity are known as Merry and Cherry.

MEREDITH. Still commonly used as a male name in Wales (it means "magnificent chief or protector" in Celtic), this is a gentle-sounding, soft-hued name that has easily segued onto the female roll call in this country and would make a good fitting-in-but-standing-out option. A new, related sighting on the namescape is MERIDIAN, first name of the psychologist, Dr. Chase, played by Nicole Kidman in the third Batman movie, *Batman Forever.*

MERLE, MERYL, MERRILL. These are three sleek, smooth, understated names. Merle is a French bird name (for "blackbird"), that was used for the surname of a slightly sinister character in Henry James's *The Portrait of a Lady*, and during the Golden Age of Hollywood was associated with India-born Merle Oberon, whose real name was Estelle. The contemporary use of Meryl is almost completely due to the fame of Meryl Streep, born Mary Louise, and its homophone Merrill has the possible advantage of being androgynous.

MIA. When Mia Farrow—actually born Maria—became an instant superstar at the age of nineteen via the TV nightime soap *Peyton Place* in 1964, her name was an obscure Scandinavian pet form of Maria, better known here as the Italian feminine possessive, as in *cara mia*. It spread rapidly through the sixties and seventies, especially liked by American families of Asian descent: It's one of the few Western names (ALISA and HANA are others) that have Asian-language counterparts. Sometimes used in modern Israel as a derivative of Michaela, Mia is still liked by parents but is no longer on the cutting edge of style.

MICHAELA, MICHAEL, MICHAL. Thanks to the popularity of *Dr. Quinn Medicine Woman*, Michaela has suddenly started to take off, actually approaching the Top 25 in a few states. With all the attention drawn to Michelle, these other Michael-related names have been neglected. Michael itself has been used by girls for years—there was a writer (married to John Barrymore) who called herself Michael Strange in the twenties, and Michael Learned played the mother of the Walton clan. Now, in the current climate, when females are appropriating rather than feminizing men's names, we expect to see more girls named Michael. Michal is the independent biblical name of the youngest daughter of King Saul and the wife of King David.

MICHELLE, MICHELE. It was the Beatles song that did it, of that we have no doubt. The tender sound, the loving half-French lyrics "ma belle." The name had certainly been heard before 1966, in fact it was already number twenty in 1960, but we're sure that the soft, sentimental ballad was the key factor in propelling it up to the Top 5. And although it is still widely used, it is definitely, after an unusually long run, on its way out of favor, although Michelles Pfeiffer and Phillips still keep it in the public eye.

MILDRED. When scientists do research on the effects of an unpopular name, we're afraid that Mildred is one of the first examples they cite, often in tandem with Bertha and Gertrude. A medieval name (a holdover from the era of ETHELRED and ETHELREDA) revived by the Victorians and quite popular here in the first couple of decades of the century, the last time it really made any impression was in *Mildred Pierce*, the melodramatic film noir starring Joan Crawford in her one Oscar-winning role. The bottom line: This is not a name that will make your daughter's path in life any smoother.

MILLICENT. Sort of a combination of the mild and the innocent, Millicent is sweet and feminissima (quite a contrast to its literal German meaning of "strong worker"), and if that is the kind of name you are seeking, it would make a much more original choice than Melissa or Michelle. The name came from Germany to France in the form of **MELISANDE**, which was borne by a daughter of Charlemagne. This mellifluous version is associated with the romance of Pelléas and Mélisande, later made into an opera by Debussy. There is also a charming fairy-tale princess named Melisande, who was cursed at birth with baldness by an evil fairy but later battled the opposite problem: too much hair. The upbeat nickname MILLY/MILLIE serves both Mildred and Millicent, and is sometimes used on its own.

MIMI. Another nickname name—both for Miriam and Maria—Mimi is the heroine of Puccini's opera, *La Bohème*, whose real name, she reveals to us in song, is neither of the above, but Lucia. Not really recommended for use on its own, Mimi has appeared as a character on *All My Children* and also belongs to actress Mimi Rogers.

MINDY. See MANDY.

MINERVA. This is one classic we don't expect to be making a return engagement. It has something to do with that *erv* sound, heard also in such other unfashionable names as Irving and Mervin, that just doesn't make music to the modern ear. A shame, in a way, as Minerva, in Roman myth, was the goddess of wisdom and invention, the arts and martial strength.

MINA, MINNA, MINNIE. Mina (rhymes with Tina) and Minna are a pair of rarely used short forms of Wilhelmina, the former made familiar as the name of the unfortunate love of Count Dracula, the latter also meaning "mother" in some West African languages. Minnie, another Wilhelmina offshoot, as well as being short for several *M* names, has comical overtones due to its associations with Minnie Mouse, Grand Ole Opry singer Minnie Pearl, and the Cab Calloway song, "Minnie the Moocher." Still, some parents see Minnie as a cute, slightly dizzy nickname name—akin to Tillie and Maisie—with an unpretentious charm.

MIRABEL, MIRABELLE. We see signs of a definite resurgence of bel names, including Belle itself, Isabel, and this more unusual, elegant example, which comes from the Latin meaning "marvelous" and is also the name of a delicate French plum. The Italian MIRABELLA is, in addition to being a fashion magazine, another attractive option.

MIRANDA. A shimmeringly lovely name with nothing but attractive associations, Miranda was invented by Shakespeare for the beautiful and admirable young heroine of his play, *The Tempest*. It also has a hint of Latin rhythm left from its association with the fiery Brazilian entertainer Carmen Miranda. Be warned, though, that this name is no longer unique—more and more parents are becoming aware of its attributes. Many are using it as an alternate for the overused Amanda, with the result that Miranda is in danger of overuse itself.

MIRIAM. Though this name plays a prominent role in the Old Testament, its sphere has remained more limited than that of other biblical names like Sarah and Rebecca, although Miriam does have some prominence among the Muslims of Somalia and Ethiopia. The oldest known form of Mary—the Old Testament version of the Hebrew MARYAM—it appears in Exodus as the elder sister of Moses and Aaron, a prophetess who led the triumphal song and dance after the crossing of the Red Sea and deliverance of the Israelites from the Egyptians. And in secular literature, Miriam was the hero's first great love in D. H. Lawrence's *Sons and Lovers*. It is a name to consider if you are looking for a pleasant sounding, not overly used biblical name. In modern Israel, the form MIRA/MIRRA has become quite popular.

MISTY. To be used in descriptions of picturesque landscapes rather than as a proper name.

MITZI. This spunky German pet form of Maria might appeal to someone who is drawn to the whole genre of period chorus girl names that proliferated in 1930s musicals. The entertainer Mitzi Gaynor was originally named Francesca—a pair of opposites if we ever saw one.

MOLLY. A name with a lot of strength and spirit, Molly, the long-independent English pet form of Mary, has a distinctly Irish feel as well, arising from such Gaelic associations as "Sweet Molly Malone" and the martyred Pennsylvania coal mining reformers known as the Molly Maguires. Old-fashioned without being sentimental, Molly has appealed to such parents as Erica Jong, Cybill Shepherd, and Mary Beth Hurt. Incipient trendiness is its only drawback. Other determined heroines with the name have been the Revolutionary period Molly Pitcher (born Mary McCauley), the unsinkable Molly Brown, and TV's Molly Dodd. MALI is the Welsh spelling.

MONA. This Gaelic name doesn't have the most optimistic sound in the world, and it is one we would be surprised to find chosen for a contemporary baby girl. It was last noticed as the name of the coquettish Grandma on the series, *Who's the Boss?*

MONICA. Monica had some flair in the forties and fifties, when it was used primarily in Catholic families, but it has just about faded away at this point. Not that we would write it off completely for the future. After all, the fourth-century St. Monica was the very paragon of maternal patience, who helped turn her son, the brilliant scholar Augustine of Hippo, into one of the greatest of Christian teachers. In recent years we have seen tennis star Monica Seles and Monica Quartermaine, a staple on the soap opera *General Hospital*. The French version, MONIQUE, has been in the Top 40 names used by African-American parents for the past several years.

MORGAN. A lean, silvery, and sophisticated ambigender name that began as a traditional Welsh male one, Morgan is definitely falling more and more into the girls' side of the equation. There are ancient precedents: In Arthurian legend, Morgan Le Fay was the not very nice stepsister of King Arthur who did, nevertheless, serve as the leader of the queens who carried him away to cure his wounds. In modern times, sexy Morgan Fairchild has played a significant role in promoting the name—one wonders what would have happened if she had kept her original name of Patsy. But let's be frank: Morgan's star is dimming almost before it really had a chance to shine, and some other androgynous choice—Murphy or MAGEE or Michael—might prove more interesting and durable.

MURIEL. This onetime poetic name of Celtic origin, the name of the angel who governs the month of June, is now showing signs of age, relegated to playing grandmas on TV sitcoms.

MURPHY. One of the boldest, brightest, and breeziest of the Irish surname names, thanks to the character played so convincingly by Candice Bergen on *Murphy Brown*—and to then-Vice President Dan Quayle for keeping it in the headlines for so long.

MYRA and MYRNA. They come from different places, but their tarnished images have a lot in common. Myra was invented in the seventeenth century by a poet called Fulke Grenville as a short form of Miranda, and it quickly caught on with other poets and romantic novelists. It was later used by a very different kind of novelist—Gore Vidal—for the female half of his protagonist, Myra Breckenridge. Myrna, on the other hand, is a traditional Irish name related to the strong-scented myrrh, used in preparing perfumes and incense, and was found in significant numbers among secretarial staffs of the twenties and thirties. Its most well-known bearer was the sparkling portrayer of Nora Charles, Myrna Loy.

MYRTLE. This name is so far out of style that we can conceive of some intrepid, lionhearted parents taking on the challenge of resurrecting it. Myrtle is also the name of a shrub with shiny green leaves and sweet-smelling white blossoms used to make perfume, a plant that in Greek myth was sacred to Venus, and therefore a symbol of love.

N

∿∿∿∿∿∿∿∿∿∿∿∿∿∿∿ ◉ ∿∿∿∿∿∿∿∿∿∿∿∿∿∿∿

NAAMA, NAAMIT, NAAVA. The meanings of these three related Hebrew names encompass many of the traditional female attributes: beauty, grace, pleasantness, charm, tenderness, and kindness.

NADIA. This exotic Russian and Slavic name—which means "hope"—took on added energy and charm when it became attached to the Rumanian Olympic gymnast Nadia Comaneci in 1976. Its French offshoot, NADINE, hit Paris in the early years of this century when the success of the Ballet Russe set off a fad for all things Russian. It has had some usage in this country, reinforced by Chuck Berry's sixties rock classic, "Nadine," but is rarely heard now.

*

NANCY. Even though it's no longer in style, Nancy still has a pleasantly light and airy feel. Originally a pet form of Ann and Hannah, it peaked about 1940, when it was the seventh most popular girls' name in America. Around that time it was closely linked with girl detective Nancy Drew and with Frank Sinatra, who crooned the haunting song "Nancy With the Laughing Face" for his newborn daughter. More recently it has evoked the image of the First Lady in red, Nancy Reagan, who was actually christened Anne Frances, and the high-profile ice skating silver medalist at the 1994 Winter Olympics, Nancy Kerrigan.

NANETTE. This harks back to the time when anything French sounded chic, and there was a rage for such names as ANNETTE, CLAUDETTE, JEANETTE, GEORGETTE, Paulette, SUZETTE— and Nanette. But if you're considering it for a nineties baby, I'm afraid we'd have to say "No, no, Nanette."

NAOMI. Unlike other Old Testament female names such as Sarah, Rachel, and Rebecca, Naomi has never been widely used in this country except in Jewish families, and even there it has not had sweeping popularity. Which is too bad, we think, because it has such a soft, melodic sound, and an all-encompassing positive meaning in Hebrew—"delightful," "beautiful," "charming," "tender," and "gentle." Its biblical referent is the wise mother-in-law of Ruth, and because of this it is a symbolic name given to girls born on Shavuot when the Bible story of Ruth is read in the synagogue. Naomi moves out of the temple and into secular life with singer Naomi Judd and model Naomi Campbell. NOEMI is the mellifluous Italian variation of the name.

NATALIE. This French form of a Russian name has become completely Americanized, and a new generation of parents is reviving it along with former canasta partners like Sophie, Belle, and Molly. Since its literal meaning is "birthday of the Lord," it is sometimes given to girls born on Christmas Day. For years it was associated with Natalie Wood (born Natasha), who became famous as a child star in the 1940s; more recently it's been linked to singer Natalie Cole, whose full name is Stephanie Natalie Maria, but chose to use the middle name in honor of her father, Nat "King" Cole. In London, where the name has been more consistently fashionable, the forms NATALIA, NATALYA, and NATANIA are occasionally used.

NATASHA. Audrey Hepburn's incandescent performance as Natasha in the 1956 movie of Tolstoy's *War and Peace* inspired some adventurous parents to import this Russian beauty to our shores. But while European iconoclasts like Vanessa Redgrave and Klaus Kinski used the name for their daughters in those pre-Perestoika days—spawning actresses Natasha Richardson and Nastassja Kinski—it wasn't until the end of the Cold War that the name achieved widespread acceptability here. Today, Natasha makes an exotic and appealing choice. Variant spellings include NATASSIA, NASTASSIA, NATASHIA, and NATASSJA, and the prevailing short form is TASHA.

NEAL, NEIL. Instead of using one of the obscure feminizations of Neil (NEILA, NEALA), we say why not appropriate the boy's name itself? It's one of those names, like SYDNEY and Seth, that immediately sound zippier as the result of a gender change. Neila (pronounced

Neh-ee-la) is also the name of the closing service on Yom Kippur, and can be a symbolic choice for girls born on that day. In the same family is NELIA, an attractive diminutive of Cornelia sometimes used on its own.

NELL. A name with a good deal of sweet, old-fashioned charm is Nell, which is officially a nickname for Helen, Ellen, or Eleanor but is most fashionably today a name used in its own right. Nell was the pet name FDR always called his wife Eleanor; the famous Little Nell in Dickens's *Old Curiosity Shop* was Elinor; and the infamous mistress of Charles II, Nell Gwynne, was born Eleanor as well. NELLIE (or NELLY) also recalls the Gay Nineties and bicycles built for two and songs like "Wait till the sun shines, Nellie."

NERISSA. An offbeat possible substitute for overused names such as Melissa and Vanessa, Nerissa, whose meaning relates to sea sprites, was the name of Portia's witty confidante in Shakespeare's *The Merchant of Venice*.

NESSA. Like its cousin TESSA, Nessa is a nickname—most often for Vanessa—that can stand on its own.

NETTIE. This is a real knitting and crocheting Grandma name that might work for a contemporary little girl in search of relief from a more formal and less wieldy name—maybe inherited from her own grandma—like Henrietta or ANNETTE.

NEVADA. Named for the snow-capped mountains of that state, Nevada is a fresh possibility for parents interested in place-names—with the usual caveat that today's undiscovered place-name could well be tomorrow's trampled tourist attraction. Another option is NEVA, which derives from the Spanish word for "snow" and has an evocatively exotic aura.

NIA. A more modern-sounding alternative to the somewhat dated Mia, Nia has become a favorite among African-American parents for whom the name has special meaning as one of the days of the holiday Kwanza, and is also a heroine of Welsh legend. Nia Peeples is an emerging young actress.

NIAMH. One of the ancient Gaelic names restored to favor in modern Ireland, Niamh is sometimes spelled NIAV to more closely reflect its pronunciation, neev. In Irish mythology, Niamh was the Princess of the Land of Promise.

NICOLE. Nicole was one of the most popular girls' names of the seventies and eighties (it reached number four in 1980), with parents responding to its French flair, just as they did to other French names like Danielle and Michelle. It has now become a teenaged name, (except perhaps on Staten Island, where it still tops the list), seen on television as the girl with *My Two Dads*. Those who have known a few too many Nicoles might want to consider NICOLA (pronounced like Nicholas without the *s*). This elegant Italian form of Nicholas (it's used for males in Italy) has long been standard issue for English girls, but for some reason has rarely made it across the Atlantic. Both names, by the way, come from the Greek Nike, which means "victory" as well as sneakers. Another, more feminine, possibility beginning to come into play is NICOLETTE, which was the name of an enchanting princess in the medieval French romance *Aucassin et Nicolette*, as well as being associated with the contemporary actress of *Knot's Landing* fame, Nicolette Sheridan. NICOLETTA may also be used; NICO is a much more modern nickname for any of the above than the overused NICKI.

NINA. This is a name that's about as cross-cultural as you can get. In Spanish, it is the word for a "young girl." In Assyro-Babylonian mythology, Nina was the goddess of the oceans; to the Incas, the goddess of fire. And in Russia it's a common name used as a pet form of ANTONINA, JANINA, and everything else ending in *ina*. The most famous American Nina, jazz singer Nina Simone, was born Eunice. Today, Nina is a stylish possibility that has not approached overuse.

NIXIE. If you think Dixie, Trixie, and PIXIE are outlandish, consider Nixie. This is the name of a mermaidlike water sprite in German folklore, half woman, half fish, who could be glimpsed only by lovers in the light of the full moon.

NOELLE, NOEL. *middle name* The French word for "Christmas" has been given to children of both sexes born on that holiday ever since the Middle Ages. These days, the male spelling might be considered preferable for girls as well, and its usage certainly doesn't have to be limited to any particular time of year. There is a character called Noelle on the soap opera *All My Children*.

NOLA. A name with a haunting, sensual quality, it belonged to the woman everyone wanted, and vice versa, in Spike Lee's groundbreaking 1986 film, *She's Gotta Have It*. In the same family are NONA, a Welsh name that in the Victorian era was sometimes given to the ninth child in a family, and NOVA, which, in astronomy means a star that suddenly increases in brightness, then returns to its normal state (and which might work better for a TV science show than for a child).

NORA. This lovely old Irish name, originally a nickname for HONORA, is being rediscovered after a hibernation of close to a century. Soft and refined, it calls up images of women in velvet and fur collars ice skating in Central Park at the turn of the century—although it was certainly borne by any number of humble washerwomen as well. The most famous Nora in drama is the heroine of Ibsen's *The Doll's House*, who was finally able to slam the door and start a life of her own. Nick and Nora Charles were the sophisticated martini-sipping couple created by Dashiell Hammett and featured in *The Thin Man* series of movies, and Nora Ephron is the witty writer and director of *Sleepless in Seattle*. NORAH is acceptable, but pointless. The diminutive form NOREEN is much more of the Mickey Mouse Club era and is rarely used today.

NORMA. At this point, Norma is a real Mom name—as it was used in *The Wonder Years*—pleasant, but not too clued in about what's really going on in today's world. Invented by the librettist of Bellini's opera,

Norma, its fame was spread by two early real movie Normas (Talmadge and Shearer) and two later fictional movie Normas, Norma Desmond, the legendary silent screen star in *Sunset Boulevard*, and Norma Rae, for which Sally Field gratefully received an Oscar. And then of course there was Norma Jean, the chrysalis that metamorphosed into Marilyn Monroe.

NORRIS. An English surname that had been used only for males until Mrs. Norman Mailer, Norris Church (born Barbara), came on the scene.

O

ᴧᴧᴧᴧᴧᴧᴧᴧᴧᴧᴧᴧᴧᴧᴧᴧᴧᴧᴧᴧᴧᴧᴧᴧᴧ ◉ ᴧᴧᴧᴧᴧᴧᴧᴧᴧᴧᴧᴧᴧᴧᴧᴧᴧᴧᴧᴧᴧᴧᴧᴧᴧ

OBA. The evocative Nigerian name of an ancient river goddess, this is one African choice unfamiliar here but definitely worthy of attention.

OBEDIENCE. It may have been popular among Puritan families, but if you are interested in a "virtue" name, we suggest you stick with Hope, Faith, or Honor and not test your child's character by giving her a name like Obedience or Chastity.

OCTAVIA. A Latin name meaning "eighth"—and was at one time given to the eighth child born into a family—Octavia was very common in Roman times (it belonged to the daughter of Claudius and pre-Cleopatra wife of Marc Antony), and is interesting for its combination of classical and musical overtones.

ODELIA, ODELE. Odelia is a pretty Hebrew name that would make a truly distinctive choice. Odele has Greek roots and a melodic meaning, and is sometimes heard in the South.

ODESSA. An exotic, original, and attractive place-name. The Russian port city was given the name by Catherine the Great, inspired by Homer's *Odyssey*.

ODETTA, ODETTE, ODILE. One of the first single-name celebrities was fifties folksinger Odetta, who carried the name into the limelight. Odette and Odile, on the other hand, are two French names that appear in the ballet *Swan Lake*; Odette, a lighter, more upbeat name, is the good swan, while Odile, a more sinuous, sensuous one, represents the side of evil.

OKSANA. This Russian name was virtually unknown in the West before the extraordinary young Ukranian orphan figure skater Oksana Baiul won first place in the World Championships and then the gold medal at the 1994 Winter Olympics. Her charm and grace just might inspire some American parents to adopt the name.

OLA. This simple but distinctive name has an unusual diversity of origins—both Norse and Polish as well as being a Nigerian name meaning "wealth."

OLGA. Whatever exotic oomph this Russian name may have had in the past is pretty much faded by now so at this point it sounds rather drab and dull. Olga was one of Chekhov's Three Sisters, the name of the saint who was instrumental in spreading Christianity in Russia and the name of one of the USSR's most famous and popular gymnasts, Olga Korbut.

OLIVE. Right now it's greatly overshadowed by the far trendier Olivia, but Olive has a more subtle, evocatively shaded appeal all its own—especially if we ignore the fact that its most famous bearer is the elastic-limbed Olive Oyl, Popeye's steady. One of the first botanical names to be applied to people, it has nothing but positive associations: The olive branch has been the symbol of peace since ancient times and an olive wreath celebrates honor and success. Trivia note: Olive is the real first name of Marie Osmond.

OLIVIA. Olivia, a name with an ideal balance of strength and femininity, is now the number five girl's name in England and catching up quickly in this country as well. It was popularized by Shakespeare in *Twelfth Night* as the name of the pampered, wealthy countess. Its prime representative was Olivia DeHavilland until Olivia Newton-John made it big in the seventies, and since then it's been a regular on TV: as the mother of the Walton clan, on soap operas *As the World Turns*, *General Hospital*, and *The Young and the Restless*, for the little girl played by Raven Symone on *The Cosby Show*, and for the baby born to one of the *Designing Women*. In real life, Denzel Washington chose it for his twin daughter. LIVIA is a shortened form sometimes used on its own—particularly in Italy. The nickname, LIVVY, is what Mark Twain always called his wife Olivia.

OLWEN. This name is as common in Wales as the more familiar Bronwen, although it's extremely rare here. In Welsh legend, the beautiful giant's daughter Olwen (which literally means "white footprint") had the magical power of causing white clovers to spring up wherever she walked.

OLYMPIA. Because of its relation to Mt. Olympus, home of the Greek gods and to the Olympic Games, this name has an athletic, goddesslike aspect. It was brought into the spotlight in recent years by Oscar-winning actress Olympia Dukakis.

OONA, OONAGH. Any name beginning with double *o*s (and this is the only one we know of) has, almost by definition, a lot of oomph. The Anglicized form of the Gaelic name Una, which means "unity," Oona was made famous in this country by the woman who was both daughter of playwright Eugene O'Neill and wife of the immortal Charlie Chaplin.

OPAL. Opal has lost its luster, a pity, we think, because of the shimmering opalescence this name can reflect on its bearer. There is a long-running character named Opal on the soap opera *All My Children*.

OPHELIA. Poor Ophelia. Ever since the beautiful young maiden went mad and drowned herself in *Hamlet*, the name has carried an unfortunate stigma. It actually means "help" in Greek, and if you can put Shakespeare aside, is a lovely sounding name.

ORA, ORAH, ORALIA, ORALIE, ORIANA, ORIEL, ORLA. All these names relate to the light of dawn and are therefore bathed in a golden glow. Oriana has been used a great deal in Spanish and English poetry; in fact two queens, Elizabeth I and Anne, were both referred to as Oriana by poets. Oriel is considered the angel of destiny. Possible problems with it: Many adults would think it was a mispronunciation of Ariel, and kids might be tempted to make Oreo-cookie jokes. Orla, Celtic for "golden lady," is used quite commonly in Ireland.

ORPAH. The Orpah Winfrey Show? No, we didn't misspell the biblical name (Orpah was an in-law of Naomi and Ruth); OPRAH's namers did. As a result, Oprah's the name that has become famous and, if you name your child Orpah, everyone will think you're the one who's wrong. The bottom line, however, is that neither name is really a viable choice. The mega-talk show hostess herself once said, on her own show, "People call me Ophrie, Okrie, Ackrie, Little Grand Ole Oprah . . . Okra the vegetable . . . but after a while you just sort of get used to people not respecting you."

OTTALIE, OTTILIE, OTTOLINE. All three of these French and German feminizations of Otto are a lot more appealing than the original. And the whole trio is used much more among the English elite than they are in this country.

OUIDA. This is one of the only names we know of that arose out of baby talk—it was a mispronunciation of the name Louise, as is the even rarer **OUISA**, used in John Guare's play *Six Degrees of Separation*, not to mention **OUISER** in *Steel Magnolias*. (The famous French novelist known only as Ouida was born Marie Louise.) Ouida's image is anything but babylike, however; it has an exotic and mysterious air.

P

〜〜〜〜〜〜〜〜〜〜〜〜〜〜〜〜 ◉ 〜〜〜〜〜〜〜〜〜〜〜〜〜〜〜〜

PAGE, PAIGE. A sleek and sophisticated name (especially with the now-preferred spelling Paige, as used by the editor of tony *Architectural Digest* magazine and the Nicolette Sheridan character in *Knots Landing*) that is growing in popularity. In 1993, there were 322 Paiges born in the State of Pennsylvania. It was also chosen by director Ron Howard as the name of his twin daughter.

PALLAS. This rarified Greek name—in classical mythology, the title Pallas Athene was given to Athena, goddess of wisdom, industry, and the arts—might just attract literary-minded parents; it did best-selling-writer-couple Louise Erdrich and Michael Dorris, who named another daughter Persia.

PALMA. This appealing Latin name is both geographical (the romantic Spanish island city of Palma de Majorca) and botanical: It derives from the palm frond, a symbol of happiness, success, and victory, and has sometimes been given to girls born on Palm Sunday.

PALOMA. Thanks to the high-profile daughter of Pablo Picasso, this Spanish name has taken on a vibrant, ruby-lipped image and is definitely being short-listed by certain trendy types—Emilio Estevez, for one, chose it for his daughter. Picasso herself gives it a lot of credit. As she once said, "I think my name Paloma, which means dove, is the most beautiful gift I was ever given. . . . It's very striking and memorable, and that's good for business."

PAMELA. Pam was a prom queen in the sixties, and a little bit pampered at that—who was never, ever called by her full name. Which is a pity, because Pamela (originally pronounced Pameela) is so mellifluous, and so rich in literary tradition. It was first used by Elizabethan poet Sir Philip Sidney in his sixteenth-century pastoral epic, *Arcadia*, but it was Samuel Richardson's enormously popular novel, *Pamela, or Virtue Rewarded*, two centuries later, that really promoted it. Although it reached the Top 10 in 1970, Pamela is rarely used now, except for TV characters like the prosperous Pamela Ewing on *Dallas*.

PANDORA. In England, this name is sometimes taken up by the more eccentric gentry (for horsey girls with brothers named PEREGRINE); in America it's all but unheard of, except for the mythological Pandora's box. In case you've forgotten, in classical lore, Pandora was the first woman on earth, sent to bring about the downfall of man, which she did when curiosity caused her to lift the lid of the box that released all the evils of the world.

PANSY. This was one of the flower names (its much weightier derivation is the French *pensee*, meaning "thought") that came into fashion in the nineteenth century, found in novels such as Henry James's *Portrait of a Lady*. But its widespread employment as a derogatory slang term for gays from the 1920s on pretty much canceled whatever limited currency it had.

PARKER, PAXTON, PAYTON, PEYTON, PORTER. These are all surnames that initially became male first names and now are used for girls as well. They each have a nice crisp contemporary edge and any of them would make a creditable choice for your little prospective CEO.

PATIENCE. Not a bad virtue as virtues go, but not a particularly easy name to grow up with either, assuming your child's strong points do not include sitting quietly waiting for something to happen. It was another story in the seventeenth century, when it was quite the fashion to name girls after the Seven Christian Virtues. Patience was also the eponymous heroine of a Gilbert and Sullivan comic operetta.

PATRICIA. Patricia still sounds patrician, though the many nicknames it spawned definitely don't. It began not in Ireland, as you might think, but evolved in Scotland, going on to become mega-popular in Britain after the christening of Queen Victoria's granddaughter, known to one and all as Princess Pat. Patricias—though rarely called that except in the classroom or at choir practice—ran rampant from the forties (it was the fourth most popular girls' name in 1948), through the sixties (it was still number nine when the First Lady was Pat—born Thelma—Nixon), but it was the short forms that took on lives of their own. There was PATSY, used mostly for Irish girls (and sometimes for Irish and Italian boys as well), which was the sassiest, spunkiest name for the jump-roping, freckle-faced, pigtailed girls of the twenties and thirties, and which then faded fast. Patsy was replaced by PATTI/PATTY, the pervasive, peppy baby-sitter name of the next generation, epitomized by Patty Duke, who pleaded in the title of her autobiography *Call Me Anna* (her real name). In another ten years or so, Patti was dropped in favor of more upwardly mobile nicknames TRICIA, TRISHA, TRISH, TISHA, and TISH. The one form that hasn't been picked up here, but which is widely used in England on its own is the fresher-sounding PATIA. The French form, PATRICE, which is a male name in France, is occasionally heard here.

PAULA, PAULINE, PAULINA, PAULETTE. All these are, of course, various feminizations of the classic male name Paul. Most promising of this Paul-girl group right now is Paulina (the Italian spelling is PAOLINA), thanks in large part to the appeal of Czech model/actress Paulina Porizkova. Paulina has been attached to an enterprising, spirited wife in Shakespeare's *A Winter's Tale*, and a character on the soap opera *Another World*; it is also the name chosen by hockey superstar Wayne Gretzky for his daughter. The first of the Paul feminizations on the scene was Paula, the name of a fourth-century saint who became the patron saint of widows; the name later reappeared as a rock song inspiration (as in "Hey Paula"). There are more recent representatives, such as choreographer/singer Paula Abdul and *This Morning* host Paula Zahn, but the name is now relatively colorless and rarely considered for girls of the nineties. Then there was Pauline, the title of the first poem published by Robert Browning and popular in this country in the era of silent films like the classic Saturday-afternoon serial, *The Perils of Pauline*. Paulette was part of the French fad of the twenties and thirties, and was long associated with Paulette Goddard. A new addition to the list is PAULE, brought into the mix by writer Paule Marshall, whose roots are in the West Indies.

PAZ and **PAZIA** (pronounced Pah-ZEE-uh). These are two exotic and unique Hebrew names that mean "sparkling" or "golden." In Spanish, of course, paz means "peace"—a worthy message for a name to carry.

PEACHES. This is one of those litmus test type names that define the limits of just how far you are willing to go in your search for a name that is hip, outrageous, never-to-be-mainstream. Irish musician and organizer of Live Aid Bob Geldof pushed the envelope on this one, naming one daughter Peaches, the younger sister of—who else?—Fifi Trixiebelle.

PEARL. Pearl, like Ruby, is a name that's beginning to be polished up for use for a new generation of fashionable children, after nearly a century of storage in the back of the jewel case, despite the persistence of such phrases as "She's a pearl" and "pearls of wisdom." Parents not quite brave enough to choose Pearl as a first name might want to consider it as a fresh-sounding middle name alternative to the becoming-overused Rose. PERLA is an occasionally used variant.

PEGGY. Peggy still carries with it the wholesome, pug-nosed, happy-go-lucky image it had from the 1920s and into the 1950s Peggy-Sue-got-married era: perky and pure, the perfect date for the prom. It originated as a pet name for Margaret (moving from Margaret to Maggie to MEGGIE to Peggy) and has been the subject of any number of songs, from "Peg O' My Heart" to, yes, "Peggy Sue." But can you remember the last time you heard it applied to an infant? PEGEEN is the dated Irish diminutive.

PENELOPE, PENNY. Penelope has a kind of straitlaced, stodgy, starchy feel, perhaps because it has for so long been associated with the faithful, long-suffering wife of Odysseus in Homer's *Odyssey*. New parents will probably run into it if they consult the works of British child-rearing maven Penelope Leach. Penny, on the other hand, is, like PATSY and Peggy, the kind of zesty moniker the young Judy Garland would don for her early Andy Hardy and let's-put-on-a-show movies of the thirties and forties. It has scarcely been heard from since, except on the screen where it says "directed by Penny Marshall."

PEONY, POPPY, POSY, and PRIMROSE. A bouquet of seldom seen, sweet-smelling, Victorian-valentine flower names you might find worth considering. The peony is thought to have healing powers, the poppy's brilliant red flowers have narcotic properties, Posy is also used as a pet name for Josephine, and PRIMROSE is still found in quaint British novels. All four are stylishly used for little girls in England, where gardening is a national pastime; of the four, Poppy is probably the most popular.

PEPITA, PEPPER. These are two names with so much energy—or should we say pep?—they almost bounce off the page. Pepita is the diminutive of JOSEFINA, just as PEPE is the nickname for the male GIUSEPPE.

PERDITA. To anyone who ever took a Latin language, this name will, unfortunately, sound lost. It was invented by Shakespeare for an abandoned baby princess in *The Winter's Tale*, but those of us in touch with our childhoods are more likely to recall it as one of the canine characters in Disney's *One Hundred and One Dalmatians*.

PERRY. Perry is a relaxed male name that has begun to be used for girls over the past few years—a fresher alternative to shopworn favorites such as Kerry and Sherry. Spelled PERI, it is a Hebrew name meaning "fruit," "abundance."

PERSIA. This place name, first used in the pre-Iran days, still retains the brilliant coloration of an ancient Persian miniature, which must have appealed to writers Louise Erdrich and Michael Dorris, who chose it for their daughter. PERSIS is a related name, meaning "coming from Persia," and mentioned in the Old Testament.

PETA, PETRA. Two modern English feminine forms of Peter. One-time Bee Gee, Andy Gibb, named his daughter Peta. PETULA, which means "saucy" or "impudent" in Latin, surfaced here briefly in the swinging London days of singer Petula ("Downtown") Clark, as did PETULIA in the memorable 1968 film of that name starring Julie Christie.

PHILIPPA, PIPPA. There is a whole group of boys' names adapted for girls that are used in England far more than here (e.g., JACOBA, JOSEPHA, Georgina, ROBINA), and Philippa is one of the prime—and most accessible—examples, as common as crumpets in Cornwall, as rare as reindeer meat in Miami. Philippa, like Philip, is from the Greek, meaning "lover of horses," and has been fashionable in England since the fourteenth century when King Edward married Philippa of Hainault. One of its nicknames (others are FLIPPA and PIP) is now used on its own: the effervescent PIPPA, made famous in Browning's poem, "Pippa Passes."

PHILOMENA. An earthy Greek name, used now in various Latin countries, that belonged to a mythological Athenian princess who was transformed by the gods into a nightingale to save her from the advances of a lecherous king. But the story's much lovelier than the name.

PHOEBE. A captivating name looked upon with great affection by anyone who's ever read *The Catcher in the Rye*, as it's borne by Holden Caulfield's sympathetic younger sister. A mythological, biblical, and Shakespearean name, Phoebe means "the pure, shining one" and is one of the titles given by the ancient Greeks to the goddess of the moon. The name of one of the linchpins of the soap opera, *All My Children*, Phoebe is also the name John Lithgow chose for his daughter. We predict that others will follow suit.

PHYLLIS. It may have a stolid, middle-aged image now, but at one time Phyllis was the very essence of lyrical grace. The name of a mythical Greek princess who pined away for love until she was transformed into an almond tree, it was used by classical poets to represent the idealized country maiden. Phyllis was in the Top 30 in 1925, but has been sinking ever since, helped along by the cloying character played by Cloris Leachman on *The Mary Tyler Moore Show*, and Phyllis Diller in her wild-hair days. On the other hand, Phylis Wheatley, the poet who was brought over as a slave from Africa in 1761, is a major Black American writer and a worthy name inspiration. One of Phyllis's variants, PHILLIDA is occasionally heard on *Masterpiece Theater* or *Mystery!* And PHYLICIA, as in *The Cosby Show* mom actress Phylicia Rashad, which looks like a variation of Phyllis, is really just the phonetic spelling of FELICIA.

PIA. A soft name in the Mia-Nia-RIA family, Pia is heard in several languages: in Italian, where it means "pious," and in Swahili and Hindi, where it means "loved one." In the case of telecaster Pia Lindstrom, it came from the combination of her parents' initials, Peter Aaron + Ingrid (Bergman, the movie star).

PILAR. The fact that this Spanish name does not end in the conventional letter *a* imparts to it a special sense of strength and elegance, in keeping with its meaning of "pillar of the church." The name of a memorably heroic character in Hemingway's *For Whom the Bell Tolls*, Pilar seems eternally stylish and would make a worthy choice.

PIPER. A light, musical name associated with actress Piper Laurie, whose birth name was Rosetta. It was recently chosen by actress Gillian Anderson.

POLLY. Polly projects the innocence of an earlier time, which may explain why it hasn't been revived as enthusiastically as Molly. We think the *P* gives it a peppier sound, combining the home-style virtues of an old-fashioned name with the bounce of a barmaid. Polly and Molly are both offshoots of Mary (it went from Mary to MALLY to Molly to Polly). Polly Peachum was the guileless heroine of *The Three-penny Opera* and POLLYANNA went down in literary history as the eternal optimist.

PORTIA. This is the perfect role model name for feminist-oriented parents, since, as far back as Shakespeare's time, Portia was portrayed as a brilliant, independent minded lawyer (albeit disguised as a man) in *The Merchant of Venice*, a model perpetuated on a long-running radio serial, *Portia Faces Life*. Some parents have corrupted the spelling of the name to PORSHA, and even (perhaps this is wishful thinking), PORSCHE.

PRISCILLA. Its very construction tends to make this name sound prissy, but thinking of Priscilla Presley could give it a completely different spin. The Brits sometimes get around this by accenting the second part of the name, CILLA, as a nickname or even on its own. Priscilla is a New Testament name (the apostle Paul stayed with her while spreading the gospel in Corinth), also made famous in the Longfellow poem, "The Courtship of Miles Standish" as Priscilla ("Why don't you speak for yourself, John?") Alden.

PRUDENCE. Like Hope and Faith, this is one of the Puritan abstract virtue names that is still viable today, possessing a quiet charm and sensitivity. The name might present difficulties, however, during the adolescent years, when young Prudence would be continually asked whether she is a prude. The related PRUNELLA, which means "little plum" and is used in England, might have an even tougher time here because of the disagreeable connotations of prunes.

Q

〜〜〜〜〜〜〜〜〜〜〜〜 ◉ 〜〜〜〜〜〜〜〜〜〜〜〜

QUEENIE. If you like cheeky chorus girl-barmaid names like Fifi and Trixie, here's another one of that ilk. Originally a nickname for girls christened Regina (the Latin word for "queen") and for those named Victoria during the long reign of that regent, it is, we must warn you, much more often used for dogs.

QUIANA. A melodious synthetic name (also spelled CHIANA) that has become increasingly popular purely by virtue of its sound.

QUINN. This was one of the first post-Ryan Irish surnames to become accepted for both boy and girl babies, and still has a lot of style and strength. It means "intelligent" in Gaelic, and also harks back to the Old English word *cwen*, which means "queen." Quinn Cummings was a child actress of the 1970s.

QUINELLA, QUINETTA, QUINTA, QUINTANA, QUINT- ESSA, QUINTILLA, QUINTINA, and **QUINTONA** are all related to the number five. At one time they were given to the fifth child in the family, but they can also be given to one born on the fifth day of the month or in May, the fifth month of the year. Joan Didion and John Gregory Dunne's now-grown-up daughter is named Quintana Roo, after the Mexican province.

R

~~~~~~~~~~~~~~~~~~~~ ◉ ~~~~~~~~~~~~~~~~~~~~~~

RACHEL, RACHAEL. It is probably the delicacy and softness of the name—it does mean "little lamb" in Hebrew—that has made Rachel one of the most consistently popular biblical girls' names since the late 1960s, when parents started to turn back to basic sources like the Bible. At a much earlier time Rachel was considered characteristically Jewish—it wasn't used as a Christian name until after the Reformation—but the fact that it is now the thirteenth most common name given to baby girls in America demonstrates that it has been widely embraced by all ethnic groups. In the Old Testament, Rachel was the beautiful and cherished wife of Jacob, and mother of Joseph and Benjamin. Celebrities who have chosen the name for their kids include Jane Pauley and Garry Trudeau and Kathleen Turner. Among the variants are the 17th century **RACHAEL**, the 20th century **RA- CHELLE** and the Spanish **RAQUEL**, Raquel Welch being half Bolivian. The diminutive **RAE** is also used independently, more often than not as a middle name.

RAINE. This unusual name popped into the headlines a few years ago when it was attached to Countess Spencer, stepmother of Princess Diana and daughter of novelist Barbara Cartland. And Richard Pryor has an actress daughter named RAIN. Andie MacDowell's daughter is RAINEY. For RAINA, see Regina.

RAISA. The name Raisa entered the American consciousness in the person of Mme Gorbachev, the Imperial wife of the former head of the former USSR. A possibility for parents of Eastern European descent (or interests) who want to move beyond the more familiar NATALIAs, Natashas, and Nadias.

RAMONA. Ramona, which fits into the desirable category of being not too popular and not too bizarre, came into prominence in the 1880s via the beautiful half-Native American heroine of the best-selling romance novel *Ramona*, by Helen Hunt Jackson. Since then it's been immortalized in a Nat "King" Cole song and was chosen for his daughter's name by director Jonathan Demme. Kids will associate it with the clever character of Ramona Quigley in the series of books by Beverly Cleary.

RANDI, RANDY. Like Mandy and CANDY, Marnie and Mindy, in the late sixties and early seventies, Randi was out to show the world just how laid back a name could be. Point proven, there are few Randis still hanging around—though the waitress-older man couple on television's *Northern Exposure* named their baby Randi, short for the infinitely more fashionable Miranda.

RAPHAELA, RAFFAELLA. This euphonious and exotic name, with its dark-eyed, long-flowing-haired image, is, like GABRIELLA and other such Latinate names, beginning to be drawn more into the mainstream.

RASHIDA, RASHEEDA. An evocative and alluring name meaning "righteous" in Turkish; less familiar than its male counterpart RASH-ID.

RAVEN. A recent trend among African-American parents has been to seek out name words that celebrate the beauty of blackness, in particular Ebony and Raven. The latter, which got a big boost from the popularity of young Raven Symone when she appeared as Olivia on *The Cosby Show*, has rated as high as number seven for Black girl babies in some states, such as Texas.

REBECCA. A name that has represented beauty in both the Bible and secular literature, Rebecca is as popular now as it was in the days of the Pilgrims. In the Old Testament, the bearer of the name, the wife of Isaac and mother of Jacob and Esau, was renowned for her loveliness, as was the Rebecca in Sir Walter Scott's *Ivanhoe*. Then there was the haunted Rebecca in the Daphne du Maurier novel of that name, and the BECKYs Sharp and Thatcher in *Vanity Fair* and *Tom Sawyer*. While BECKY is still the most common nickname, many modern Rebeccas are becoming known as BECCA. Another variation is REBA, which has garnered a country and western flavor, thanks to megastar Reba McIntire. Trivia note: When the Native American Princess Pocahontas was baptized, she took the name Rebecca.

REGAN. This vibrant last-name-first Irish name, while a strong, straightforward choice, does have a few unsavory literary connotations you might want to keep in mind: Regan was the nastiest of King Lear's three nasty daughters and the Regan character played by Linda Blair in *The Exorcist* got pretty nasty herself.

REGINA. This queenly name—Queen Victoria like other British queens had Regina appended to her name—has a certain regal elegance. On the other hand, the Regina played by Bette Davis in *The Little Foxes* can only be described as a ruthless vixen. RAINA, the Slavic form of the name, was introduced to the English-speaking world by George Bernard Shaw in his play, *Arms and the Man*, in 1894.

REMINGTON. This ultramasculine-sounding surname—whose macho image is only heightened (or is it deepened?) by TV's *Remington Steele*—takes an interesting 360-degree turn when assigned to a girl, something actress Tracy Nelson might have considered when naming her daughter Remington Elizabeth.

RENA, RINA, RENATA. Three names that evolved from the Hebrew word meaning "joyful song." Renata, the only fashionable version of the three, is used in Germany, Czechoslovakia, and Poland, as well as Italy. Writer Renata Adler has made the name semifamous among the literati.

RENÉE. Remember the Four Tops song, "Walk Away Renee"? Well, the name Renée walked away a few decades ago, along with such other French names as Roxanne and ROSALIE. But it might be trying for a comeback via Rod Stewart and Rachel Hunter, who have bestowed it on their baby girl. RENÉ, traditionally the male spelling, is now often used for girls. RENNY is a sometime nickname or variation.

RHEA. This melodious name is rich in mythological ambiance. The ancient Greeks believed Rhea to be the mother of the gods Zeus, Poseidon, Hera, Hestia, Hades, and Demeter and the goddess who personified the earth; to the Romans she was the mother of Romulus and Remus, legendary founders of Rome. In more modern times, the name is associated with actress Rhea Perlman, who played waitress Carla on *Cheers*. The similarly pronounced RIA is the short form of Maria, and sometimes used on its own.

RHIANNON. If your family has Welsh roots, you might want to consider this lovely name—it's pronounced ree-anon—which is almost unknown on this side of the Atlantic. In Celtic folklore, it is linked to the moon.

RHODA. The 1970s TV character Rhoda Morgenstern, played by Valerie Harper, put a pretty powerful Bronx accent on this name that actually means "rose" in Greek. It was widely used from the thirties to the fifties.

RHONDA. Rhonda is, talk about surprising origins, a place-name of southern Wales. In the forties it was attached to red-haired Rhonda (born Marilyn) Fleming, in the sixties to the Beach Boys tune, "Help me, Rhonda" and now, finally, to the campiest of late-night television hostesses. Warning: If you're considering this name for your child, you should know that its original meaning is "noisy one."

RICKI, RIKKI. This is one of the earliest of the relaxed, unisex names that were so faddish a few decades back, immortalized in the Steely Dan song, "Rikki Don't Lose That Number." The song and the name are both now restricted to classic rock stations and daytime talk shows like Ricki Lake's.

RILEY, REILLY. This is a lively Irish name that projects a particularly upbeat, cheerful feel. And just think, any child given that name will be sure to lead the life of Riley. Comedian Howie Mandel chose it for his daughter.

RIMA. Anyone who had to read *Green Mansions* in grade school will remember Rima the Bird Girl, the wild and beautiful creature of the jungle, played by Audrey Hepburn in the movie, and for them this name will always retain that image.

RIPLEY. A bold, intrepid surname choice; the name of the action heroine Sigourney Weaver played in *Aliens*.

RITA. Rarely used now, this was a hot name in the forties, the heyday of sexy Rita Hayworth (whose full name was Margarita), but is rarely given to babies today. The domain of the saint named Rita covers some pretty contemporary concerns—she is the patron of those in matrimonial difficulties and other desperate situations, as well as of parenthood. Rita is also a Hindu name, and was immortalized by the Beatles in "Lovely Rita, Meter Maid."

RIVA. This creative name means both "maiden" in Hebrew and "shore" in French. The related RIVKA (the Hebrew form of Rebecca) belonged to the wife of Isaac and mother of Jacob and Esau in the Old Testament.

ROBERTA. Roberta is, of course, the male name Robert feminized in the simplest way—with the addition of a final *a*. The title of a Jerome Kern operetta, it harks back to the day when Roberta sat around discussing the newest Sinclair Lewis novel with her friends Lois and Lorraine.

ROBIN. Robin—originally a male nickname for Robert—sounded bright and chirpy when it began to be used for girls in the fifties and sixties, but by now the name has definitely lost much of its lilt. One Robin still on the scene is the ex-Mrs. Michael Tyson, Robin Givens; another is Howard Stern's sidekick, Robin Quivers.

ROCHELLE. Although the meaning of this French name relates to rock, its image is much more feminine, fragile, and shell-like. And while its popularity peaked in the forties and fifties, it still retains a fragrant sweetness and sounds a bit fresher than some of the more current French favorites, like Michelle. Its nickname, Shelley, took on a life of its own, due largely to Shelley Winters.

ROMA. An old-fashioned place-name—the Italian name for its capital city—Roma has been in use since the 1880s, although it never achieved the popularity of that other Italian city, Florence. ROMY, actually a short form of Rosemary made famous by actress Romy Schneider, was the unusual name choice of Ellen Barkin and Gabriel Byrne for their young daughter. Going even further afield, the related ROMULA was created by George Eliot for her novel, and ROMAINE is also occasionally heard, for people as well as salads.

RORY. Buoyant and brimming with Irish spirit, Rory has a delightful red-headed, freckle-faced, slightly tomboyish image. But let's not be coy: One of us has a daughter named Rory, so we're only too familiar with the real-life ups and downs of the name. On the positive side, a female Rory (or even a male one, on this side of the ocean) always feels special because of her name. The negatives: confusion over one's gender, a serious issue when you're four, plus having to spell your name so people don't think it's LAURIE, Marie, or Gloria. Robert Kennedy's youngest daughter, born after he was assassinated, is named Rory. In the British Isles, Rory is a fashionable (and purely male) name, made famous by twelfth-century Irish high king Rory O'Connor.

ROSALIND. Rosalind started out as a lyrical, bucolic name, probably coined by Edmund Spenser for a shepherdess in one of his pastoral poems. It was further popularized by Shakespeare when he applied it to one of his most charming heroines, in *As You Like It*. Centuries later, it toughened up when it became linked with Rosalind Russell, the epitome of the fast-talking, supercapable, woman-in-a-man's-world, thirties and forties career woman. Spelled ROSLYN, it was the name Arthur Miller gave to the character he wrote for his then-wife Marilyn Monroe to play in *The Misfits*. And today? Rosalind is a name that can go either way, feeling a bit dated but perhaps so far out it's in if used for a hip young child.

ROSAMOND, ROSAMUND. This quintessentially English name is rarely heard on these shores, a situation we think should be rectified. "Fair Rosamond" was a legendary twelfth-century beauty, the mistress of Henry II, who built a house in which to sequester her in the middle of a maze, but his jealous wife, Eleanor of Aquitaine, managed to find and poison her. ROSEMOND is the middle name of Elizabeth Taylor.

ROSE. After five centuries of being associated with the fragrant flower, Rose has suddenly become an overnight success—as a middle name. Parents (such as Michelle Pfeiffer, who named her daughter Claudia Rose; Jeff Bridges, who has a Hayley Rose; Jon Bon Jovi with his Stephanie Rose; Rickie Lee Jones with Charlotte Rose, and Olivia Newton-John with Chloe Rose) across the country are finding this the perfect connective between first and last names, with much more color and charm than old standbys like Lynn, SUE, and Ann. It was popular as a first name all through the nineteenth century, as reflected in the dozens of songs it inspired—"Honeysuckle Rose," "Rose of Washington Square," "Second Hand Rose," "My Wild Irish Rose," "Rambling Rose" et al., and it has been well used in other languages too—RAIZEL in Yiddish, ROSA in Spanish and Italian, and is found in countless combination and pet forms, including ROSALIA, ROSALIE, RO-SALBA, ROSANNA, ROSELLE, ROSELLEN, ROSETTA, ROSITA, and, in a class by itself for obvious reasons, ROSEANNE. And some cool, pioneering parents, particularly Brits, are calling their kids RO-SIE, a name currently on movie marquees followed by O'Donnell and Perez.

ROSEMARY, ROSEMARIE. This particular amalgamation of two classic names projects a sweet, solid, somewhat old-fashioned, sensibility, suggesting the aromatic fragrance of the herb (although one namesake did give birth to *Rosemary's Baby*). The French version, Rosemarie, came into favor in the United States in the 1920s, partly influenced by the heroine of the Rudolf Friml operetta (and the song, "Rosemarie, I Love You"). Both names retain some popularity in Irish and Italian families. ROMY is the German pet form.

ROWENA. A fabled storybook name, Rowena is most identified with the noble heroine of *Ivanhoe*, who marries the eponymous hero. The name comes from the Welsh RHONWEN, meaning "slender" and "fair," an infinitely more attractive choice.

ROXANA, ROXANE, ROXANNE. Roxane has a touch of the exotic, perhaps because of its Eastern origins. It belonged to the Persian wife of Alexander the Great and, even more familiarly, to the beautiful and virtuous heroine of *Cyrano de Bergerac*, to whom Cyrano says "Your name is like a golden bell." It was chosen for their daughter by *thirtysomething* couple Ken Olin and Patricia Wettig. ROXY (also spelled ROXIE) is its far more audacious offshoot.

RUBY. Of the glistening array of jewel names (Pearl, Opal, Crystal, et al.) that became popular at the end of the nineteenth century, Ruby was and still is the most colorful. After a hundred-year hibernation, and perhaps inspired by the haunting Ray Charles song, it is once more being considered by such state-of-the-art parents as Rod Stewart and Kelly Emberg.

RUE. Unusual and rather mysterious, Rue comes from the Old German meaning "fame" (which did come to Golden Girl Rue McClanahan) and is redolent of the aromatic plant of that name.

RUMER. A lot of people said, "Huh?" when star couple Demi Moore and Bruce Willis bestowed this name on their first daughter. But when Demi and Bruce explained that it was inspired by English author Rumer (born Margaret) Godden, the name didn't sound quite so weird. Now we can ask them about Scout LaRue and Tallulah Belle.

RUTH. Ruth has an air of gentleness, calm, and compassion, qualities that apply to the biblical Ruth, the loyal and devoted daughter-in-law of NAOMI who left her own people to stay with the older woman, speaking the famous lines, "Whither thou goest, I will go." Although it was the second most popular girls' name in the country at the turn of the century, and still right up there at number five in 1925, Ruth is rarely heard from now. But parents tiring of Rachel and Rebecca might just want to give it a second thought. Tidbit: Ruth was the real name of Bette Davis.

S

~~~~~~~~~~~~~~~~~~~~~ ◉ ~~~~~~~~~~~~~~~~~~~~~

SABA, SABAH. This unusual, exotic name has a dual heritage: In the Bible it is an alternative form of Sheba, and in Arabic it means "morning." It is a Muslim name that is quite popular in North Africa.

SABINA, SABINE. An interestingly sleek, but neglected name, perhaps due to the fame of the story and the painting, *The Rape of the Sabine Women*. The Sabines were an ancient Italian race raided by the Romans, who were said to have carried off the Sabine women. But when the Sabines sought revenge, it was the women who succeeded in effecting peace between the two peoples.

SABRA. A strong but sensitive name that is now used as a term for native-born Israeli.

SABRINA. A name with a great deal of bewitching, bright-eyed charm and one that might be considered as a more distinctive alternative to the ultrapopular Samantha. Sabrina was a legendary Celtic goddess and, in more modern times, the heroine of a successful play called *Sabrina Fair* and its movie clone, *Sabrina* (Audrey Hepburn at her most glowing), a teenage witch on *The Archie Show* (who got a spinoff cartoon series of her own), the Kate Jackson character in *Charlie's Angels* and, yes, even a soap opera character—Sabrina Hughes of *As the World Turns*.

SADIE. This name (which originated as a pet form of Sarah) is one of those that can be seen as a litmus test defining where you stand in girl naming. For many people, Sadie is hopelessly out, either old-fashionedly grandmotheresque or low class beyond consideration, except perhaps for a pet. But for a certain forward-thinking, hip segment of the population, particularly the British gentry, Sadie is seen as quite the opposite—the coolest of the cool, epitomized by the lovely new star, Sadie Frost, first noticed in *Dracula*. The related SADE (pronounced Sharday) was brought to public attention by the Nigerian singer of that name (who was actually born Helen) and SADIO, which means "pure," is used in the French-speaking countries of West Africa.

SAFFRON. Shades of the sixties and seventies, Woodstock, the Maharishi, orange-scented incense, and sounds of the sitar; a pretty name for the retro rebel. It is the daughter's name on *Absolutely Fabulous*.

SAGE. A distinctively fragrant name that, of course, also connotes wisdom. Bear it in mind, too, if you're seeking a short but strong middle name. And if you like spice, you might also have a taste for CORIANDER, occasionally used as a name in England.

SALLY. Suddenly Sally is bouncing back, after several decades of lying low. A name with a cheerful, fresh-faced, good-girl-next-door image, Sally was originally a nickname for Sarah. It was popular in the eighteenth century and then again from the twenties to the sixties and was the inspiration of innumerable popular songs, from "My Gal Sal" to "Long Tall Sally" to "Lay Down Sally."

SALOMÉ. One of the sexiest names in the book, Salomé is a lot for a young girl to live up to, and should be approached with caution. In the Bible, Salomé danced for King Herod and pleased him so much that he offered her anything she wanted. What she requested and received was the head of John the Baptist, thus tainting the name with an unsavory association. In Hebrew, though, the name is related to shalom, meaning "peace."

SAMANTHA. This name began its phenomenal rise in popularity in the sixties (in large part ignited by its use for the endearing, nose-twitching heroine of the TV series, *Bewitched*) and shows no signs of diminishing—it is currently number four on the hit parade of girls' names; number one in South Dakota. Part of Samantha's popularity owes thanks to the stylishness of her brother, SAM, a nickname which is the prime appeal for many parents. In popular culture, the name also got a boost from the actress Samantha Eggar and from the Cole Porter song, "I Love You, Samantha," sung to Grace Kelly (playing Tracy Samantha Lord) in the 1956 movie, *High Society*, and has since become a sitcom staple—in shows from *My Sister Sam* to *Who's the Boss?* It is also, by the way, among the Top 10 names given to female dogs in both L.A. and New York.

SANDRA and SONDRA. These twin names were born in the thirties and were among the most popular girls' name in the class of 1950, but are rarely used for babies today. Originally offshoots of ALEXAN-DRA, the original is now favored.

SAPPHIRE. Never as popular as such other jewel names as Pearl or Ruby, Sapphire (the birthstone for September), has nevertheless seen some use. Unfortunately, it was the victim of stereotyping when it was applied to George (Kingfish) Stevens's harpy of a wife in *Amos and Andy*. The related SAPPHIRA is a Hebrew name meaning "gem."

SARAH, SARA. m. N. Firmly in America's Top 5—and approaching number one when you count both spellings—Sarah has been the premiere biblical girls' name here for two decades, offering rich Old Testament associations for those parents wishing to mine their religious roots and a sweet yet strong, patrician yet straightforward image to those in search of more secular name appeal. The big question: Are there too many Sarahs? While thousands of babies of all ethnic backgrounds throughout the country are given the name—the spelling ratio is generally three with the final *h* to every one without—Sarah has weathered trendiness perhaps better than any other contemporary female example. It's like one of the classic boys' names—Daniel, for instance, or David—in its ability to retain its widespread popularity without ever feeling dated. Long popular in England as well as here, in the Old Testament, Sarah was the wife of Abraham and mother of Isaac—who actually changed her name from SARAI at the age of ninety. Probably its most famous bearer, the great actress Sarah Bernhardt, was born Rosine. Two more contemporary actresses are Sarah Jessica Parker and *Roseanne*'s Sara Gilbert. Among the international variations on the theme are ZAHARIA (Greek), SARI (Hungarian), SARKA (Russian), and SARITA (Spain).

SASHA, SACHA. This name started life as a Russian male nickname (for Alexander), but is now used as widely in this country for girls as for boys, projecting an arty and active image. Producer Steven Spielberg and mate Kate Capshaw have produced a Sasha of their own. Another interesting possibility is the Dutch SASKIA, made famous by the wife and frequent model of Rembrandt and more recently by rising young actress Saskia Reeves.

SASSANDRA. An African place-name, being a river on the Ivory Coast. She'd be sure to go through life as SASSY.

SAVANNAH. A name redolent of magnolias and other sweet smells of the Old South, Savannah is becoming one of the hottest of the currently hot place-names, as well as one of the most appealing. It got an added push from the character Savannah Wingo in the book and movie, *The Prince of Tides*, as well as from Savannah Wilder on *Days of Our Lives*. Songwriting author Jimmy Buffet is one parent who chose it for his daughter, another is Sylvester Stallone.

SCARLETT. The blockbuster book and movie *Gone with the Wind* had a tremendous effect on American baby naming: Just think of the characters Melanie, RHETT, Ashley, Brent, and Bonnie—and even the plantation setting, Tara. Somewhat left behind until recently, probably because the character was so strong and forceful that the name was forever linked to her, was that of the heroine (few people remember that she was actually christened Katie Scarlett—her grandmother's maiden name—O'Hara). Now, finally, this seductively Southern name is being looked at on its own; Jerry Hall and Mick Jagger used it as a middle name for their daughter, Elizabeth.

SCHUYLER. Once exclusively male, this Dutch-origin name has recently crossed over to the other gender. (Actress Sissy Spacek was in the vanguard when she used it for her daughter several years ago.) It retains an attractively boyish, aristocratic air. Some parents have phoneticized the name to SKYLER.

SELENA, SELINA. Smooth, shiny, and sensual, Selena is an attractive, underused name. In Greek mythology, Selene was the beautiful goddess of the moon. Every night, as she crossed the skies in her chariot drawn by two white horses, her golden crown would light up the darkness. And in modern times, Selina was the everyday name of Catwoman in *Batman Returns*.

SELMA. A Scandinavian name that got some play in this country in the twenties and thirties, Selma is a bridge-playing, tea-party kind of appellation without much contemporary charisma.

SEPTIMA. If you have six children, this name is a possibility for your next one.

SERAPHINA, SERAFINA. Although this name may be related to the word for seraphim, the highest form of angels in the celestial sphere, its image is closer to its meaning in Hebrew—"passionate one," like the lusty, sensual Serafina portrayed by Anna Magnani in her Oscar-winner performance in Tennessee Williams's *The Rose Tattoo*.

SERENA. As calm and tranquil as its meaning implies, this is a name found more often on the rosters of elite English schools than in the playground of this country, a situation we find ripe for change.

SETH. Although rarely used for girls, the soft, gentle sound of this name make it a perfect candidate for crossing over to the female camp.

SHANA, SHAYNA. Even many non-Jews know the phrase "shana maidel" means "pretty girl" in Yiddish, so a child with this creative name will have pleasant expectations set for her. The journalist Shana Alexander brought the name to the attention of the public, and soap opera fans will be familiar with Shana Vochek on *Loving*. And the Eddie Murphys named their third daughter SHAYNE Audra.

SHANNON. Could a name sound more Irish? Well, Irish it is, but in the Emerald Isle it's a surname and the name of a river, not a name for a colleen. Along with other cheery Gaelic-inflected names like Erin and Kelly it peaked in popularity in the seventies and is infrequently given to babies today. Former Beverly Hills bad girl SHANNEN Doherty publicized another spelling of the name; SHANNA and SHANI are nickname offshoots.

SHARI. One of those rebelling-against-Shirley-type names of a few decades ago, Shari probably began life as a pet form of Sharon. But energetic though it still is (just as Shari Lewis is still energetically scolding Lambchop on TV), it is decidedly dated. Shari is also the phonetic version of the Hungarian form of Sarah—SARI—the given name of Zsa Zsa Gabor.

SHARIFA. A Swahili name, found in East Africa, that means "distinguished" and lives up to that image. SHAREEFAH is another spelling.

SHARON. An Old Testament place-name (the fertile Plain of Sharon), Sharon was the sixth most popular name for girl babies born in 1940, number nine in 1950 and was still in the Top 25 in 1960. It had pretty much settled into a Mom image until the advent of Sharon Stone, whose potent persona just might lead to a revival, except in Britain, where Sharon is seen as the ultimate working-class girls' name.

SHAWN. The usual girls' spelling of the Irish boys' name, Shawn has passed its day in the sun, though SEAN has some androgynous punch via actress Sean Young. SHAUNA is a further corruption of the original, and SHANE was used for both boys and girls in the years following the release of the haunting western of that name in 1953. More interesting contemporary choices than any of the above might be SHEA, Sinead, Siobhan, or Sorcha.

SHEBA. This exotic biblical place-name for the region in Arabia now known as Yemen is occasionally given to babies, but more often and more appropriately to puppies and kittens.

SHEENA. The Gaelic form of Jane (it's spelled SINE in Ireland and Scotland) this is an animated, easily assimilated ethnic name introduced to the American public by singer Sheena Easton. SIAN, the Welsh form of Jane, looks pretty on paper, but most Americans would have no idea how to pronounce it—SHAN.

SHEILA. This is an Irish name (an offshoot of Celia or Cecilia) that peaked in popularity in this country in the thirties—although it was still clinging to the edge of the Top 40 list of 1960. Aficionados of Australian movies will be aware that sheila is the generic term down under for a girl. Modern parents would probably be more likely to select Sheena, Cecelia, or Celia over Sheila.

SHELBY. A few media usages (the tragic Julia Roberts character in *Steel Magnolias* and the Shelby on the soap opera *Loving*) have helped propel this name, quite suddenly, onto the Top 25 list for newborn baby girls. It is a throwback-to-the-seventies kind of name that we don't think will retain its popularity for long, so if you don't want your daughter date-stamped early nineties, better rethink this choice.

SHELLEY. When Shirley Schrift adopted the stage name of Shelley Winters (supposedly inspired by the poet Shelley), a naming trend was born. Previously a male nickname for the now-nerdish Sheldon, it became a faddish fifties female name, in tune with the Sharons, Sharis, and Sherrys coming into style at the same time. It is now very much a parental-generation name. Shelley is the nickname for Rochelle.

SHERALYN, SHERILYN. Some of the MARYLOUS and BETTY ANNs of yore grew up to hatch little combo-named kids of their own, and this (recently brought into the spotlight by actress Sherilyn Fenn of *Twin Peaks*) was one of their options. Nineties parents for the most part prefer to keep first and middle names separate and distinct.

SHERI, SHERRY. It's a phonetic version of the French CHERI, an alcoholic beverage, and a peppy cheerleader name of the sixties and seventies, sure to evoke the strains of the Four Seasons song of that name (in which it was stretched to three syllables). What it isn't is a likely choice for a nineties baby. The similar SHERYL began life as a variant spelling of CHERYL.

SHIRLEY. Shirley Temple almost single-handedly lifted the gloom of the Great Depression, and in tribute (and perhaps wishing for a similarly bright-eyed, curly-headed, dimpled darling of their own), thousands of parents of that generation gave their little girls her name. In an earlier time used primarily for boys, the tide turned with the publication of Charlotte Brontë's novel *Shirley* in 1849, the story of a character whose parents had selected the name for a male child, then decided to use it anyway when he turned out to be a she. Virtually never used for babies today.

SHOSHANA. In Hebrew this is a popular flower name, meaning "lily." A graceful choice, if a bit difficult to pronounce. The English translation is Susannah.

SHULA, SHULAMIT, and **SULAMITH** are all variations on shalom, the Hebrew word for "peace," and are often found in Israel.

SIBYL, SYBIL. The ancient Greeks used this as a genetic word to represent prophetesses—women who relayed the messages of the gods. It now has a rather dowdy, unfashionable image, despite the blonde gloss of the uniquely spelled CYBILL Shepherd.

SIDONIA, SIDONY, SIDONIE. These names, which are virtually unknown in America, are most widely used in England and France.

Although they might be considered eccentric, all three have a rhythmic (accent on the second syllable), novelistic appeal. SOLANGE is another evocative French name, meaning "rare jewel."

SIENA. A soft and delicate place-name, conjuring up the warm reddish brown tones of the Tuscan town.

SIERRA. This ambigender place-name, which brings to mind snowy peaks and pure air, has made great strides in popularity in the past few years, now climbing official most-popular lists. First there was the character of Sierra Estaben on *As the World Turns*, then L.A. Laker James Worthy selected it for his daughter. CIERRA is an alternate, if inauthentic, spelling.

SIGRID. This Scandinavian name that came into the American consciousness around the same time as Ingrid is rarely used in this country outside Norwegian families.

SILVER. It may not sound that way at first hearing, but Silver is a legitimate girls' name and not a flower child fabrication of the seventies. A gleaming, glistening possibility for parents seeking a creative choice. The similar sounding (especially if you have a New York accent) SILVA is a rarely used saint's name.

SIMONE. This name reverberates with Gallic sophistication (think of Simone Signoret, Simone de Beauvoir), yet its simple spelling and pronunciation make it a perfectly acceptable (and imaginative) possibility for use here. SIMONA is the equally appealing Italian version.

SINEAD. Irish for Janet and pronounced Shinade, this name may be difficult to separate from the somewhat aggressive demeanor of its one well-known bearer in this country, singer Sinead O'Connor. But if you can do that, it makes a striking choice for a child with strong Irish roots.

SIOBHAN. An Irish form of Joan (pronounced Shavaun) this name is more familiar here today in its phonetically spelled versions, which range from SHEVAUN to SHEVONNE to SHAVON ad infinitum. We admit the original spelling is bafflingly foreign to most Americans; still, using it preserves the ethnic integrity of this, one of the most lovely of the Gaelic girls' names.

SKYE. Unlike other hippie-dippy-nature names of the swinging seventies, Skye has a number of elements that make it remain viable today. It has the added attraction of being a place-name (the Isle of Skye, off the coast of Scotland) and has had some soap opera visibility (Skye Patterson on *All My Children*).

SLOAN, SLOANE. MN A gray-flannel-suit, androgynous-executive name, which seems to predict either corporate CEOship or, failing that, considerable charity ball committee activity.

SONIA, SONYA, SONJA. In all three spellings, a wintry, ice-skating name dressed in heavy red velvet and white ermine muffs. Bred in cold climates (it means "wisdom" in Norwegian and is a Russian diminutive of SOFIA), Sonia, Sonya, Sonja is/are both exotic and grandmotherly warm.

SOPHIA and **SOPHIE.** Both these names have both become ultra-trendy in the last few years, completely shedding their once dowdy-granny images (even the elderly Sophia Petrillo on *The Golden Girls* couldn't be called dowdy) for more elegant ones. In Great Britain, Sophie shot into first place among girls' names listed in the *London Times* in 1992. When Bette Midler chose it for her daughter, she explained, "We think Sophie sounds like an impoverished Austrian princess who is forced to marry a coarse member of the bourgeoisie." We agree.

SORCHA. Virtually unknown in this country, Sorcha (pronounced Sorr-a-ha) is an Old Irish name that has become very popular in contemporary Ireland. It means "shining bright."

SPENCER. Yes, Spencer for a girl. One of those "Doesn't-this-sound-as-good-or-better-for-the-opposite-sex?" names that suddenly seem completely conceivable. Ask Jaclyn Smith, who named her daughter Spencer Margaret a few years ago.

SPRING and **SUMMER.** These are two distinctive, evocative names, conjuring up images of sunshine, warm breezes, and new green growth. Summer Black was a character on *Santa Barbara*, Spring Byington a well-known character actress in movies and TV. And if you can't decide between the two, you can always consider SEASON, as in actress Season Hubley.

STACY, STACEY. Originally a boys' name (as in Stacey Keach), it became a key cheerleader in the nickname name game of the late sixties and early seventies (reaching number eighteen in 1970). A more contemporary-sounding substitute might be STACIA or, back to the original, Anastasia.

STELLA. A name that manages to be both celestial and earthy at the same time, primarily because a) it means "star" in Latin, and b) many of us can still hear Brando bellowing the name in *A Streetcar Named Desire*. The name was coined by Sir Philip Sidney in 1590, popularized more recently by the song "Stella by Starlight," and has been used for their daughters by ex-Beatle Paul McCartney and painter Julian Schnabel.

STEPHANIE. Stephanie is a name that has remarkable staying power, perhaps more than any other feminine form of a male name (the French STEPHAN); it doesn't sound dated even though it has been popular (still remaining in the top dozen) for twenty-five years. It is feminine wihout being frilly and parents seem to like its short forms—STEFFI and STEPH—never resorting to the French nickname, FANNY. Royal bad girl Princess Stephanie of Monaco certainly lends the name some class; STEFANIE is how actress Powers (born Stefania) spells the name.

STORM. A tempestuous name that might prove too much for a quiet, retiring girl to live up to.

SUSAN, SUSANNAH. Susannah (also spelled SUSANNA) is by far the most stylish version of this classic name today, with Susan reserved for Moms born during the name's heyday, 1948 to 1964, when it was consistently among the Top 5. It derives from the Hebrew Shoshana, meaning "lily," and its diminutives are found in any number of popular songs ("Sweet Sue," "If You Knew Susie," "Wake Up Little Susie," to name a few). In the New Testament, Susannah was the heroine of the story of Daniel and the Elders. The French versions SUZANNE and SUZETTE attained a certain measure of popularity slipstreaming behind Susan, Suzanne coming back briefly into prominence as the name of the high-profile Delta Burke character on TV's *Designing Women*. We've heard the interesting SANNA or ZANNA as a nickname for the versions that end in an *a* sound. More original than SUSIE or SUZY, in any case, is the old and charming SUKIE or SUKY.

SYDNEY. When given to a girl, Sydney takes the somewhat nerdy image it has as a boys' name and turns it inside out: The female Sydney is polished, poised, creative, elegant, and intelligent, qualities more and more parents have begun to recognize. It has been the name of a running TV character portrayed by Mariel Hemingway as well as a not-very-nice young woman on *Melrose Place*. And just in case we think this is a new development, Katharine Hepburn played a woman named Sydney in her film debut in 1932. SYDELLE is the Bronx-Brooklyn version of the forties.

SYLVIA. Many of us have had an Aunt or Great-Aunt Sylvia and so might be quick to relegate this name to Purgatory, but if we could shake away the dust and listen to the pure sound of Sylvia, we might rediscover its musical, sylvan qualities. Sylvia Plath was the Tragic Heroine of modern poetry. SILVIA was the mother of the twins Remus and Romulus, who founded Rome. SILVIE/SYLVIE is the livelier French version.

T

〰〰〰〰〰〰〰〰〰〰〰〰 ◉ 〰〰〰〰〰〰〰〰〰〰〰〰

TABITHA. Ever since 1965 when the cute little girl with supernatural powers was introduced on the long-running TV series *Bewitched*, the name Tabitha has had a slightly off-center, occult charm. But it never took off the way Samantha—the name of her mother's character—did, perhaps because the nickname TABBY was considered too feline. (One of Beatrix Potter's storybook characters is a cat called Tabitha Twitchet.) Tabitha appears in the New Testament in the form of a charitable woman who was restored to life by St. Peter. Tabitha Sorin is a high-profile MTV personality.

TAFFY. A member of the Tawny-Tammy-Taffy sorority of names that project sweetness, sexiness, and not much substance. Taffy is in fact the female form of David in Wales, where it is also used as a male nickname.

TALIA. A neglected Hebrew name that means "the gentle dew from heaven." In the mythology of one ancient sect, Talia was one of ten angels who attended the sun on its daily course. A prominent bearer of the name is Talia Shire, doomed to go down in cinema history as the mousy girlfriend ("Yo, Adrienne!") in *Rocky*. TALI is a variation singer Annie Lennox chose for her daughter.

TALLULAH. For years this name was taboo because of its ironclad link with the blowsy, acid-tongued actress of the thirties and forties, Tallulah Bankhead. Now, since most prospective parents have hardly heard of the lady, it's time for a reappraisal of this resonant, rhythmic Choctaw Indian name—which means "leaping water"—especially since one of Hollywood's power couples, Demi Moore and Bruce Willis, chose it for their third daughter. Spelled TALLULA, it is also a traditional Irish name, belonging to two early saints.

TAMAR. A strong, rich, out-of-the-ordinary Hebrew name borne by several Old Testament women, including a daughter of King David. Its literal meaning is "date palm," which suggests beauty and grace. In the Jewish culture it is sometimes given to girls born on the holiday of Sukkoth, because palm branches are used in constructing the roof of the sukkah. The Russian form of the name is TAMARA, the final vowel adding a more sensual, Slavic tone; it belonged to a famous twelfth-century Georgian queen. TAMORA is the version Shakespeare used in *Titus Andronicus*, and TAMA is also heard, as in the name of the art-scene novelist Tama Janowitz.

TAMMY. A nickname-name that skyrocketed to popularity in the late fifties with the appearance of the Tammy movies, starring first Debbie Reynolds, then Sandra Dee, as a wholesome, barefoot backwoods gal, and a theme song that went to the top of the hit parade. Tammy was still among the leading twenty-five names of 1970, but by now it's completely lost its verve. The best-known people to have answered to the name are actress Tammy Grimes (who inherited it from her Scottish great-great-grandmother), country singer Tammy Wynette (born Virginia), and tearful evangelista Tammy Faye Bakker. TAMIKA is a recent creation.

TAMSIN. An offbeat name that originated as a contraction of THOMASINA. Quite popular in Britain, it is just waiting to be discovered on this side of the Atlantic. The same might be said of TANSY, the name of a yellow wildflower and herb, found in a number of English novels.

TANYA, TANIA. A Russian name that has been fully integrated into the American name pool, while retaining a good measure of its ethnic flavor. It started life as a pet form of TATIANA, which is beginning to be used in this country as well—by Caroline Kennedy Schlossberg for one—and that has a more delicate, feminine appeal to the contemporary ear. TITANIA was the name of the fairy queen in Shakespeare's *A Midsummer Night's Dream*. And then there's TONYA, a name that got more than its share of headlines before, during, and after the 1994 Winter Olympics. It's also the name of one of the young stars of *All My Children*, Tonya Pinkins. TANISHA is a new version.

TARA. It seems that every name associated with *Gone with the Wind*, including this name of the O'Hara plantation, has shared in some of the book and movie's popularity. The additional advantage of an Irish accent (a geographical name there as well: Tara is the ancient capital of the Irish kings, also the wife of one of them), plus a prominent soap opera character, Tara Martin in *All My Children*, combined to propel this windswept name into the Top 50 in the early eighties, but it has pretty much blown away by now. TARYN is an offshoot created in the Sharon-Karen period.

TATUM. Like Shaquille, a unique name that may be prime for wider use, especially if your last name is as congenial as O'Neal.

TAWNY. See Taffy, then add to its image a golden tan.

TAYLOR. In the last couple of years, this name has shot past all the other androgynous surname names to reach the national girls' Top 10. Its strikingly sophisticated and successful image has been projected onto the TV screen in such daytime dramas as *All My Children*, *As the World Turns*, and *The Bold and the Beautiful*, and has been further publicized by singer Taylor Dane (whose name at birth was Leslie). Used about four times more often for girls than boys, it was chosen by Garth Brooks for his daughter.

TEAL. A really offbeat color name, this could make an interesting middle-name choice.

TEMPEST. This stormy-sounding name was brought to public attention by the young Tempestt Bledsoe (the double *t* is her unique variation) who played the sweet-tempered Vanessa on *The Cosby Show*, making it seem like a contradiction in terms.

TERESA, THERESA, THÉRÈSE. A Greek classic, made famous by the sixteenth-century Spanish St. Teresa of Avila, a strong, witty, and intelligent Carmelite nun who combined the active life of establishing and running seventeen convents with mystical contemplation and writing. In more contemporary times, Mother Theresa has added to the image of selfless hard work fused with compassion. Thérèse, pronounced *Terez*, is the French form. American parents—particularly Catholics—favored this name from the twenties to the early seventies, by which time it had exploded into a panoply of friendlier forms: TERRY, TERI, Tracy, and the one most apt to be chosen today, Tess.

TERTIA. (pronounced Tersha). An unconventional possibility for the third child in a family.

TESS. An earthy, windblown name with Irish overtones. Once a scullery maid favorite, it has now definitely moved up in the world and is more likely to be on the rosters of Park Avenue play groups. The name has an odd conglomeration of associations: Thomas Hardy's naive *Tess of the d'Urbervilles*, Dick Tracy's significant other, Tess Trueheart, the spunky Tess McGill character played by Melanie Griffith in *Working Girl* and Shirley MacLaine in *Guarding Tess*. Primal not-ready-for-prime-time player Jane Curtin is the mother of a Tess. TESSA, also on the rise, is a more elegant, creative spin on the name, while TESSIE moves in the other direction—raucous and ribald.

THALASSA, THALIA, THEONE. Three rarely used Greek names. Thalia is one of the Three Graces in Greek mythology, and also the Muse of Comedy (she's the one holding the smiling mask).

THEA. A name that paints an artistic picture; sensitive and serene. Thea makes a hip choice on its own or short for Theodora/Dorothea.

THELMA. Invented by a late nineteenth-century writer named Marie Corelli for the Norwegian heroine of one of her novels, this name is now as dated as her book, although it did gain some latter-day notoriety through the movie *Thelma and Louise*. Trivia trifle: Thelma was Pat Nixon's given first name.

THEODORA. It's already hot in some urban playgrounds, and we predict that this long-neglected, softly evocative, yet serious name is in for a widespread revival (as is its syllable reversal, Dorothea). It was borne by the beautiful ninth wife of the Emperor Justinian, who became the power behind his throne, and, more recently, selected by the Daddy of cool, Rolling Stone Keith Richards, for his daughter. Variations include THEODOSIA, FEODORA, and TEODORA.

THIRZA. A Hebrew Old Testament name meaning "pleasantness," rarely used perhaps because of its association with thirst.

THOMASA, THOMASIN, THOMASINA. These three female derivatives of Thomas are not used very often in these days when women would prefer to take on men's names rather than sweeten them with feminine endings.

TIA. With the waning of Mia, similar-sounding names like Tia, Nia, Pia, BRIA, and LIA have come to the fore. All of them are sprightly alternatives. Newly coined names with a related base are TIANA, TIARA, and TIERRA. Be aware that these recent inventions, though pretty, do not carry much weight.

TIFFANY. This was a quintessential name of the Booming Eighties, the nominal personification of prosperity, luxury, and extravagance, of *Breakfast at Tiffany's* and dinner at an expensive trattoria every night. It was worn by gorgeous women in James Bond movies, soap operas, and *Charlie's Angels*. But when the economy plummeted at the end of the decade, it dragged the image of the name down with it, so that while Tiffany still may be lingering at the lower edges of the popularity lists, it has definitely lost its silvery sheen. (Apparently unaware that the eighties are over, Marla Maples and Donald Trump called their baby girl Tiffany. Trump was quoted as saying he chose the name to commemorate his purchase of the air rights above the famed jeweler, Tiffany & Co., which cleared the way for his Trump Tower on Fifth Avenue.) At one time in history Tiffany, which is Greek for "manifestation of God," was reserved for girls born on the Epiphany (January 6th or Twelfth Night).

TILLIE, TILLY. This name hasn't been used in so long that it's beginning to sound cute again. Writer Tillie Olsen is a feminist favorite.

TINA, TITA. Tina, the pet form of such names as Christina and MARTINA, had its moment in the early seventies, but these days is more likely to be replaced by the more elegant originals. Tina's image is petite, quiet, and ladylike—unless you think about Tina Turner (born Anna Mae). Similarly, Tita is short for MARTITA, and recently reached the best-seller list as the heroine of *Like Water for Chocolate*.

TISA. The Swahili word for the number "nine," Tisa was once used primarily for ninth-born children. In this era of the shrunken nuclear family, though, it's a possible choice for even a first child.

TOBY. One of the earlier unisex names, Toby, when used for a girl, retains its tomboyish quality. It originated as a nickname for the male name Tobias.

TONI, TORI. In the forties, the nickname Toni began to supercede its progenitor, Antonia. (In ensuing decades, girls named Toni were plagued by the ubiquitous advertising slogan, "Which twin has the Toni?") Now, although Nobel and Pulitzer Prize–winning novelist Toni Morrison (born Chloe) has heaped honors on the name, modern parents would probably be better advised to reassess the pioneer strength of the original. Tori came along a couple of decades later, replacing, VICKY, the other pet name for Victoria. It is now represented in the cast of *Beverly Hills 90210* by Tori Spelling.

TOVA, TOVAH. A lively modern Hebrew name meaning "good."

TRACY, TRACEY. After taking a typical place-name-to-last name-to-male-first-name route, Tracy's ascent as a girls' name was due almost solely to the vibrant character Tracy Lord, portrayed first by Katharine Hepburn in *Philadelphia Story* (1940) and later by Grace Kelly in the musical version, *High Society* (1956). By the late sixties it was one of the most popular of the laid-back ambigender names, but is rarely used in these tighter times, although still visible on such public figures as Tracey Ullman, singer Tracy Chapman, and tennis player Tracy Austin. A more modern choice would be Grace or GRACIE.

TRIXIE. A sassy, spunky name for the bold parent who doesn't connect it solely with Mrs. Ed Norton on *The Honeymooners*. Trixie Delight was the name of the Madeline Kahn character in *Paper Moon*, and Damon Wayans selected it for his daughter. The more formal name, if only for the birth certificate (and future résumé): Beatrix.

TRUDY. Innocent, sincere, and bright-eyed, Trudy is nevertheless almost as outdated as Gertrude, the name it's short for.

TUESDAY. Days of the week, unlike months of the year, are rarely used as names in this country, but when Susan Kerr changed her name to Tuesday Weld, she brought it into the realm of possibility.

TWYLA. A Middle English name whose meaning has to do with weaving, ultra-arty Twyla is largely associated with choreographer Tharp.

TYNE. Sharp and creative, this name was introduced to the public by actress Tyne (born Ellen) Daly.

TYLER and **TYSON.** A pair of handsome male surname names that have begun to be appropriated by females. Tyler, rising fast in the boys' popularity charts, retains a definite masculine edge, with Taylor the name becoming more usual for girls. Singer Nenah Cherry chose Tyson for her daughter, though some moms may not want to honor fighter Mike by using his name for their daughters. Another possibility is TYRA, as in the single-named model/actress.

U

〰〰〰〰〰〰〰〰〰〰〰〰 ◉ 〰〰〰〰〰〰〰〰〰〰〰〰

UMA. This throaty, exotic name is one of the more than one thousand appelations for the Hindu goddess Sakti (a fact that surely inspired the father of Uma Thurman, a Columbia University professor of eastern religion. Thurman's middle name, KARUNA, is equally exotic). In Hebrew, Uma means "nation," and is therefore often used for girls born on Israeli Independence Day.

UNA. An ancient Irish name, Una can also be spelled Oona (as in the case of the daughter of Eugene O'Neill and wife of Charlie Chaplin) or the even more authentic Oonagh. The poet Edmund Spenser used Una for *The Faerie Queene*, daughter of a legendary king and the quintessence of truth and beauty. The name, which symbolizes unity, hasn't been used much in this country since the thirties. Another Irish form of the name is Juno.

UNITY. Puritan virtue names like Unity, VERITY, and Prudence seem to be on the verge of a comeback, embodying as they do qualities we would all like to impart to our children. And this is a more unusual one than Grace or Hope—its only well-known bearer was British author Unity Mitford.

URSULA. Today's kids will probably associate this name with the exaggerated actions of the campy, corpulent octopus sea witch in Disney's *The Little Mermaid*, while yesterday's adults will recall the sex goddess, Ursula Andress. It was also used for the intelligent and spirited heroine of D. H. Lawrence's novel, *The Rainbow*, Ursula Brangwyn, while St. Ursula is the patron saint of schoolteachers, and the name Ursula K. LeGuin is often seen on fiction best-seller lists. In any case, however, its slighty heavy, Germanic feel makes it a poor bet for popularity.

UTA. Pronounced Oota, this is another rarely used three-letter *U* name. This one originated as the diminutive of yet another rarely used (but more attractive) name: Ottalie.

V

∧∧∧∧∧∧∧∧∧∧∧∧∧∧∧∧∧∧∧∧∧∧ ◉ ∧∧∧∧∧∧∧∧∧∧∧∧∧∧∧∧∧∧∧∧∧

VALDA, VANDA, and VARDA. Three names with different roots but a similar, occultish aura. Valda is from the German meaning the "heroine of a battle," Vanda is a variant of Wanda, and Varda, which means "rose" in Hebrew, is widely used in Israel.

VALENTINA. An interesting possibility for parents seeking a viable alternative to the more common Victoria and Vanessa. Meaning "strong," "healthy" woman in Latin, Valentina also has an artistic, slightly exotic image. **VALENTINE,** the usual male form of the name (though nearly unthinkable for use on a modern boy), is too closely tied to the saint and holiday.

VALERIE. Steadily popular since the forties, Valerie never made any Top 20 lists, and so still doesn't sound all that dated. Its image is strong (maybe because of the association with valor), has the slight suggestion of a French accent, and is often seen on TV credits, preceding such surnames as Harper, Perrine, and Bertinelli. Still, in tune with the overall trend toward versions of names that end with *a*, the Italian **VALERIA** sounds more modern.

VANESSA. A pretty, ultrafeminine name, Vanessa hit its peak in the late eighties—getting a lot of exposure from actress Vanessa Redgrave as well as a character on *The Cosby Show*—along with other frilly three-syllable names like Melissa and Tiffany, and has managed to retain its freshness longer than the others. It was invented by Jonathan Swift for a young woman named Esther Vanhomrigh—he combined the first syllable of her last name with the pet name ESSA. The nickname Nessa may be viable on its own, but VANNA is doomed to a lifetime of playing *Wheel of Fortune*.

VELMA. Like Thelma and Selma, gone with the wind.

VELVET. How could a name possibly be softer or more luxuriant? It is primarily associated with the character played by twelve-year-old Elizabeth Taylor in *National Velvet*: Velvet Brown, an intrepid young woman willing to masquerade as a boy in order to race her horse in a dangerous steeplechase.

VENETIA, VENITA, and VENICE. All three call to mind the radiance of that fabled Italian city, and are among the most evocative and exotic of the place-names rising to prominence today. VERONA, an hour's drive to the west of Venice, provides another name with the same antique, Italianate charm.

VENUS. This name falls into the too-much-to-live-up-to category, conjuring up as it does the supreme Roman goddess of beauty and love, the incarnation of female perfection. Venus Williams is an outstanding young tennis star.

VERA. Vera was the height of flapper chic in the twenties but now it's almost impossible to picture it embroidered on a baby blanket or Magic Markered onto a child's lunchbox. Still common in several Slavic countries, its meaning is associated with the Latin for "truth." Two other, infinitely more appealing names with the same root are VERENA and the Puritan virtue name, VERITY.

VERNA. Another V name that, despite its springlike etymology, is not particularly pleasing to the modern ear.

VERONICA. This name has a dual image: saintly (Veronica was the name of the compassionate woman who wiped Jesus' bleeding face when he was on his way to Cavalry and whose cloth was miraculously imprinted with his image; she is now the patron saint of photographers) and sensuous (there was Veronica Lake, the peekaboo blonde of the forties, and the sultry, dark-haired rival of Betty in the *Archie* comics).

If the sexy image is the one you want, you could clinch it by choosing the seductive French version, VERONIQUE.

VICTORIA. The epitome of gentility, cultivation, and refinement, the name Victoria derived this image from the queen who reigned over England from 1837 to 1901, and who lent her name to a controlled and corsetted era. In the United States it has been popular since the forties; in the sixties and seventies, its short form, VICKY/VICKI/VIKKI became one of the energetic nickname names most often used on its own. Today, Victoria retains some fashion value (it's currently the ninth most popular name in Texas) along with other formal, traditional names, such as Alexandra and Caroline, and is most stylishly used in its entirety.

VIENNA. One of the most promising of the newly discovered place-names, with a particularly pleasant sound. Few people remember that way back in 1954, Joan Crawford played a character with this name in *Johnny Guitar*.

VIOLET. A sweet but colorful flower name just on the brink of rediscovery, Violet was used as far back as the Middle Ages, so it certainly predated the flower-name vogue of the turn of the 20th century (Lily, Daisy, etc). We see it now as an attractive possibility: familiar but not faddish—the one possible handicap being the expression "shrinking violet." Violet was the name of the character twelve-year-old Brooke Shields played in the controversial 1978 film, *Pretty Baby*, and also Lily Tomlin's in *Nine to Five*. VIOLA is the Italian and Scandinavian version, used both by Shakespeare in *Twelfth Night* and by the writers of the soap opera *The Guiding Light*. VIOLETTA is a frillier, more operatic rendition.

VIRGINIA. For parents tiring of such trendy classics as Elizabeth and Katherine, Virginia is another traditional name worth considering, one that is beginning to sound new again after a forty-year hiatus. Its geographical association gives it a slightly Southern flavor and its Latin derivation adds a virginal quality. The state was given its name by Sir Walter Raleigh in honor of Elizabeth I, known as the Virgin Queen, and the first child to be born of English parents in the New World in

1597 was called Virginia Dare. It is the real name of both Ginger Rogers and Tammy Wynette. One advantage if you do choose it: You'll really be able to say, "Yes, Virginia, there is a Santa Claus"—for a few years at least. One disadvantage: virgin jokes.

VITA, VIDA, VIVA. The Latin word for "alive" is *vivus*, and all three of these names share that meaning, although none of them is very much alive at this time. VIVECA, the Scandinavian version à la actress Lindfors, definitely sounds more contemporary.

VIVIAN, VIVIEN, VIVIANNE, VIVIENNE. This name, which also means life, actually shows signs of coming back to life—it was the name of Julia Roberts's character in *Pretty Woman* and was chosen as her daughter's name by trendy choreographer-performer Debbie Allen. Although in Arthurian legend it was the name of an enchantress who was the mistress of Merlin, for centuries it was used more for boys than girls.

W

WALLIS. Wallis has the force of a masculine name, while its distinctive spelling sets it apart from the boys. Recent-history buffs will remember it as the name of the American woman, Wallis (born Bessie) Warfield Simpson, for love of whom a British king was willing to sacrifice his throne in the thirties.

WANDA. Rarely heard these days, Wanda has an old-fashioned Slavic or German feel and has been used as a witch's name in several children's books. Not a good omen. And then there was a fish called. . . .

WENDY. Wendy has the date stamp of the fifties imprinted all over it, as well as an unfortunate fast-food connection. A bouncy, peppy, perfect-baby-sitter name, it was invented by Sir James Barrie in 1904 for the big sister character in his play, *Peter Pan*. The story goes that he took it from the nickname "Fwendy-Wendy" used for him by a young girl acquaintance.

WHITNEY. Whitney took the path from place-name to last name to high fallutin' male first name to popular girls' name in record time, thanks in part to the phenomenal popularity of singer Whitney Houston. At this point it has lost its efficient-executive edge and is more pretty than powerful. The related WHITLEY came to the fore via the spoiled *A Different World* character played by Jasmine Guy, and is used primarily by African-American families.

WILHELMINA. Standing stolidly in its heavy Dutch image of thick blonde braids and clunky wooden clogs, Wilhelmina does not share the panache of new favorites Willa and Will.

WILLA. Willa combines the strength and tradition of a pioneer name (through its association with frontier novelist Willa Cather) with the coziness of a grandmotherly name and the slender beauty of the willow tree. Originally a pet form of Wilhelmina, it was chosen for their daughter by playwright David Mamet and actress Lindsay Crouse, and as a middle name for Meryl Streep's daughter Mary. Willa is definitely beginning to be discovered by vanguard parents.

WILLOW. This name has transcended its onetime hippie aura to move into the realm of reappraised and appreciated nature names. Among the most graceful of trees, the willow is believed by Gypsies to possess magical powers to heal the sick and revitalize the aged. The name was selected by The Who rock immortal Roger Daltrey for his child, and by actress Gabrielle Anwar for hers. Supermodel Willow Bay has accentuated its willowiness.

WILMA. Yabba-dabba-doo, we're afraid Wilma is still fossilized in Bedrock.

WINIFRED. One of those once-out-of-the-question nineteenth-century great-grandmother names that is decidedly ready to be reconsidered by the twentieth-century parent. You might not guess it, but its roots are in Wales and it was in fact the name of a legendary Welsh saint. Its nickname WINNIE has a decidedly sassy charm of its own and on its own. Forget *Winnie-the-Pooh* and think instead of the sweet, sensitive girl on *The Wonder Years*.

WINONA. No, this rhythmic, resonant name wasn't invented by Ms. Ryder's parents. She was named after the Minnesota town in which she was born and which in turn is a Sioux Indian word (often spelled, as it was by the mother of Hiawatha, WENONAH), meaning "first-born daughter." Another of its many variant spellings is WYNONNA, as in Judd, although she was born Christina.

WYNN, WYNNE. Spelled with or without the final *e*, Wynn means "white" or "fair" and is, like GWYN and Bryn, an attractive ambisexual Welsh name. All three are especially worth considering if you are seeking an original one-syllable middle name.

X

∿∿∿∿∿∿∿∿∿∿∿∿∿∿ ◉ ∿∿∿∿∿∿∿∿∿∿∿∿∿∿

XANTHE. As in most words starting with *x*, the first letter of this name has a *z* sound (pronounced zan'the), a concept most children's friends might have trouble with until they reach the point of being able to spell *xylophone*. It comes from the Greek meaning "golden yellow," and conjures up the picture of an exotic, otherworldly being. XENA and XENIA are two more Greek-derived names with a *z* sound and that same siren allure. (But you can also consider whether it might make your child's life easier to just spell them Zena or ZENIA.)

XAVIERA. The female version of Xavier, this name came into prominence awhile back when it was attached to the author of the best-seller *The Happy Hooker*.

Y

〜〜〜〜〜〜〜〜〜〜〜〜〜〜〜〜 ◉ 〜〜〜〜〜〜〜〜〜〜〜〜〜〜〜

YAEL. If you're looking for an unusual (in this country if not in Israel), and appealing Hebrew name, this might be it. Just ignore the fact that its derivations have to do with wild mountain goats and remember that it is pronounced with two distinct syllables.

YAFA, YAFFA. A modern Hebrew translation of SHAYNA, which means "beautiful."

YASMINE. A name whose sweet and delicate essence, like that of the jasmine flower it represents, is widespread across the Near Eastern world, in a wide variety of different spellings. In America, it has recently taken on a supermodel image, and was chosen by Meshach Taylor, late of *Designing Women*, for one of his four daughters.

YETTA. Too close to yenta for our taste.

YOLANDA. This name conjures up the costume epics of the forties and fifties, (e.g., *Yolanda and the Thief*), complete with gauzy veils, harem pants, and invisible navels. It is actually Greek, meaning "violet," the flower of the sign of Aquarius.

YVONNE and **YVETTE.** Two French names that bring to mind the kind of dark and sultry actresses who might have starred in the movies mentioned above. (Like Yvonne De Carlo, who was actually born the far less exotic Peggy.) If you are seeking an *ette*-ending French name, a few preferable, fresher-sounding alternatives might be ARLETTE, BLANCHETTE, MUSETTE, NICOLETTE, or VIOLETTE.

Z

wwwwwwwwwwwwww ⊙ wwwwwwwwwwwwww

ZAHARA. Although it sounds desertlike, this is actually a Muslim and Swahili name meaning "flower." In Hebrew, it denotes "brightness."

ZANDRA. When iconoclastic British fashion designer Zandra Rhodes changed the first initial of her name from *S* to *Z*, she legitimized what had formerly been a diminutive of Alexandra. And, indeed, Zandra is much more creative and fresh-sounding than the now dated Sandra.

ZARA. Princess Anne defied British royal convention by giving her daughter this exotic Arabic name in 1981, thus bestowing on it instant upper-class status. And unlike many other foreign-sounding names, it has the advantage of being completely accessible in terms of spelling and pronunciation.

ZELDA. This name has been in label limbo for several years but there are signs that it is due for a comeback. One of them is that the zany Robin Williams, who appears to like the letter *Z*, named two of his children Zachary and Zelda. Other strong associations with the name are that of F. Scott Fitzgerald's tortured wife and one of Dobie Gillis's more ardent pursuers in the sixties TV series.

ZELIA. An appealing name almost unknown in our culture but with roots in several others including Latin, French, and Hebrew.

ZENA, ZINA. Another multicultural name: In Persian it means "woman," in Hebrew it signifies "stranger," and in Africa Zina refers to a child's secret spirit name. It was used for the character played by Rhea Perlman in *Taxi*. The similar in feeling ZITA was the name of a thirteenth-century Tuscan saint, who is the patron saint of housewives.

ZENOBIA. Clearly this is not a name for everyone, but, for the daring, it does have a rhythmic sound and some rich historic and literary associations. It was the name of a beautiful and intelligent third-century queen who for a time ruled the eastern Roman Empire, and it can be found in the novels of both Nathaniel Hawthorne (*A Blithedale Romance*) and Edith Wharton (*Ethan Frome*).

ZILLA, ZILLAH. Although this name is soft and delicate, it runs the risk of being associated with the monstrous Godzilla.

ZOE. Short but with a lot of creative character, Zoe is a member of that select group of names that are both inventive and interesting, yet acceptable and accessible. But using the umlat, Zoë, propels it into the realm of the pretentious. Most cultures have a name signifying the life force (e.g., Chaim, Viva, FAYOLA, VIDAL), and in Greek it is Zoe, the equivalent of Eve, the mother of all life. Henry Winkler, Lisa Bonet and Lenny Kravitz are all parents of Zoes.

ZORA, ZORAH. A biblical name, representing a place rather than a person. It also signifies "dawn" in the Slavic vocabulary, and appeared as a character in the Gilbert & Sullivan operetta, *Ruddigore*.

ZULEIKA. A challenging name but not out of the question. Its most famous association is with the eponymous heroine of the satirical 1910 Max Beerbohm novel, *Zuleika Dobson*, who is so drop-dead gorgeous (its meaning in Persian is in fact "brilliant beauty") that all the young men at Oxford University kill themselves for love of her. African-born model Iman spells her daughter's name ZELEKHA.

BOYS' NAMES

A

AARON. In its own quiet way, Aaron has been one of the most popular biblical names of the last twenty years, the softness of its initial double vowel giving it an appealing gentleness. In the Old Testament, Aaron, older brother of Moses, appointed by God to be his brother's spokesman, was the first High Priest of Israel, and of late it has been attached to singer Aaron Neville. The Hebrew version is AHARON. Elvis spelled his middle name ARON.

ABBOTT. Both a fairly common surname and a noun meaning the head of a monastery. Although some people might associate it with slapstick comedian Lou Costello bellowing the name of his partner, as in "Hey, Aaabottt!", it is an attractive, offbeat possibility, and the first name of activist Abbie Hoffman.

ABDUL. This name, which means "servant of Allah" in Arabic, has been widely used by American Black Muslims since the early eighties.

ABEL. The bad news is that this was the name of the second son of Adam and Eve and the world's first fratricide victim. The good news is that the name/word connotes someone supremely capable and competent, ready and willing.

ABIAH. A highly unusual Old Testament name—it belonged to Samuel's second son—which also appears as ABIJAH, it can be used for both boys or girls.

ABNER. Finally, after some sixty years, this name is beginning to throw off its L'il Abner Yokum-yokel, country bumpkin comic strip stigma enough to be reevaluated on its own merits as a perfectly respectable Old Testament name, that of the commander of Saul's army. It is also associated with the founding father of baseball, Abner Doubleday. The modern Hebrew form is AVNER.

ABRAHAM. Originally named ABRAM (the syllable *ah*, meaning "father of many," was added after he accepted the idea of a single God), Abraham was the first of the Old Testament patriarchs and is considered the founding father of the Hebrew people. In the nineteenth century, President Lincoln hung a beard on the name that a young child still might find difficult to pull off. But with many Old Testament names reaching the heights of fashion over the past few decades, and the American ear now attuned to hearing such sonorous names as Joshua and Benjamin and Nathaniel echoing through the playground, we think such weighty names as Abraham and Moses and Isaiah will begin to feel lighter and more modern over the coming years. ABE is an honest, homey nickname, sometimes used on its own; a more contemporary and hip short form is BRAM. The frequently used Arabic version is IBRAHIM.

ABSALOM. More common on the printed page (Absalom was the handsome and favored son of King David in the Bible, and the name appears in the works of Dryden and Faulkner as well) than in real life, this name projects a serious, even solemn image.

ADAIR. A name with flair, the panache of Fred Astaire. Just don't think about the fact that it's the Scottish version of Edgar. ADARE is a town in western Ireland.

ADAM. Adam is one of those names that galloped in with the posse of TV cowboy shows of the sixties (Adam Cartwright being the eldest of the *Bonanza* boys), then went on to become a soap opera staple. In the twenties, the name was associated with the D. H. Lawrence novel, *Aaron's Rod*, in the forties with the Tracy-Hepburn film, *Adam's Rib*, and in the sixties and seventies with the TV cop series, *Adam-12*. At this point, the name of the first man to be created by God in the Book of Genesis is feeling a little faded from overuse and might deserve a rest. A more modern-sounding (if less biblical) spin would be ADDISON, which actually means son of Adam, and that came to prominence as the surname of the wisecracking Bruce Willis character on *Moonlighting* a few seasons back.

ADLAI. Grandparents will link this name with the unsuccessful 1952 and 1956 Democratic presidential candidate and later UN representative, Adlai Stevenson, but we see it as an interesting and distinctive Old Testament/personal hero name ripe for discovery. (And Murphy Brown *did* consider it for her son before she settled on Avery.)

ADOLPH. This was a fairly prevalent name among German-Americans prior to World War II (it was also the real first name of Harpo Marx), but the rise of Hitler made it absolutely verboten not only here but in most countries throughout the world: Several nations—France and Norway are two examples—literally outlaw its use. A somewhat more acceptable variation would be the Latinized ADOLPHUS or the short form DOLPH, now linked to action hero Dolph Lundgren.

ADRIAN. Very popular in England for at least fifty years, Adrian never really caught on here, perhaps because the female version Adrienne has the same pronunciation and is more commonly heard. If you're not bothered by the gender confusion, it can be an appealing choice, one you would share with Edie Brickell and Paul Simon, who picked it for their baby boy. In the past it's been tied to the only English pope, Adrian IV; the Hollywood golden age costume designer who was one of the original single name celebrities; and the real-life Adrian Cronauer played by Robin Williams in *Good Morning, Vietnam*, as well as basketball star Adrian Dantley.

AHMAD, AHMED. One of the five hundred or more names used by Mohammed. It is currently a favorite Black Muslim name (among its best known bearers are former football player-sports commentator Ahmad Rashad and jazz pianist Ahmad Jamal), perhaps due to the adage that angels pray in any house where an Ahmad or Mohammed resides. In Swahili it means "praiseworthy."

AIDAN. An appealing Irish name introduced into the American melting pot of nomenclature by Aidan Quinn when he appeared opposite

Madonna in the 1985 film, *Desperately Seeking Susan*. Particularly recommended for families with Irish roots, it was the name of a famous seventh-century Irish saint, and is related to the Irish word for "fire."

ALAN, ALLAN, ALLEN. A name whose burst of popularity paralleled the rise of taciturn tough guy Alan Ladd in the forties. Right now it's kind of faceless, making it hard to picture a nineties baby being given the name. The Welsh spelling, **ALUN**, while more attractive, might seem contrived here.

ALBERT. This name became extremely fashionable in both England and America after Queen Victoria married Prince Albert in 1840, and it managed to stay in style for eighty-odd years. With its serious, studious image (think of Einstein and Schweitzer), however, it hasn't shown any signs of enjoying the revival that other British classics have, nor have its short forms, **AL** or **BERT**.

ALDO. A spirited Germanic name very popular in Italy and occasionally used in this country, especially during the period when gravel-voiced Aldo Ray was making movies. In Italy it can be short for such names as **RINALDO**. **ALDOUS** is the original German form, as in Huxley.

ALEXANDER, ALEXIS, ALEX, ALEC. The whole constellation of Alexi-related names has become tremendously popular for both boys and girls in the past few years, to the point where Alexander has just entered the Top 25 list of boys' names. (It's currently number three in England.) As opposed to many here-today, gone-tomorrow trendy names, however, Alexander has a solid historical base dating back to Alexander the Great, and has been born by such legendary figures as the liberal Russian Tsar Alexander II, Alexander Hamilton, and Alexander Graham Bell, who laid the first foundations for the information superhighway. Alexis was a strong, Russian male alternative until the influence of the unscrupulous Alexis Carrington on *Dynasty* established it as an almost exclusively female name. Alec (thanks to the eldest Baldwin brother) has recently come to be seen as a sexier short form in this group than Alex, the image of which was colored by the violent hero of *A Clockwork Orange*, the reliable Alex Rieger on *Taxi* and the buttoned-up Michael J. Fox character on *Family Ties*. Some possible foreign variants: ALESSANDRO (Italian), ALEJANDRO (Spanish), ALEXEI and Sasha/Sacha (Russian).

ALFRED. Although Alfred the Great was a wise, compassionate and scholarly king of old England, contemporary kids might sooner envision the grinning Alfred E. Neuman of *Mad* comics fame or the jowly contours of Alfred Hitchcock when they hear the name. If you like the nickname FRED, a more stylish choice would be Frederick.

ALGERNON. Originally a nickname meaning "with whiskers," this just might take the prize as the jellyfish name of all time.

ALI. An Arabic name that really does mean "the greatest" (as in Mohammed Ali). A shortened form of ALLAH, it is used by Muslims in Turkey, Egypt, Iran, Jordan, India, Arabia—and now the United States. It is also associated with Ali ("Open sesame.") Baba in the ancient Arabic tales, *A Thousand and One Nights*.

ALISTAIR, ALASTAIR. That's the way the British spell it; the Scots prefer ALASDAIR—but they are all Gaelic versions of Alexander. To most Yanks, thanks primarily to the longtime host of *Masterpiece Theater*, it represents ultra sophisticated Britishness.

ALOYSIUS. See LOUIS.

ALPHONSO and its more palatable Spanish form ALONZO. They have given rise to one memorable nickname, FONZIE, and two more usable ones, LON and LONNIE. Alonzo has been associated with several star athletes, including Alonzo Stagg and Alonzo Mourning. ALPHONSE is the real name of Alan Alda.

ALVIN. A Germanic name literally meaning "noble friend loved by all," Alvin has, alas, taken on quite a different meaning due to all the nerdy characters given that name in movies and television over the years. Not to mention the association with those screeching chipmunks.

A more distinguished bearer was Alvin Ailey, founder of the Alvin Ailey American Dance Theater.

AMADEO. A euphonious Italian name, often associated with the painter Modigliani. It was chosen for his son by actor John Turturro. The Latinate version is AMADEUS, as in Mozart. Another intriguing form of the name is AMYAS or AMIAS, which can be pronounced Amy-us or a-MY-us.

AMBROSE. An upper-class-British-sounding name, which carries with it an air of blooming well-being. It belonged to one of the four great Latin teachers of Christianity, who also developed the use of music in church services. Television fanatics might be interested to know that in 1961, Ambrose was designated the patron saint of educational TV by Pope John XXIII.

AMORY. It comes from the Latin amor, suggesting a loving person, and is, like Avery and Emory, the kind of executive-sounding family name that is growing in popularity as a first name. Amory Blaine was the hero of F. Scott Fitzgerald's *This Side of Paradise*.

AMOS. A strong biblical (it means "strong" in Hebrew) name that has suffered since the thirties from its association with the racially stereotyped characters on the radio and TV show, *Amos and Andy*, But that was then and this is now and we suggest it's time it was liberated from that association and looked at with fresh eyes. After all, any child could become a Famous Amos. Trivia tidbit: Amos was the real name of comedian Danny Thomas.

ANATOLE. This French name has a decided touch of the creative, the exotic, perhaps verging on the exaggerated, conjuring up an image of artist's beret, smock, and pencil-thin moustache.

ANDREW. The eleventh most popular name for boys born in the United States today, Andrew is that rare combination of being both classic and trendy, widely used yet still retaining a large measure of strength and character, reflecting its literal meaning of strong and manly. Of all the leading boys' names, it's the one most favored by highly educated mothers, according to a Harvard research study. Most of the many little Andrews around these days are called by their full name, or sometimes Drew, less and less frequently by the relaxed and friendly ANDY, exemplified by Raggedy Andy, Andy Hardy, Andy Rooney, Andy Griffith, and Andy Williams. It's also been connected to two of America's most famous artists, Wyeth and Warhol. In the New Testament, Andrew was the first disciple to be called by Jesus and, although the origins of the name are Greek, Andrew is the patron saint of both Scotland and Russia. It also has several pleasant foreign manifestations that are sometimes used in this country, including ANDRÉ (French), ANDREI (Russian), ANDRES (Spanish), ANDREA (Italian), ANDREAS (German, Dutch, and Greek), and ANDERS (Norwegian and Swedish). ANDERSON is the surname-name option. We must add that the name does have a couple of minor negative associations—"Randy Andy," the nickname for the present Duke of York and the devastating hurricane of 1992.

ANGEL. The saintly associations of this name make it difficult for a boy, in particular, to carry, except in Latino families, where it is quite commonly used. Angel Clare was the name of the decidedly non-angelic husband of *Tess of the d'Urbervilles* in the Thomas Hardy novel. ANGELO is the Italian version.

ANGUS. The image of this name was, not that long ago, that of a fusty, fuddy-duddy old Scot dressed in kilts and playing the bagpipes. To us it has recently started to sound novel and new, with enough robust character to make it a plausible choice, particularly for parents with bloodlines that can be traced back to Glasgow or Edinburgh. In Gaelic it means "unique choice," one that was made by Amanda Pays and Corbin Bernsen for one of their twin sons. In Irish folklore, Angus Og is a chieftain-lord who used his magical powers and treasures for the pleasure and prosperity of mankind. And on top of all that, Angus is also a breed of fine cattle. The surname Maguiness or Macinnes means "Son of Angus"—perfect for the next generation or two.

ANSEL, ANSELM, and **ANSON.** Three names so distinctive that their bearers would never be met with the question, "Ansel (or Anselm or Anson) who?" Ansel is associated with the great western photographer, Ansel Adams, St. Anselm was the Archbishop of Canterbury in the twelfth century, and Anson Williams will go down in posterity as "Potsie" on *Happy Days*.

ANTHONY. This name's social setting ranges from da street corners of da Bronx to a debutante's ball, and the same can be said for its pet name, **TONY.** The name of the patron saint of Italy and of the poor, Anthony (which means "priceless" in Latin), after being popular in this country since the twenties, is still in the Top 25, a fact that can probably be attributed to its Latinate charm. **ANTON** is the version used in Russia and other Slavic countries, as well as in Germany, Sweden, and Norway; it is **ANTOINE** in France and **ANTONIO** in Italy, where the nickname name **TONIO** is also prevalent (Antonio is a Shakespearean favorite—he used it in no fewer than five of his plays) and in Spanish-speaking countries. And in England, whether it's spelled Anthony or **ANTONY**, it's often pronounced à la Noël Coward, without the *h*—just as it is on some sidewalks of New York.

ARA and ARAM. Two common Armenian names, the latter having become familiar in this country through the works of writer William Saroyan, who named his son Aram, and the former via Notre Dame football coach Ara Parseghian.

ARCHER. One of the more stiff and formal surname names.

ARCHIBALD, ARCHIE. These are more apt to be attached to a Beagle than a baby these days, but you might want to think about resurrecting them, especially if your last name is Campbell or Douglas, the families they have long been associated with in Scotland. Archie is actually very fashionably used in England, where all things Scottish carry an undying charm, but Americans would have to obliterate the image of *All in the Family*'s resident bigot, Archie Bunker, and the hapless hero of *Archie* comics.

ARIEL (and its energetic short form, **ARI**). Very popular in Israel, Ariel has several appealing associations: It is one of the Hebrew names for God, a symbolic name for Jerusalem, it is the name of a great Hebrew leader, and also the witty and clever spirit in Shakespeare's *The Tempest*. Ari was the heroic character Paul Newman played in *Exodus*. Major drawback: In America, Ariel is much more often used as a girls' name, and now relates very strongly to Disney's *Little Mermaid* character.

ARLO. Names ending in the letter *O* have a unique aura of friendliness and cheer, and Arlo is no exception. It came on the scene in the seventies in the person of the shaggy singer Arlo Guthrie and is still infrequently enough used to remain distinctive.

ARMAND. This French name has long been considered one of the world's most romantic, from the lover of Camille to such smoldering modern bearers as Armand Assante.

ARNOLD. Arnold started life as a powerful Teutonic tribal chieftain name (it means "strong as an eagle" in German), but its strength has been sapped until it verges on the nerdy when seen as a name for a nineties child—Mr. Schwarzenegger to the contrary. But if you have a beloved Uncle Arnold you'd like to honor in your baby's name, you might consider the livelier ARNO or the Scandinavian ARNE.

ARTEMAS, ARTEMUS. Whatever the spelling, this name has a mythological, historical ring, perhaps because ARTEMIS was the Greek goddess of the hunt and wild animals. Artemas is also mentioned in the New Testament, and Artemus Ward was the pen name of a renowned American humorist.

ARTHUR. Arthur once shone as the legendary head of the Knights of the Round Table in Camelot. Now the name leaves a much quieter, more intellectual impression and is very rarely used. Vintage television was full of Arthurs and ARTS—from Godfrey to Linkletter to Arthur "Fonzie" Fonzarelli on *Happy Days*. More recently, tennis champion Arthur Ashe, the first African-American to win the U.S. Open, restored some dignity to the name.

ASA, AZA. The name of a long-reigning biblical king of Judah for more than forty years, Asa means "physician" in Hebrew. Its soap opera image is that of a strong patriarch (Asa Buchanan in *One Life to Live*), so using this name would require a bit of foresight.

ASHER. This might be a viable choice if you're looking for an Old Testament name—Asher was a son of Jacob—that's less widely used than, say, Aaron or Adam. Its diminutive, ASH, also has an overlay of Rhett Butlerish Southern charm.

ASHLEY. Even if the sensitive Ashley Wilkes was your favorite character in *Gone with the Wind*, bear in mind that Ashley is at this moment the number one most popular name given to girl babies in America, making it not the most viable or virile choice for a boy.

AUBREY. This is an upperclass British name rarely used on this side of the Atlantic. One handicap it has is its similarity to and possible confusion with the female name Audrey. Its most famous bearer was the turn-of the-century artist-illustrator Aubrey Beardsley. Similar in feel is AUBERON, transformed into Oberon by Shakespeare in *A Midsummer Night's Dream*.

AUGUSTUS and AUGUSTINE. Neither of these has been heard very often in the last hundred years, but they are exactly the kinds of names trendsetters are looking at with fresh eyes, considering whether they might be ripe for revival—Mick Jagger and Jerry Hall did use Augustine as the third name for their son. GUS, of course, is the more user-friendly nickname. The German form, AUGUST, is also suddenly in the air. It was chosen by actress Lena Olin for her son in honor of Swedish playwright August Strindberg, and it belongs to another famed playwright, Pulitzer Prize–winner August Wilson.

AUSTIN (sometimes spelled **AUSTEN**). This name is hot, hot, hot, combining an unbeatable number of desirable elements: It's got a sexy southwestern feel, place-name panache, and the solid base of having long been an Anglo-Saxon surname. Austin Reed is a current dreamy romantic lead character on the daytime drama *Days of Our Lives*, and

Austin Devereaux is the name of Michelle Philipps's son. Austin is currently at the top of the list in one state—Utah.

AVERY. Growing in popularity as a last-name-first name, Avery got a giant boost from its use for Murphy Brown's baby. (He was named after Murphy's mother; the creator of the show has a known penchant for giving her female characters strong male names.) Parents should note, however, that there are a fair number of little girl Averys around these days as well.

AVI. This is the short form of several Hebrew names, including AVIAV, AVIDOR, AVIDAN, AVIEL, AVIRAM, and AVITAL.

AXEL. The Scandinavian form of the Hebrew Absalom has been brought out of obscurity and into the spotlight by two distinctive contemporary characters: rocker Ax'l Rose and Axel Foley, the policeman portrayed by Eddie Murphy in the *Beverly Hills Cop* series. It's a name with the strength of ten Ashleys.

B

BAILEY. An extremely amiable, open sounding surname (it originally signified a bailiff) that hails from Britain, not—as it might sound—from Ireland. Other occupational surname-names worth a moment's thought: BAKER, BARKER (it meant shepherd or tanner), BREWSTER.

BALTHASAR, BALTHAZAR. This is a choice recommended only for the intrepid baby namer—it has been used in the oil-rich Getty family, for example. Balthasar was one of the three Wise Men of the Orient who brought gifts to the infant Jesus, and it was also the name assumed by Portia in her disguise as a male lawyer in Shakespeare's *A Merchant of Venice*.

BARNABY. Barnaby fits into that golden triangle of names that are neither too common nor too bizarre, but strike the happiest of mediums. Its genial and exceptionally attractive image make it the perfect blind date name. Barnaby has been in the corner of the public eye since the sixties, as a TV cowboy (on *Wagon Train*), detective (*Barnaby Jones*), and a syndicated comic strip character (*Barnaby*). BARNABUS is a weightier, more somber version, having been both one of the first Christian converts and missionaries and the lead character on the cult series, *Dark Shadows*.

BARNEY. This name has gone through many incarnations, the latest of which is as a mega-popular purple dinosaur. Before that there was Barney Google, with the "goo-goo-googly eyes," Barney Rubble, Barney Fife, and Barney Miller. Until the dinosaur craze dies down, it could be somewhat difficult for a child to live with this otherwise warm and friendly name.

BARRY. Barry dates from the Gary-LARRY-Carrie-Shari fifties and is showing no signs of a nineties rerun. And although its roots are Irish, its best-known bearer, Barry Manilow, is not.

BARTHOLOMEW. This a pretty heavy moniker to hang on a child, but for the bold parent (actor Timothy Bottoms is one) this apostle's name may have some unorthodox appeal. But then there's the nickname BART to consider. Until the *Simpsons'* popularity subsides, especially among elementary school kids, a child might feel the terrible obligation to live up to that little wise guy character's reputation. Unless you could direct his admiration toward someone like the great Green Bay Packer quarterback, Bart Starr. BARTON—as in the unfortunately named "Barton Fink" —is a decidedly unstylish relative.

BASIL. Although Greek in origin (in the fourth century, a bishop by that name established the principles of the Greek Orthodox Church), it has taken on the aura of aquiline-nosed upper-class Britishness ever since Basil Rathbone was cast as Sherlock Holmes. And in recent years, the Pesto Generation has added the fragrant aroma of the herb to its image. Trivia note: St. Basil bore the distinction of having a grandmother, father, mother, older sister, and two younger brothers who were all saints as well.

BAYARD. An Old English red-haired name—one of the few that doesn't begin with the letter *R*. Its first syllable can be pronounced either as *bay* or *by*.

BEAUREGARD. This name harks back to the old plantation and would not be easy for a child of today—northern or Southern—to pull off. Its short form, **BEAU**, is another story, suggesting as it does someone devilishly handsome (it originally was a nickname meaning just that); and has been used for characters fitting that description in novels, in the old TV westerns (*Maverick*, *Wells Fargo*), and in soap operas such as *As the World Turns*. Its best-known contemporary bearer, Beau Bridges, was actually born Lloyd Bridges III.

BENJAMIN. This soft and sensitive Old Testament name was for centuries used primarily by Jews. In modern times, it came into more general favor in the sixties, partly through the influence of the character Dustin Hoffman played in *The Graduate*, and has been used by many celebrities for their sons, among them Carly Simon and James Taylor, Richard Dreyfuss, Harrison Ford, Raul Julia, and Jeff Daniels. In the Bible, Benjamin was the youngest of the twelve sons of Jacob, and there have been numerous other notable Benjamins in the past, from Benjamin Franklin to Benjamin Spock. Though the use of Benjamin has been widespread for thirty years, it is still a strong and viable choice.

BENEDICT has quite a different history, as the name of the saint who founded the Benedictine Order and of fifteen Popes; it might be seen as a more distinctive alternative to Benjamin, except for its lasting link to Revolutionary War traitor Benedict Arnold and the use of the name as a word for a confirmed bachelor who marries reluctantly (as in Shakespeare's *Much Ado about Nothing*, where it is spelled Benedick). **BENNETT, BENTLEY, BENTON,** and **BENSON** are four pretentious last-name-first names, lacking any of the gusto of the Irishinflected surnames. BEN is the gentle short form for all of the above, which becomes more creative when spelled BENN—BENNO even more so. BENJI, alas, is in the doghouse.

BERNARD. A name with a highly intellectual image quite in keeping with that of the saint bearing that name, who was a brilliant scholar, but not one that a nineties child would be likely to thank you for. Bernard, the patron saint of mountain climbers, is also the real first name of Tony Curtis.

BERTRAM and **BURTON.** Two names hibernating in the Land of Nerd, especially since onetime macho men Burt(on) Lancaster and Burt(on) Reynolds have moved past those images. Trivia note: composer Burt Bacharach is the son of journalist Bert Bacharach.

BEVAN. A Welsh surname meaning "son of Evan," this would make a strong individual replacement for that increasingly popular name.

BEVIS. An unusual and interesting British name (pronounced with a soft *e*) that we could have recommended more highly before the arrival of the outrageous MTV animated twerps, Beavis and Butt-Head.

BIRCH. A rarely used nature name that calls to mind the attributes of the tall, strong but graceful tree. Its best known bearer is Senator Birch Bayh. The parent taken with the notion of tree names might also consider ASH, of course, as well such offbeat ideas as OAK and PINE, even perhaps HICKORY.

BIX. Like DEX and JINX and other names ending with X, Bix is distinctive and energetic. It might also be a hero name for jazz lovers who admire the great musician and composer, Bix Beiderbecke—whose birth certificate name was Leon.

BJORN. Although one of the most popular boys' names in Scandinavia, in this country Bjorn is connected to one particular individual, the Swedish tennis star and five-time Wimbledon winner Bjorn Borg. We hope it doesn't lose any of its agility when we tell you it's the Scandinavian form of Bernard.

BLAKE. A fairly bland androgynous name, Blake is still very much linked to the slick, silver-haired Blake Carrington character of *Dynasty* fame, reflecting an acquisitive eighties attitude. BLAIR is somewhat similar, although used much more for girls than boys. One attractive male with the name, however, is Blair Underwood, of both daytime (*One Life to Live*) and nightime (*L.A. Law*) TV fame.

BOAZ. An unusual Old Testament name with a lot of contemporary pizzazz. It was used by the seventeenth-century Puritans, but at this point in time, yours would surely be the only Boaz on the block. Among Jews, it is associated with the holiday Shavuot (as that is when the Bible story of Ruth is read in the synagogue, and Boaz was Ruth's wealthy second husband) and so is sometimes given to boys born on that day. Added attraction: It *does* have one of the all-time great nicknames, BO, a very popular name in Denmark, associated in this country with sports great Bo Jackson (born Vincent), musician Bo Diddley (born Ellas), and the romantic *Days of Our Lives* character Bo Brady.

BOONE. A long and lanky cowboy name, Boone can be traced back to the French, meaning a blessing.

BORIS. This Russian-inflected name has been as dead as one of Mr. Karloff's mummy characters for a long time, and shows no signs of resuscitation, despite the fame of German-born tennis star Boris Becker. Other notable Borises: the sixteenth-century Russian tsar and opera hero Boris Godunov, novelist Boris Pasternack, and political leader Boris Yeltsin.

BOSTON. An attractive and unique place-name, used for their son by the equally uniquely named Season Hubley and then-mate Kurt Russell. (In any case, it's not as far out as the place-name given to his offspring by director Jonathan Demme—BROOKLYN.)

BOWIE. An Irish surname (although not the real one of David B., who was born with the considerably less marketable moniker David Hayward-Jones), Bowie successfully combines Gaelic charm with a western drawl. The best-known bearer is onetime baseball commissioner Bowie Kuhn.

BOYD. Only slightly more contemporary than Lloyd or Floyd, Boyd has a bit of a hayseed image. In Gaelic it means "blond one," and is a well used Scottish clan name.

BRADLEY, BRAD. Inching up the current popularity charts, this name is almost always used in full by contemporary parents. Maybe that's because BRAD—despite the appeal of current heartthrob Brad Pitt—is still out on a surfin' safari with Chad, Todd, and Scott.

BRADY and **BRODY.** Two high-energy Irish surnames that have begun to be used as first names over the past few years. Brady, in fact, literally means "spirited one" in Irish Gaelic, while Brody is a well-known Scottish clan name. Brady was the name of the memorable character portrayed by Billy Dee Williams on *Dynasty*.

BRAM. Bram has an unusual amount of character and charm for a one-syllable name. It started life as a hipper-than-Abe diminutive for Abraham, but is also an independent Irish and Dutch name, made familiar to American ears by the creator of Count Dracula, Bram Stoker.

BRANDON. Brandons are suddenly appearing everywhere—on the Top 10 list of most popular boy baby names (as high as number four in some states), in the cast of characters on more than one soap opera, and as teen favorite Jason Priestley's character on *Beverly Hills 90210*. It is related to the Irish Saint's name BRENDAN, currently attached to rising star Brendan Frasier, which has one of the worst literal meanings we've ever heard (okay, if you must know, it's "stinking hair"). According to Irish legend, St. Brendan the Voyager was the first European to reach American soil. A more offbeat and softer-sounding alternative to this somewhat overused pair is BRENNAN.

BRENT, BRETT, BRET. These three names swept into the public consciousness in the wake of the smash hit late fifties–early sixties TV western, *Maverick* (in which the male family members were called Bret, BART, BEAU, and Brent). Of late, they've lost a lot of their masculine swagger, especially since Brett is equally used for girls. Bret Harte, whose given first name was really Francis, was an important novelist of the early West, and tennis great Jimmy Connors named his son Brett.

BRIAN. This was the fourth most popular boy baby name in the United States in 1975 and still manages to hang onto a large degree of its jaunty Gaelic charm, even if it no longer sounds like a fresh choice. The name of the most famous of all Irish warrior-kings, Brian Boru, it was part of the second-generation wave of Irish names to emigrate to this country, along with such compatriots as Kevin, Dennis, Darren, and Duane. In Monty Python's irreligious *Life of Brian*, the hapless Brian gets mistaken for the Messiah, and before that *Brian's Song* portrayed the true story of Chicago Bear Brian Piccolo. BRYAN is an alternate spelling, as in singers Ferry and Adams.

BRICE, BRYCE. The image here is sleek and sophisticated, elegant and efficient, perhaps to an extreme.

BROCK. A granite rock of a name derived from the Old English word for a badger, Brock has been used on the soap opera *The Young and the Restless*.

BRODERICK and BRONSON. Two surname names that have become familiar through the use of a pair of single actors—Academy Award–winner Broderick Crawford and sitcom star Bronson Pinchot. Although it sounds somewhat formal and cold, Broderick actually means "brother" in Old Norse, while Bronson, a softer sounding name, derives from the Old English for "son of the dark-skinned one."

BROWN. This name is as rich and warm as the tone it denotes, and much more simpatico than its harsher Italo/German equivalent, BRUNO, which has traditionally been used to represent a bear in children's stories. Color names like Brown and Gray are highly evocative and, we think, unfairly neglected.

BRUCE. Its somewhat sissyish image was completely turned around when a batch of ultravirile Bruces suddenly hit the large and small screens a few years back—namely B. Lee, B. Willis, B. Springsteen, and B. Jenner, although this did nothing to resuscitate it as a baby name. An earlier attachment was to Robert "the Bruce," who ruled Scotland as King Robert I in the fourteenth century, and was said to have been inspired by the perseverance of a spider.

BRYANT. Bryan with attitude.

BURL. This name has a fragrant, woodsy feel. Its only well-known owner, folk singer Burl Ives, was born with the first name of Icle.

BYRON. For centuries this name had a long-haired, windswept image due to its strong connection to the poet, Lord Byron, who inspired its use as a first name. These days it gives off a somewhat more serious, even intellectual message, one that might have appealed to *thirtysomething*'s Mel Harris, who chose it for her son. Golf legend Byron Nelson helped give it a touch of panache.

C

CAESAR/CESAR. The name of the greatest Roman of them all is rarely used outside Latino families. In the early years of this country it became a typical slave name, along with such other classical appellations as Cato and OCTAVIUS. Sonny Bono phoneticized it for his son as Chesare.

CAIN. Rarely heard outside of soap operas (*One Life to Live* and *Santa Barbara*), Cain carries the stigma of being associated with the world's first murderer, according to the Old Testament, who killed his own brother in a fit of jealousy. If it weren't for that—a very big if—Cain would be a strong, acceptable, and viable name. One way around the problem might be to sidestep the biblical connection and transform the name via spelling into the Irish surname Kane.

CALEB. A biblical name that could make a distinctive alternative to the less creative-sounding and increasingly common Jacob, now the seventh most popular boy baby name in the country. The meaning of the name is faithful, intrepid, and victorious, an apt description of the Old Testament Caleb who was one of only two ancient Israelites (Joshua was the other) who set out with Moses from Egypt to finally enter the promised land. A contemporary-sounding variant is CALE, which has the drawback of being a homonym for a vegetable.

CALVIN. Not too long ago, Calvins—thanks to Mr. Klein—was a synonym for jeans (as in the phrase, "Nothing comes between me and my Calvins"). Now that that campaign is history, Calvin can be appreciated for what it is: a slightly quirky but cozy name, which doesn't at all reflect the rigid precepts of Calvinism. There have been a number of notable Calvins past and present, including President Coolidge (born John), basketball star Calvin Murphy, and baseball's Cal Ripken. The unprepossessing short form, CAL, was also borne by James Dean in one of his most moving roles, in *East of Eden*.

CAMERON. Definitely one of the hottest names around, especially for boys, but starting to heat up for girls as well. Scottish by heritage, Cameron gives off a handsome, sensitive aura, one that's been utilized by the writers of several soap operas. It was also chosen for his son by Michael Douglas.

CARL, KARL. This no-nonsense German form of Charles is strong but lacks much sensitivity or subtlety. Its most famous bearers include poet Carl Sandburg, scientist Carl Sagan, musician "Doc" Severinsen, and track superstar Carl Lewis. The Latin forms CARLO and CARLOS have far more fire.

CARLETON. An upscale name almost to the point of caricature, as demonstrated by the preppy son in the TV show *Fresh Prince of Bel*

Air, although baseball's Carlton Fisk has done his share to bring the name down to earth. The same description would fit CHARLTON and CARLYLE, which tend to sound more like hotels than people.

CARROLL. This name, which began life as a 100 percent male name, has gradually invaded the female camp (dropping one of its *R*s and *L*s in the process), to the point where it has now lost virtually all remnants of its masculine punch. Trivia tidbit: The man inside *Sesame Street*'s Big Bird is named Carroll Spinney.

CARSON. An androgynous-executive name of the type that is rapidly growing in popularity; this one becomes more and more viable as Johnny Carson fades from public view. Although writer Carson McCullers was of course female, the name retains all its original masculinity, and feminist mothers may appreciate the symbolism of naming a son after a notable female.

CARTER. Carter is another posh and trendy surname name, à la socialite-businessman Carter Burden. Another fashionable element: the presidential association.

CARY. One of those names, like Oprah and Orson, whose popularity can be traced back to one celebrity—in this case Cary Grant (born with the name Archibald, he renamed himself after a character he was playing). But although his image was that of the quintessentially debonair man-about-town, this name, like its homophone CAREY, now sounds soft and feminine due to the preponderance of girls named Carrie and KERRY. We doubt that even the attractive star on the horizon, Cary Elwes, can turn this name around.

CASEY. A name with a big wide grin, Irish, friendly and open, Casey reflects its association with American folk heroes like Casey Jones, the engine driver of the Cannonball Express who gave his life to save his passengers (and whose given name was actually Johnathan, but who took his name from the city of his birth, Cayce, Kentucky), the legendary Casey at the Bat, and baseball's other Casey—Stengel. Though the name is now used in aboout a quarter of instances for girls, and became a tad overexposed during the free wheeling seventies, it retains a good measure of boyish vitality.

CASPER, CASPAR. After thirty years, this otherwise feasible name is still quite firmly linked to the white-sheeted image of the cartoon *Casper the Friendly Ghost*. The Dutch form of Jasper, it also belonged to one of the Three Magi who brought gifts to the infant Jesus.

CASSIDY. A lean and lanky Irish cowboy name that is in danger of being taken over by the females of the species (once Kathie Lee Gifford captures a name . . .). Presidential brother Roger Clinton said he'd give his child this name, his mother's maiden, whatever the baby's sex. The nickname CASS is sometimes used independently, as in the Sinclair Lewis novel, *Cass Timberlane*.

CATO. It may once have conjured up images of ancient Roman statesmen or Southern antebellum retainers, but now it sounds cool and jazzy; a jaunty *O*-ending name with historic substance as well.

CECIL and CEDRIC. A pair of stereotypically soft British names. Cecil, which had a lofty heritage as a famous Roman clan name and then as the surname of a prominent sixteenth-century English family, has gradually lost its color and potency over the years; it was the name of the prissy character played by Daniel Day-Lewis in the movie version of E. M. Forster's *A Room with a View*. With Cedric, a name invented by Sir Walter Scott for a character in *Ivanhoe*, this happened in one fell swoop, via the character of the long-haired, lace-collared Little Lord Fauntleroy in Frances Hodgson Burnett's 1886 novel, whose given name was, yes, Cedric, and who became an unwitting symbol of the pampered mama's boy. There are, of course, Cedrics and Cecils who have fought the stereotype and achieved success, including baseball player Cedric Maxwell, pioneer movie producer-director Cecil B. de Mille, photographer Cecil Beaton, and jazz pianist Cecil Taylor.

CHAD. Chad, like BRAD, became popular in the late fifties, and escalated even more in the era of hot TV doctor shows, when Chad Everett (born Raymond) starred on the long-running *Medical Center*.

Rarely used now, it was also the name of a seventh-century saint and a country in north central Africa.

CHAIM. Many cultures have attempted to bestow longevity on their children by giving them names that signify life—among them Viva, Zoe, FAYOLA, VIDAL—and another prime example is Chaim, the Hebrew word for "life," as in the toast "l'chaim," to life. It is a name that barely survived the first wave of Jewish immigrants, being passed on to later generations in such watered-down forms as Hyman and HYMIE. Today Chaim survives in the stories of Isaac Babel and Isaac Bashevis Singer, in Israel and in more orthodox Jewish communities.

CHARLES. The use of Charles has been so widespread in English (and French)-speaking countries for so long that it is virtually faceless—it can conjure up anyone from Dickens to Chaplin to Bronson. Arising from a Germanic word meaning "free man," it owed its initial popularity to the emperor Charlemagne, which translates as Charles the Great. It has been an elegant royal name—designating both Bonnie Prince Charlie, leader of a 1745 rebellion, and the present Prince of Wales, and also has one of the most buoyant and classless of nicknames: CHARLIE, also spelled CHARLEY, which has been celebrated in song ("Charlie is My Darling," "Charlie My Boy," "Clap Hands! Here Comes Charlie!"), on stage (*Charley's Aunt*), on film (Charlie Chan, *Charlie Bubbles*), on TV (*Charlie's Angels*) and in cartoons (*Charlie Brown*). Nowadays, when parents aren't using the full form of the name, they are also considering the jazzier CHAZ, and should also be aware of such British spins as CHAR and CHAS, as well as the Scottish version, CHAY. CHUCK is now only for dads, or beef.

CHASE. Chase is an ultra prosperous sounding name redolent of the worlds of high finance and international banking. More symbol than name, it's not surprising that it was found in the plots of such teledramas as *Falcon Crest*, *General Hospital*, and *The Young and the Restless*.

CHAUNCEY. A name halfway between its old milquetoast image and a more jovial Irish-sounding contemporary one. No such ambivalence for its sometime-short form, CHANCE, which has a dangerous swagger, a gambler's edge. Its most famous bearer is the Tennessee Williams character Chance Wayne, portrayed by a young Paul Newman in the movie *Sweet Bird of Youth*. Another is the enigmatic figure played by Peter Sellers in the film version of Jerzy Kosinski's *Being There*. And Billy Ray Cyrus recently used Chance as the middle name of his son, Braison.

CHESTER. A comfortable, solid, teddy bear of a name that we would place in the so-far-out-they-could-be-on-their-way-back-in category, one that hasn't been used in so long it suddenly sounds both quirky and cuddly. Perhaps this was what impelled Tom Hanks and Rita Wilson to use it for their son. CHET is the usual, but still dated, nickname.

CHEVY. This, like Cher and Madonna, falls into the category of who-needs-a-last-name? names. In fact, the Chevy Chase we all know and love entered the world as Cornelius and was probably nicknamed after the Washington suburb. There was, however, a medieval ballad called "Chevy Chase," and Charles Dickens called a character Chevy in his novel, *Martin Chuzzlewitt*. But be warned that any child named Chevy might be expected to do pratfalls for the rest of his days or at least as long as there are reruns of *Saturday Night Live*.

CHEYENNE. Once upon a time it was the name of the eponymous hero of a TV western; now it's being discovered in a big way by parents of various backgrounds who share an enthusiasm for all things southwestern and Native American—from furniture to food to names. Also used, as Marlon Brando did before it was fashionable, for girls.

CHRISTIAN. It is only recently that this name has come into widespread use, probably because it once sounded a bit too pious for most people's taste. But now with the swift rise of young star Christian Slater that taboo seems to be fading, and the name does sound fresher than the ever-popular Christopher. In the Middle Ages, Christian was a female name, but turned male with the introduction of the hero of John Bunyan's *The Pilgrim's Progress*. In the more recent past, most

Christians of note have had a French accent—the lover of Roxane in *Cyrano de Bergerac*, for instance, and the designers Dior and Lacroix. It is the real first name of Buddy Ebsen and, in the category of star babies, Mel Gibson is the father of a Christian.

CHRISTOPHER. This fashionable classic is more popular than ever—it was second only to Michael for well over a decade, probably because parents like the combination of its strong, sincere, straightforward image with a rhythmic three-syllable sound. A Greek name meaning "bearer of Christ," it is sometimes used to honor St. Christopher, a third-century martyr who became the patron saint of travelers because of the medieval belief that anyone who looked at his image would be protected all day. The almost ubiquitous American nickname is CHRIS, but there are British variations that might add a more individual spin to the name—Kit, Kip, and CHRISTY, the last of which is more common in Ireland and may be too feminine for use here. Two Christophers known to every school child: Christopher Robin and Christopher Columbus.

CLANCY. A lively, almost pugnacious Irish surname; full of moxie and more distinctive than Casey.

CLARENCE. This name pops up on TV every year around Christmastime, in the guise of Clarence Oddbody, Jimmy Stewart's sagacious guardian angel in the perennial classic, *It's a Wonderful Life*, and is rarely if ever heard from the rest of the year. Nor do we expect it to be, even though Clarence was the name of the character played by Christian Slater in *True Romance*. It was also the improbable real name of suave actor Robert Cummings.

CLARK. In the heyday of Clark Gable, this name had a smooth, debonair charm, but it now sounds rather stiff and outdated—more like Clark Kent.

CLAUDE. A soft-spoken French name that conjures up the pastel colors of Monet and the harmonies of Debussy. Still used for women in

France, it was ambisexual everywhere in its early history. The attractive Italian version, CLAUDIO, is also sometimes heard in this country.

CLAY. A rich one-syllable name that has been a soap opera staple—from the current *Guiding Light* and *Loving*, to the dearly departed *Search for Tomorrow* and *The Edge of Night*. Its Southern-inflected handsome-rogue image does not carry over to the longer forms, CLAYTON and CLAYBORNE.

CLEMENT. If Clement has a papal ring, that could be because there have been fourteen heads of the Catholic church by that name, as well as several early saints. It also has a mild, pleasant feel, as in the phrase "clement weather." The short form, CLEM, is homey and humble, with a distinctive down-home charm.

CLEON. A rare and distinctive name with historic and literary over-tones: Cleon was the leader of the Athenians during the Peloponesian War and a character in Shakespeare's *Pericles*.

CLEVELAND. An old place-name not nearly as interesting as some of the more recently coined ones. The short form, CLEVE, used on its own, has a more individual, original sound.

CLIFFORD. Clifford is beginning to overcome a slightly stodgy, intellectual impression and is showing signs of a revival—ex-*thirtysome-thing*'s Ken Olin and Patricia Wettig, for example, chose it for their son. CLIFTON, on the other hand, is showing no signs of life. There have been quite a few CLIFFs on television in the past few years, in particular Bill Cosby's Cliff (short for HEATHCLIFF) Huxtable and the verbose Cliff Claven on *Cheers*. Kids will also be familiar with a big red dog named Clifford in a series of juvenile books.

CLINTON. The fate of this old English family name probably will depend on the ultimate reputation of president Bill, or on your political point of view. Its short form, CLINT, associated as it is with the legendary Mr. Eastwood (born Clinton), has a much steelier image.

CLIVE. We can't think of any name that could be more clipped or British than Clive—conjuring up as it does a terribly couth chap in high boots and khakis and a pencil-thin moustache. An old English family name, it was launched as a Christian one by the nineteenth-century novelist William Thackeray for a character in his novel *The Newcomes*.

CLOVIS. An aromatic, unconventional name, Clovis is of German descent, related to the later forms LUDWIG and Lewis. Clovis I was the first Christian ruler of the Franks and Clovis Ruffin was an inventive clothing designer.

CLYDE. A cross between a nerd and an outlaw, this name's reputation rested for years on the imprint of Clyde Barrow of Bonnie and Clyde fame. The name of a river that runs through Glasgow, it has somewhat been redeemed by the achievements of Clyde Drexler, a member of 1992 Olympic basketball "Dream Team."

CODY. Lest you think that Kathie Lee Gifford single-handedly invented this name and spread it across the land, be reminded that before little Cody Gifford there was Buffalo Bill, there was the hero of the TV series *Riptide*, there was Cleveland Browns tackle Cody Risien (after whom baby Gifford was named), and the name has been used for their sons by other celebrities, including Kenny Loggins and Robin Williams. But it cannot be denied that Regis's cohost's day-by-day reports on her son's accomplishments did ignite the name's meteoric success—it's now number fourteen on the national list and well into the Top 10 in several states. So although Cody still sounds very appealing, be aware of how modishly Western it is, and how dated it might become. You might just want to consider something less trendy like, say, BRODY.

COLE. A short name that manages to embody a lot of richness and depth, perhaps because of its association with the great, sophisticated songwriter Cole Porter combined with the outlaw quality of the Cole member of the infamous bank-robbing Younger brothers. Cole Gioberti was a character on the nighttime soap *Falcon Crest*, and, daytime viewers will be aware of a hunk-of-the-month character named Cole on *The Young and the Restless*. And in case you've ever wondered, Old King Cole (originally spelled COEL) refers to an early Welsh ruler.

COLIN. This name has skipped across the Atlantic, its dashing World War II RAF image and British accent intact, and has made a triumphant landing in America. The one point of contention is its pronunciation. Traditionally, it is sounded with a soft *o*, but American flying ace Colin Kelly promoted the Cole-in version later emulated by General Colin Powell, the first Black Chairman of the Joint Chiefs of Staff. Originally a short French form of NICOLAS, Colin was a popular name for shepherds in English pastoral poetry (and retains some of that lyrical quality), was a favorite of the MacKenzie and Campbell clans in Scotland, and was chosen by Tom Hanks and Rita Wilson for one of their sons.

COLUM and **COLM** are two highly unusual names in this country—but widely used in Ireland—that mean "dove," the symbol of peace. **COLMAN** is a surname form.

CONAN. In the first edition (1988) of *Beyond Jennifer & Jason*, this name was pretty much a no-no, being so closely associated with the Barbarian. In the intervening years, the memory of Schwarzenegger's character has faded and Conan's image has softened, partly due to the amiable persona of late-night host Conan O'Brien, and also because of the acceptance of lesser-known Irish names in general. Conan, which means "intelligence" or "wisdom" in Gaelic, was the name of an illustrious seventh-century Irish saint.

CONNOR, CONOR. An appealing, up-and-coming, (there were 733 Connors born in the State of California alone in 1993) Irish name that has already made its mark on daytime drama (in not one, not two, but three soaps: *The Bold and the Beautiful*, *General Hospital*, and—as a female—on *As the World Turns*). It was frequently found in Irish myth and has been particularly used by families named O'Brien and (of course) O'Connor in the Old Sod, as well as by actor Patrick Duffy for his boy.

CONRAD. This is a somewhat neglected English version of the German KONRAD that some see as intellectual and manly, but others view as nerdy and old-fashioned. Your call.

CONSTANTINE. A rather bulky and unwieldy name for a modern child to bear, despite—or because of—its heavy historical associations. It was the name of the first Christian Emperor of the Roman empire, as well as three Scottish kings. In Ireland, it's traditionally used by the Maguire clan.

COOPER. An upscale, somewhat preppy yet genial surname (as reflected in the character of *Loving*'s resident prepster, Cooper Alden), this name is beginning to proliferate among trendsetting types. An occupational name—it originally referred to a barrel maker—it was chosen by Hugh Hefner for one of his young sons.

CORD. A severe, soap operaish name without much soul. Not surprising, then, that Cord Roberts has been a character on *One Life to Live*.

COREY. A name with energy but not much muscle. There seemed to be an epidemic of Coreys (Haim, Feldman, Parker) in eighties teen entertainment, but, along with other nickname-type names like JAMIE and Jody, Corey's image has definitely dimmed. A possible substitute might be CORIN, an unusual Shakespearean name found in *As You Like It*.

CORMAC. This traditional Irish name was brought to the attention of the American reading public in recent years via best-selling author Cormac McCarthy. An Irish version of Charles, it's an evocative name that runs through Celtic mythology as the legendary king of Tara.

CORNELIUS. As soon as the word *corny* came into the slanguage, this name was in trouble. Even before that, it had come to sound pompous and pretentious—perhaps through its association with newspaper mogul Cornelius Vanderbilt. CORNELL and CORNEL are short forms.

COSMO. A friendly, expansive Greek name, that seems to embrace the whole world—or cosmos. The name of the patron saint of doctors, Cosmo could make an exotic, creative choice.

CRAIG. A once-popular one-syllable baby boomer name (frat brother of Kirk, Clark, Scott, et al.), Craig has Scottish origins (it's still the third most common name in that country) and an overly smooth image. Modern parents would probably tend to prefer Kyle.

CRISPIN. Introduced into the mainstream by young actor Crispin Glover, this name which means "curly-haired" in Latin, has an image very much like its first syllable, crisp, autumnal, and colorful. CRISPIAN is an interesting, rarely used variation, as is CRISPUS, associated with Black hero Crispus Atticus, the first American to die for independence in the Boston Massacre.

CROSBY. A laid-back Irish surname, reflecting the nonchalance of crooner Bing Crosby and David Crosby of Crosby Stills Nash & Young. A mellow musical choice made by fellow singer Kenny Loggins for his son.

CULLEN. An Irish Gaelic surname meaning "handsome one" that might make an appealing alternative to Colin—although it could also be confused with it. To avoid that, you might consider the related CURRAN, which means "champion" or "hero."

CURTIS. A rather elegant Old French name that actually does mean "courteous." One notable bearer of the name is music great Curtis Mayfield. The short form CURT is a lot more macho, and has been borne by several outstanding athletes, including Flood (baseball) and Strange (golf), as well as sportscaster Curt Gowdy.

CYRIL. A name with a monocle in one eye, wearing an ascot in place of a tie. Despite its Greek roots, Cyril definitely has a British accent, and an upper-class, intellectual one at that.

CYRUS. An old-fangled, sitting-on-the-porch, smoking-a-corncob-pipe kind of name that might just be funky enough to appeal to parents looking for a so-far-out-it's-in possibility. Its origins were far more lofty—Cyrus the Great was a sixth-century founder of the Persian empire. Cybill Shepherd named her twin son Cyrus ZACHARIAH, in honor of two ancestors, but he is known to the world as Zack. CY is the very short form.

D

〜〜〜〜〜〜〜〜〜〜〜〜〜〜 ◉ 〜〜〜〜〜〜〜〜〜〜〜〜〜〜

DAKOTA. This geographic and Native American tribal name is currently very trendy for both girls (as used by Melanie Griffith and Don Johnson) and boys (chosen by Melissa Gilbert). And no wonder—it's got lots of spirit and charisma, though you may decide you want your little cowboy to live in a less crowded name territory.

DALE. A pleasant-sounding nature name, evocative of shaded glens and valleys, the androgynous Dale tipped slightly toward the girls' side with the fifties fame of cowgirl Dale Evans. Though *Twin Peaks'* FBI agent Dale Cooper (played by androgynously named Kyle MacLachlan) gave the name some modern masculine attention, it would still be a somewhat risky choice for a boy.

DALLAS. An attractive, attention-catching, cowboy place-name that's become more visible in recent years, partly due to the influence of baseball's Dallas Green and, to a lesser degree, newscaster Dallas Townsend. A literary reference is Dallas Winston, the character Matt Dillon played in the 1983 film, *The Outsiders*, based on the popular S. E. Hinton novel. But none of these western place names—Dallas, Austin, Dakota—packs the same style power it did even a few years ago.

DALTON. A classic English surname with a roguish western overlay—which could be related to the legendary Dalton brothers, two of whom were killed while trying to rob two banks at once. Though screen writer Dalton Trumbo was for a long time the only known bearer of this name, it is gathering some momentum and may well gallop as a dark horse onto the popularity charts in the next decade.

DAMIAN, DAMIEN. A Greek name with exotic, other-worldly overtones, mainly because of its links to the possessed child in *The Omen* movies and the priest, Father Damien Karras, in *The Exorcist*. Black magic notwithstanding, Damian has a flip side—Irish and antic, with considerable charm. It is the name of four saints, including the patron saint of doctors, chemists, barbers, and the blind, and is also the name of a slippery wheeler-dealer character on *General Hospital*.

DAMON. A name with a strong, pleasing sound and extremely positive ancient associations. In classical mythology, Damon and Pythias are the symbols of true friendship, as Damon risked his life to save his friend from execution. In Latin pastoral poetry, Damon is often used to denote a young lover. And Damon of Athens was the fifth-century B.C. philosopher who taught both Pericles and Socrates. Damon Runyon wrote *Guys and Dolls*, and, in more recent history, Damon Wayans was a key player in the groundbreaking *In Living Color*.

DANA. It was the forties movie star Dana Andrews who made this name viable for boys. Then, as his influence faded and Dana became almost completely feminized, along came Dana (*Wayne's World*) Carvey to re-inject it with a little masculine punch. Still, not too long ago, a *Wall Street Journal* reporter wrote a whole feature story on the trials and tribulations of being a male Dana.

DANIEL. A perennial favorite, Daniel was popular in the days of Daniel Webster and Daniel Boone and is still the twelfth most prevalent name for boy babies in America today. And its appeal is international— not only is it found all over expected places like Israel and Ireland, but it is currently number three in Germany as well. What is it that makes this name so attractive to so many different kinds of parents? A prime factor is that although it was the name of one of the greatest biblical heroes (what child has not thrilled to the story of the prophet whose faith protected him when he was thrown into a den of lions?), it does not seem at all solemn or pretentious compared, say, to Ezekiel or even Abraham. Daniel is, in fact, one of the very few male names that's both traditional and modern-sounding, that has charm as well as weight. And its nicknames—DANNY and DAN—make it sound even friendlier, although, as with other classics, more and more parents are opting to use the name in full.

DANTE. An Italian name strongly associated with the thirteenth-century poet (whose full name at birth was Durante), who described, in the epic poem *The Divine Comedy*, his journey through heaven and hell. Warning: There have been an inordinate number of beauty-parlor owners and operators who have shared this name.

DARBY. A light-hearted, light-footed name that conjures up the whimsy of the fifties Disney film, *Darby O'Gill and the Little People*. In British folklore, Darby and Joan represent the ideal loving elderly couple.

DARCY, D'ARCY. A handsome, roguish kind of appellation that combines elements of French flair, aristocratic savoir faire, and a soft Irish brogue. It was the surname of an appealing character in Jane Austen's *Pride and Prejudice*. But Darcy's problem is a big one: It sounds more like a girls' name than one for boys.

DARIUS. Darius is a name that is increasing in popularity, especially among African-American name givers. In fact, it was the ninth most popular name for Black babies born in Texas in 1992. The name of several Persian Kings—including the one responsible for throwing Daniel to the lions—it now has a creative, artistic image, and would not look out of place on a concert program or art gallery announcement.

DARRELL, DARRYL, DARRIN, and DARREN. These are a quartet—or pair—of beach-boy names that have been around since the fifties and sixties and have pretty much ridden their last wave—as males, anyway. Darryl comes from the Old English meaning "darling," and has been attached, in recent years, to movie mogul Zanuck, Hall (of Hall & Oates), Strawberry (of Mets/Dodgers fame), Jack Nicholson (Daryl was his seductive devil name in *The Witches of Eastwick*), and the two idiot brothers, Darryl and Darryl, on the former *Bob Newhart Show*. Darrin/Darren are members in good standing of the Karen-Sharon-Taryn-Darren coalition of the fifties. The Irish surname Darren entered American first name nomenclature via the character of Darrin Stevens, the confused (maybe because he was played by two different actors) husband of Samantha, the beguiling witch on *Bewitched*. Like the other members of the club, Darren is currently out of favor. Spelled DAREN, it is a West African name meaning "born at night."

DASHIELL. This name has a great deal of dash and panache, and although it's always been linked to a single personality—Dashiell Hammett (whose given first name was actually Samuel), creator of Sam Spade—it is now up for general grabs, as evidenced by the fact that it was used by comedian Harry Anderson for his son.

DAVID. David is the kind of name, like Michael and Stephen, that girls have been writing in the margins of their notebooks for generations, because Davids sound so sweet, serious, and simpatico. It has deep biblical roots as well, David being the Hebrew name (meaning "beloved") of the second king of Israel in the Old Testament, who, as a boy, slew the mighty warrior Goliath with his slingshot, then grew up to become a wise and highly cultivated leader who enjoyed music and was a poet, as well as becoming the inspiration of such great sculptors as Michelangelo and Donatello. The name has a special resonance for Jews, the Star of David being the symbol of Judaism. A sixth-century David became the patron saint of Wales—where there are several different pet forms, such as DAI and TAFFY. There have been countless Davids of note in history, entertainment, sport, and fiction, including Bowie, Cassidy, Copperfield, Crockett, DeBusschere, Jones, Letterman, and Winfield. DEVLIN is an appealingly devilish Irish form of David, while DEWEY, an anglicized version of the Welsh form, DEWI, is no more popular than HUEY or LOUIE. DAVIS is an attractive surname linked with David, and also with old Southern traditions via confederate president Jefferson Davis. It was used in the sitcom *Davis Rules* and for the characters Steve Martin played in not one but two movies, *Housesitter* and *Grand Canyon*. DAWSON is another David relative.

DEAN. Dean is a fifties kind of name with something of a goody-goody image, associated with such period personalities as Dean Jones, Dean (born Dino) Martin, Dean Stockwell, and Secretaries of State Acheson and Rusk. The Italian version, DINO, is sometimes used in this country as well, although we know one little Dino who was mercilessly teased about his connection to Dino the Dinosaur on *The Flintstones*.

DECLAN. Very popular in the Emerald Isle, but hardly known here, Declan—the name of an Irish saint and the real first name of Elvis Costello—might just be ripe to join such recent Irish imports as Connor and Kieran.

DELANEY and **DEMPSEY.** These are two good old Irish family names that would translate well into strong, singular given names.

DENNIS. Although it sounds to us like one of the older Irish names, Dennis is actually of French derivation (St. Denis is the patron saint of France) and harks back even further to DIONYSIS, the Greek god of wine and debauchery. It was considered a pretty cool name for an adult through the fifties and sixties, but once Dennis the Menace took hold, first as a comic strip, then as a TV show, and finally as a movie, any six-year-old with that name had major problems.

DENVER. A place-name that suggests high altitudes and clean air, becoming familiar via the versatile character actor, Denver Pyle.

DENZEL, DENZIL. This old Cornish family name has taken on a whole new identity in the person of the dashing and talented actor Denzel Washington, and we predict that many new little Denzels will follow.

DEREK, DERRICK. This name, with its sophisticated, slightly British accent, has been growing in popularity since the seventies, and is now at the point where it is trendy, verging on overused. A mainstay of soap opera scripts, various debonair Dereks have played out the plot lines of *All My Children*, *General Hospital*, and *The Guiding Light*. The

Nets basketball star prefers the spelling Derrick Coleman. DIRK, the Dutch form of the name, is also used in this country, although Dirk Bogarde, the most famous bearer of the name, was born in Scotland of Dutch descent, and was originally named Derek. The more Irish-sounding DERRY is another possibility.

DERMOT. Definitely part of the new Irish invasion, marching briskly along with Liam, Conor, Cormac, and Conan. Its Celtic meaning is "free from envy," an enviable quality to impart to any child, and its most visible bearer at the moment is up-and-coming actor Dermot Mulroney.

DESMOND. A debonair British/Irish name now taking off in this country. It is strongly associated with Desmond Tutu, the Black South African bishop who won the Nobel Peace Prize in 1983 and also, for some, with the character of Desmond Hamilton on the soap opera, *Loving*.

DEVON. A handsome, windswept place-name that is used almost equally for boys and girls, although at the moment it's making great strides in the boys' camp. When Vanessa Williams chose it for her son, she spelled it DEVIN, which means "poet" in Celtic. The original geographical Devon is a beautiful seaside county in southwest England.

DEWEY. See DAVID.

DEXTER. Names with Xes (except maybe Xavier) have a lot of energy and sex appeal and we see this one as a retro name waiting to re-happen. Over the years, it's been attached to a varied assortment of public personae—C. Dexter Haven, the witty Cary Grant character in *The Philadelphia Story* (which gave the name a sparkling, sophisticated, upper-class twist), jazz tenor saxophonist Dexter Gordon, and gridiron star Dexter Manley. The short form, DEX, has even more pizzazz. It was the name of a character on *Dynasty*, and was also the bold choice Dana Carvey made for his son's name.

DIEGO. This name, which is a Spanish form of James, has a lot of verve when combined either with a Latin or an Anglo surname. It belonged to Diego Rivera, the Spanish leftist muralist who was the husband of Frida Kahlo.

DIMITRI, DMITRI, DHIMITRI. This is a name dressed in high boots and high collars, one that conjures up feverish czardas and ballet dancing and impassioned orchestra conducting. It is the name of one of the Brothers Karamazov and—from the sublime to the ridiculous—a major character on the soap *All My Children*. Ursula Andress and Harry Hamlin spelled their son's name Dimitri. DEMETRIUS, a Greek form now occasionally heard, means lover of the earth.

DION. Short for DIONYSIS (a name that would be too much for any child to handle), the Greek god of wine, Dion (usually pronounced DEE-on) would make a creative choice. Classic rock 'n' roll buffs might associate it with the sixties group Dion and the Belmonts, responsible for such hits as "A Teenager in Love."

DOLAN. Although it has never officially entered the main stockpot of first names as, say, Nolan, has, Dolan (which means black hair) is definitely another energetic Irish surname possibility.

DOMINIC, DOMINICK. Until the twentieth century, this was a name used almost exclusively by Roman Catholics, often for children born on Sunday, "The Lord's Day." It is utilized more frequently and fashionably in England than the United States, where it still feels a little solemn, although it has always been prevalent in Italian-American families. Basketball star Dominique Wilkins—" the human highlight reel"—prefers the French spelling.

DONALD. Used for centuries in Scotland, where the McDonald clan is one of the most ancient and there have been six kings by that name, Donald was also the eighth most popular boys' name in America in the mid-twenties, and managed to hold its place in the Top 20 through 1950. But first there was Donald Duck to distort its image, and then there was The Donald Trump, until now there's not much potential for it as a nineties baby name. More promising and more authentically Celtic-sounding is DONAL, which is quite commonly used in Ireland. Then there are the related surnames, DONNELLY and DONOVAN. The latter was one of the earliest Irish surnames to take off as a given name in this country, thanks largely to the sixties folk-rock ("Mellow Yellow") singer, who dropped his last name of Leitch. It has also appeared in the titles of several movies, e.g., *Donovan's Brain*, *Donovan's Reef*, and *Donovan's Kid*.

DORIAN. Since it means "child of the sea" in Greek (the Dorians were a division of early Greeks that included the Spartans), Dorian is often given to boys born under water signs—Pisces, Cancer, or Scorpio. It was introduced as a first name by Oscar Wilde in *The Picture of Dorian Gray*, the story of a dissolute character who retains his youthful good looks while his portrait in the attic ages hideously. A more recent bearer is African-American actor Dorian Harewood. Rhythmic and unusual, Dorian is a distinctive choice—made by Lindsay Wagner for her son—but one that to some may sound slightly feminine.

DOUGLAS. Douglas, and more particularly its nickname, DOUG, had a real romantic swagger in the fifties and sixties—relics, perhaps, of the swashbuckling image of Douglas Fairbanks, combined with the wartime heroics of General MacArthur. Originally a Celtic river name, it became attached to a powerful Scottish clan, renowned for their strength and courage. In its earliest incarnation Douglas was used equally for girls and boys. The variant DOUGAL is heard in the Scottish highlands, and a substitute for the nickname Doug was introduced on the 1989 TV show, *Doogie Howser, M.D.*

DOV. A Hebrew name that means "bear," Dov is frequently heard in Israel.

DRAKE. A sleek surname name with roots that link it to dragons and ducks. It was the name of the character Ronald Reagan played in the movie *King's Road*—his greatest (or perhaps second greatest) role.

DREW. Drew gives off a polished, somewhat intellectual impression. It's used as a name in its own right and often, these days, as a nickname for the popular classic Andrew—ANDY being deemed somewhat retrograde. Actress Drew Barrymore has feminized the name to some degree.

DUANE, DWAYNE. This name bears a date stamp of the fifties and sixties, and carries with it twangy echoes of Duane Allman, Duane Eddy, and the haunting Jeff Bridges character in *The Last Picture Show*.

DUDLEY. This is a name with a sense of humor, maybe because of its association with cute little Dudley Moore, or maybe because it's easy to love a name that rhymes with cuddly and has a nickname like DUD. And then there was Dudley Do-Right, the inept hero of a sixties Sunday morning cartoon spin-off from the *Bullwinkle* show. All this contradicts Dudley's origins as an aristocratic surname.

DUFF. A somewhat rough, rowdy, ragged Celtic name, at home in a noisy pub or out walking on the moors. In Scotland, it was originally a nickname for someone with dark hair or a swarthy complexion. The MTV generation will identify it with bassist Duff McKagen (born Michael), one of the more visible members of Guns N' Roses.

DUNCAN. Jaunty, confident, and open, this name is brimming with friendly charm, and definitely makes it into our golden circle of ideal names that are neither too ordinary nor too far-out. Duncan was the name of two Scottish rulers, one of whom was the well-loved and beneficent king killed by Macbeth. Other Duncans of note: America's most famous furniture maker, Duncan Phyfe (who was born in Scotland), TV's original Cisco Kid, Duncan Renaldo; Duncan Idaho, the hero of Frank Herbert's classic sci-fi *Dune* series; and the character Duncan MacKechnie of the soap opera *As the World Turns*.

DUNSTAN. It could sound like a confused cross between Duncan and Dustin, but Dunstan is very much a name of its own. Its best known bearer was the exceptional tenth-century English saint who was the Archbishop of Canterbury and principal adviser to the kings of Wessex. Also a skilled metal worker, calligrapher, and harpist, Dunstan is the patron saint of locksmiths, jewelers, and the blind. If there are too many Dustins in your neighborhood, you might consider this alternative.

DUSTIN. There suddenly appears to be an epidemic of Dustins and we're sure it's not because masses of parents idolize Dustin Hoffman (who was, it turns out, named by his movie-fan mother in honor of silent screen star Dustin Farnum). We have two guesses for the sudden spurt: It might be a response to the character Dustin Donovan on *As the World Turns*, and it might be its similarity in sound to Justin, which is even higher on the popularity charts.

DWIGHT. This Anglo-Saxon name that means "white" was big in the Eisenhower years, but hasn't been heard from much since. A sports hero who brought more recent fame to the name is New York Mets megastar pitcher, Dwight Gooden.

DYLAN, DILLON. One of the most poetic and romantic of boys' names, and one that is zooming up the popularity charts these days, Dylan can no longer be considered a rebellious or iconoclastic choice. A Welsh name tied to the sea, Dylan was a legendary sea god for whom all the waters of Britain and Ireland wept when he died. It also belonged, of course, to the great Welsh poet, Dylan Thomas, whose name Bob Dylan adopted in tribute. It has lately been linked to Dylan MacKay, the sexy good boy-bad boy played by Luke Perry on *Beverly Hills 90210*, up-and-coming actor Dylan McDermott, and Dylan Shayne Lewis on the soap opera *The Guiding Light*. Dillon, another spelling frequently used, removes it from the poet/folk-singer context.

E

EARL. It may have started out as a noble name—ranking right between a marquis and a viscount—but Earl has plunged from that lofty perch and is rarely given to babies these days. It had its American moment of glory in the twenties, when it was one of the Top 40, and another claim to fame with basketball Hall of Famer Earl "The Pearl" Monroe. In a different spelling, it belonged to the creator of Perry Mason, ERLE Stanley Gardner.

EBENEZER. Old Mr. Scrooge pretty much annihilated this biblical name (actually used for a stone in the Good Book rather than a person) for all time. On the other hand, the short form EBEN would make an unusual and creative choice.

EDGAR. Probably the least fashionable of the ED names, Edgar is more recognized today as the name of the award given for the best mystery book of the year (in memory of Edgar Allan Poe) than as a viable baby name. In addition to Poe, there have been some other notable Edgars in the past. There was Edgar the Peaceful, the first recognized king of England; a commendable character in *King Lear*; Edgar Rice Burroughs, creator of Tarzan; Edgar Bergen, father of Candice and godfather of Charlie McCarthy; and flaxen-haired singer, Edgar Winter.

EDISON. A last-name-first name that invokes all the creativity and inventiveness of Thomas A., without whom we wouldn't have our CD players or halogen lamps.

EDMUND. "There is nobleness in the name of Edmund," says a Jane Austen character, and we would have to agree. And the unhappy poet John Keats once bemoaned, "Had my name been Edmund, I would have been more fortunate." Perhaps he knew that its literal meaning is happy, fortunate and rich. Edmund is a name that is heating up in England (where it's been the name of three kings) and we can conceive of its having a minirevival over here—it's already a soap opera hero name on *All My Children*. EAMON is its quintessentially Irish equivalent.

EDWARD. EDDIE and ED are out, Edward is in. This Anglo-Saxon classic, one of the most frequently used names for British kings (there were eight of them), is definitely back in vogue, either used in full or, possibly, with the nostalgic Nancy Drew nickname, NED, or the further afield Ward. Strong evidence of its return is its visibility in recent films, such as *Edward Scissorhands* and the self-contained power businessman played by Richard Gere in *Pretty Woman*. There is no such rosy prospect for EDWIN.

EGAN. The sound of this Irish surname, related to the word "eager," gives it a ready-to-please, effervescent energy.

ELDON/ELDIN. This English place-name has recently come to the fore in the person of the solid, dependable housepainter cum confidant cum nanny of Murphy Brown. Its cousin ELTON is associated with someone who took it on as a nom de rock (Elton John was born Reginald Dwight) in tribute to saxophone great Elton Dean. Another related name is ELVIN, a variant of Alvin and associated with basketball's Elvin Hayes and pianist Elvin Jones.

ELDRIDGE. The best-known bearer of this name is Eldridge Cleaver, author of *Soul on Ice* and well-known civil rights radical and Black activist. Its meaning in German is "wise, mature counselor." The somewhat similar ELDRED, in case you're interested, is the real name of Gregory Peck.

ELEAZER. (el ē az′er) Four-syllable names are not the easiest for a child to handle (or pronounce), but this rarely used Old Testament name (Eleazer was a son of Aaron), has distinct possibilities, as long as some fourth-grade wise guy doesn't dissect it to get at some devastating nickname.

ELI, ELY. This solid but not heavy biblical name (Eli was the high priest and last judge of Israel, who trained the prophet Samuel), might just be due for a comeback, especially among Yale alumni.

ELIJAH. Another venerable Old Testament prophet name—he was the one who went to heaven in a chariot of fire—as well as the name of Elijah Muhammad (born Robert), founder of the Nation of Islam, Elijah was suddenly rejuvenated when Cher and Greg Allman bestowed it on their son Elijah Blue in 1976, and it has had a hip nuance ever since, now being attached to up-and-coming young actor Elijah Wood. ELIAS, the German and Dutch version and Bo Diddley's real name, is equally attractive and as strong a possibility for a modern boy. Other forms include: the Greek ELIHU, the Greek and Italian ELIA—ELIO is another Italian form—and the French ELIE. An Anglicized, somewhat adulterated version is ELLIS, the name Emily Brontë took as a male pen name and that of the father of the musical Marsalis brothers.

ELISHA. This creative name belongs to yet another Hebrew prophet, the successor to and disciple of Elijah. Its limitation is that it might sound too much like a girls' name, i.e., Alicia or ELISSA.

ELIOT, ELLIOT. This name got a bit of a boost in popularity after the release of *E.T.* in 1982, probably because of the haunting calling of the name of the young human hero by the endearing extra-terrestrial—but not much has been heard of it since. Before that its two main associations were FBI good guy Eliot Ness and actor Elliot Gould. It was also the name of one of the key characters on *thirtysomething*.

ELLERY. This is one of those interesting names that we would like to liberate once and for all from its limited single-note identity. In this case, of course, it's that of mystery writer Ellery Queen, who never even existed—it was the pen name of two cousins called Frederic Dannay and Manfred B. Lee. The rhythmic, three-syllable sound of the name corresponds to such popular female names as Mallory, Brittany, and Stephanie—not easy to find in a boys' name. But alas, that very association might limit its success.

ELMER. Thanks to Elmer Fudd, Elmer the Cow, and maybe even Elmer's glue, this name has become something of a joke, the quintessential so-far-out-it-will-never-be-in nerd name that we don't see ever coming back into favor. It is actually a variant of the Old English name, AYLMER.

ELMO. This name calls to mind the image of St. Elmo's fire—the light show sometimes visible around ships' masts during storms at sea—quite appropriate since St. Elmo (another name for ERASMUS) is the patron saint of sailors. *St. Elmo's Fire* was also the name of a popular Brat Pack movie of the eighties. Toddlers of today will link the name with the most popular Muppet to hit Sesame Street since Cookie Monster.

ELVIS. Prospective parents who are considering this name probably have a motivation so strong that they don't want or need any professional advice. And, in fact, as powerful as its association is, the name is not taboo to ordinary mortals. In fact, 52 New York City babies were given the name in 1993. Elvis Costello, who changed his name from Declan in tribute to The King, has certainly sustained a successful career, and Anthony Perkins and Berry Berenson had no qualms about using it for their sons. The name also has roots beyond Memphis— there was a sixth-century Irish St. Elvis—who was also known as ELWYN, ELWIN, ELIAN, and Allan.

EMANUEL, EMMANUEL. In the Bible, this is the name given to the promised Messiah, in the prophecy of Isaiah. Commonly used by Jewish families from the twenties to the forties, it was somewhat devalued by its reduction to the nickname MANNY. But it is now beginning to be reevaluated in its complete form and has in fact been chosen by such high-profile parents as Debra Winger and Timothy Hutton, who named their son Emanuel Noah.

EMERY, EMORY, and **EMERSON.** Three sturdy, rather serious surnames sometimes used as first names.

EMIL, EMILE, EMILIO. Emilio, the Spanish form, is the winner of this trio, thanks to actor Emilio Estevez. Despite the charm of the children's classic *Emil and the Detectives*, Emil and Emile are just too close to the mega popular girls' name Emily as well as to other current female favorites such as Emma and Amelia.

EMLYN is a common Welsh name that holds the danger of being perceived as feminine in this country. The renowned Welsh actor and playwright Emlyn Williams was actually christened George, which he used as the title of his autobiography.

EMMETT, EMMET. This name—which comes from the Hebrew meaning "truth"—has an honest, sincere, long-legged, laid-back, creative quality. Its most famous bearer was America's best-loved clown, Emmett Kelly, and it was also the first name of the weird Dr. Brown character played by Christopher Lloyd in *Back to the Future.*

ENOCH and ENOS are two unconventional names from the Book of Genesis. Enoch, which has a sound that is not very appealing to the modern ear, was the eldest son of Cain, born after he killed his brother, Abel. Enos was another direct descendant of Adam and Eve, but the image of the name today is more bucolic than biblical, associated with such old TV shows as *The Dukes of Hazzard.* The only notable Enos in modern times has been baseball star Enos Slaughter.

ENZO. Originally a nickname for VINCENZO, Enzo is very popular in Italy right now and beginning to be used in this country as well. And not only by Italian-Americans—actress Patricia Arquette chose it for her son.

EPHRAIM. A neglected biblical name (Ephraim was the second son of Joseph), it has a uniquely creative yet distinguished ring. EFREM Zimbalist Sr. (violinist) and Jr. (star of *The FBI* TV series and father of Stephanie), preferred the phonetic spelling.

ERIC, ERIK. This is the most popular Scandinavian boys' name ever in the United States—it was as high as number eight for babies born in 1982, and although it has now begun to fade, some parents are still attracted to its Norse strength, reminiscent of Viking hero Eric the Red. The *k* ending definitely emphasizes the Nordic connection. Noteworthy bearers of the name include sports figures Dickerson and Heiden and musicians Nelson (known as Rick) and Clapton. The spelling ERICH adds a more Germanic spin.

ERNEST. This is probably the only name a whole play was based on—Oscar Wilde's *The Importance of Being Earnest*—in which one character says, "There is something in that name that seems to inspire absolute confidence. I pity any poor woman whose husband is not called Ernest." Well, not many women in the year 2030 will have husbands named Ernest, because it is rarely given to babies of today, despite the fact that it does conjure up positive associations—Hemingway, Ernie of the Bert & Ernie team, Ernie Kovacs, even the doofus played by Jim Varney in the *Ernest Goes to Camp* movies. But perhaps earnestness is a dated virtue in today's world.

ERROL. Unknown in this country until Errol Flynn made his smashing, swashbuckling debut in *Captain Blood* in 1935, this Scottish place-name has been used quietly since then, especially by African-Americans, perhaps to honor jazz great Errol Garner.

ESAU. This falls into the category of rarely used Old Testament names, possibly because of its hirsute connotations ("for Esau was an hairy man"), Esau being the twin of Jacob, son of Isaac and Rebecca. That aside (and the fact that a child might have to put up with the jingle "he saw Esau on the seesaw" a few hundred times), it's a perfectly usable name.

ETHAN. Ethan is a biblical name that has played around the edges of the popularity lists for a couple of decades but has not been used enough to sound terminally stale. Its history includes ties to such real and literary heroes as Ethan Allen and Ethan Frome, and in the seventies was thought of as a cowboy name. In the more recent past, it was attached to the appealing but troubled young boy on *thirtysomething*. ETAN and EITAN are modern Hebrew spellings; in that language the name is pronounced ay-tahn and means "firm and strong."

EUGENE. This Greek-based name, which belonged to no less than four popes, had a long run of popularity—from about 1875 to the forties—but it's definitely in limbo now. As Jim Carrey said in an interview, "My middle name is Eugene. I always figured my parents named me that to keep me humble. You can never get too cool with a name like Eugene." If you like the sound, though, some more modern alternatives might be the British EUAN, or EWAN or EWEN, which are Scottish and Welsh forms of John.

EUSTACE. As sedate and stuffy as the monocled Eustace Tilley of *New Yorker* magazine fame, Eustace is a Greek name that belonged to a saint who was said to have been converted to Christianity by the vision of a crucifix between the antlers of a stag as he was hunting. Its twentieth-century claim to fame is that it gave birth to Stacy, one of the prime androgynous nickname names of the seventies.

EVAN. This Welsh version of John has a mellow nice-guy image, and seems to be rising in popularity. The best-selling novelist Evan Hunter (who also writes mysteries under the name Ed McBain), was born Salvatore Lombino. The longer form EVANDER was a name prominent in Greek and Roman mythology; in classical lore he was an Arcadian hero who founded the city in Italy that preceded Rome. And of course the legendary Evander of today is boxing champ Holyfield.

EVERARD. Hardly ever used here, Everard is a decidedly upper-class name in England. Decidedly. EVERETT is a somewhat formal and stately surname name spin-off, chosen by writer John Irving for his youngest son.

EZEKIEL. The name of this visionary Old Testament prophet is most often reduced to the nickname ZEKE when used by modern parents.

EZRA. A Hebrew name that is both heroic and somewhat quirky. According to the Bible, Ezra led a group of fifteen hundred Israelites out of slavery in Babylon and back to Jerusalem. A more familiar Ezra is poet Pound.

F

FABIAN. Fabian still has a sixties teen-idol aura, reminiscent of beach blanket movies—even though the singer was never in one—and songs like "Hound Dog Man." Before that it was the name of a third-century pope, and a socialist society associated with George Bernard Shaw.

FABIO, on the other hand, has long leonine hair, a seductive Italian accent, and glistening biceps, just like the model of that name.

FARRELL. Farrell is a strong Irish surname—it means "man of courage" in Gaelic—that would be far preferable to the outdated Darryl at this point.

FELIX. A very adult yet feline name, from the Latin meaning "happy and fortunate," Felix is definitely on the upswing: it's already made inroads with the swank Sloane Rangers of London. In the past, it belonged to no less than four popes and sixty-seven saints, and for a while suffered from its affiliation with the overly fussy Felix Unger character in *The Odd Couple*.

FERDINAND. Somewhat bulky and unwieldy (maybe because of Ferdinand the Bull), this name is very rarely used except in Latino families. In Shakespeare's *The Tempest*, though, Ferdinand was a handsome young prince shipwrecked on Prospero's island. Ferdinand was also the real name of Jelly Roll Morton. The sexier FERNANDO was for years associated with the quintessential Latin lover, Fernando Lamas, as well as baseball hero Fernando Valenzuela.

FERGUS. A traditional name in both Scotland and Ireland, Fergus made an impression on American moviegoers via the heroic character in the film *The Crying Game*—and indeed it sounds much better when spoken with an Irish brogue. In Celtic lore, Fergus was the ideal of manly courage, and it was also the name of ten Celtic saints.

FINIAN. As Irish as Irish can be, this lilting saint's name shone in neon lights on Broadway, via the classic musical, *Finian's Rainbow*, later made into a film staring Fred Astaire as Finian McLonergan. Finian O'Toole is a character on *General Hospital*. FINNIAN is another spelling; either version may be abbreviated to the even more appealing FINN.

FINLAY. This Scottish royal name (it belonged to the father of Macbeth), which sounds a tad fusty, is rarely heard on these shores but may be considered along with other surnames.

FINN. A name with enormous energy and charm, Finn has a rich and vivid heritage, having belonged to the greatest of all Celtic, mythological heroes, Finn Mac Cool, an intrepid warrior with mystical, supernatural powers, noted as well for his wisdom and generosity. The name, which means "fair-haired" in Irish Gaelic, is now also used in Norway and Denmark, and is the name of the soap opera actor—Finn Carter, who plays the dynamic Sierra Esteban on *As the World Turns*.

FITZ+. Any number of Fitz- names—Fitzroy, Fitzgerald, Fitzpatrick, Fitzwilliam—have been used as Christian names, but be warned that there used to be a tradition that Fitz- names were given to the illegitimate sons of royalty. Fitzwilliam was the Christian name of the dashing Mr. Darcy in *Pride and Prejudice*.

FLANN. A friendly, freckle-faced Irish name that started life as a nickname meaning "red-haired." Flann O'Brien (born Brian O'Nolan) was a well-known Irish columnist and novelist. Potential problem: Too reminiscent of the Spanish custard? Flannery, also a girls' name via writer O'Connor, is another, non-food-related possibility.

FLETCHER. A straitlaced surname with a touch of quirkiness— mainly because of the nickname FLETCH, used for the protagonist of a couple of clever Chevy Chase movies, based on novels by Gregory McDonald. Fletcher Christian was the hero of *Mutiny on the Bounty*, Fletcher Henderson was a great jazz pianist, composer, arranger, and bandleader, and Fletcher Reade is a character on *The Guiding Light*.

FLINT. You can't find a much tougher, steelier sounding name than this; macho to the max. Unfortunately, it also has over-the-top soap operaish overtones.

FLORIAN. Its first syllable gives this name a blooming, flowery, almost feminine feeling. Florian is the patron saint of those in danger from water, be it from floods or drowning.

FLOYD. Somewhere along the line, Floyd has developed an almost comical hayseed persona—quite a contrast to its origins as an Anglicization of Lloyd, said to have come from the inability of the English to pronounce the double *l* of the Welsh name. Floyd Patterson was a World Heavyweight boxing champ and Floyd Parker is a character on *The Guiding Light*.

FLYNN. An Irish family name, Flynn has an easygoing, casual, cowboy kind of feel. It was chosen by James Earl Jones for his son.

FORREST. A sylvan name made famous by the redoubtable Forrest Gump, Forrest's strong but sensitive, down-to-earth yet distinctive image is furthered by newsman Sawyer, actor Whittaker, ex-Green Bay Packer Gregg, and the sympathetic lawyer-father figure on *I'll Fly Away*. If you can't shake the sound of Tom Hanks's Gump-accented voice from the otherwise appealing Forrest, you might consider two other virile surname names with the same touch of gentility: FOSTER, which like Forrest was originally an occupational name meaning woodsman, and FERRIS, used in France and Ireland to indicate an iron worker and associated with the high-spirited hero of *Ferris Bueller's Day Off*.

FRANCIS. This name, which was in the Top 10 at the turn of the last century, has been pretty much confined to Irish and Italian Roman Catholics in the past decades (e.g., Francis Albert Sinatra, F. (rancis) Scott Fitzgerald, Francis Ford Coppola), and still has something faintly sacrosanct about it. The fact that it means "Frenchman" in Latin accounts for the name change of St. Francis of Assisi, who was born Giovanni, then nicknamed Francis because his wealthy businessman father had taught him to speak French. A deeply spiritual man, he devoted himself to caring for the poor and infirm, established the Franciscan order, was said to have been able to communicate with animals, and was made the patron saint of ecology. Another Francis, St. Francis de Sales, is the patron saint of writers and editors. Now, despite the bad rap the name got in the fifties with all those talking mule movies, the name is being reconsidered by parents looking for a conservative, traditional option.

FRANK, FRANKLIN. Frank, a diminutive of Francis and Franklin, has been standing on its own since the seventeenth century. On the Top 20 list in this country from 1875 through the thirties, it is now a warm and friendly grandpa name, a conceivable style heir to Max and Sam. Franklin, the name of two Presidents, is much less approachable (and usable), more the name of a distant ancestor, though Roosevelt admirers may find it an honorable choice.

FRASER, FRASIER, FRAZER, FRAZIER. In its various spellings, this is an up-and-coming surname name, thanks largely to the character who successfully spun off from *Cheers* into his own hit series. In the past, it's been used primarily by families of Scottish origin, but that restriction no longer holds.

FREDERICK, FREDERIC. When that somewhat pretentious but voguish couple, the above-mentioned Frasier and Lilith Crane, tagged their telebaby Frederick, a lot of people sat up and took notice, and a name that had hardly been used for forty years suddenly started to sound kind of spiffy again. Before that it had taken on a rather forbidding, foreign, uptight, military air, reminiscent of Frederick the Great, the enlightened King of Prussia who laid the foundations of the powerful Prussian empire. For African-Americans, it can be seen as a hero name, honoring Frederick Douglass, who rose from slavery to power as a political activist. But most Fredericks inevitably wound up as FREDs, a far more genial, neighborly moniker, as in Flintstone, MacMurray, Mr. Rogers, and even Astaire. Fred could, like Jack and Henry, be revving up for a comeback, but the nickname FREDDY will have to wait till everyone stops having Freddy-Krueger/Nightmare-on-Elm-Street nightmares. The German diminutive, FRITZ, is also occasionally used, usually in families of German or Swedish origin.

FRISCO. A swaggering, frisky, roguish place-name, which many daytime-drama watchers will associate with the character on *General Hospital*.

G

GABRIEL. A hearty, upbeat name with multiple religious overtones: Gabriel is an archangel who appears in Christian, Jewish, and Muslim texts, the angel of mercy, life, joy, judgment, truth, and dreams, who presides over Paradise. In addition to all the above responsibilities, Gabriel is the patron saint of broadcasters and diplomats and governs Mondays and the month of January. An appealing alternative to the ubiquitous Michael as well as to some of the more common biblical boys' names, such as David and Daniel, it has recently been connected to the brooding Irish-born actor Gabriel Byrne, as well as to the acclaimed Colombian novelist, Gabriel García Márquez. It was also used by *Seinfeld*'s Jason Alexander for his son.

GALEN. Galen was the great second-century physician who formed the basis of early European medicine—and the name still projects a scholarly image, though perhaps is too close in sound to Gail for comfort in these gender-sensitive times.

GAMAL. An Arabic name meaning "camel" that is sometimes used by African-American parents.

GANDY. A novel, rarely used name that fairly dances off the page— perhaps because of the phrase "gandy dancer," which is railroad slang for a person who lays tracks.

GARETH. This name, which is from the Welsh meaning "gentle," is both romantic (Gareth was a knight who sat around King Arthur's Round Table in Camelot) and endearing (maybe it's that lispy last syllable). It was popular in England in the eighties, is still hot in Wales, and is now beginning to be discovered over here. The related **GARTH** has taken on a pronounced country twang since becoming attached to Nashville megastar, Garth (born Troyal) Brooks (mixed with a little goofiness, thanks to *Wayne's World*), while GARRETT has a distinct Irish inflection. It was the name of Jack Nicholson's ambivalent astronaut character in *Terms of Endearment*, of one of the original "The Not Ready for Prime Time Players," Garrett Morris, and was chosen for his son by Bo Jackson.

GARFIELD. This name is probably too tightly tied to the fat cartoon cat right now to be realistically considered for a human-type child.

GARY, GARRY. In 1950, the top nine names for boy babies were Robert, Michael, James, John, David, William, Thomas, Richard—and Gary, making it probably the first nonclassic name ever to crack the Top 10. The rise in popularity of the name can be traced directly to the rise in popularity of Gary Cooper who, ironically, was born Frank. His agent, who hailed from Gary, Indiana, suggested he adopt the name of her hometown. Now, forty years later, Gary/Garry has lost its glitter, although it is still borne by two of our most prominent cartoonists, Trudeau (born Garretson) and Larsen, and cable sitcom star Garry Shandling.

GASTON. A gallant Gallic name chosen by Jaclyn Smith for her son but, less attractively, also used for the vain antihero of Disney's *Beauty and the Beast*.

GAVIN. A Scottish-Welsh name that's less overused and fresher sounding than the Irish Kevin, Gavin's best known bearer, *Love Boat* Captain Gavin MacLeod, was actually born Allan.

GENE. A nickname name sometimes used in the past on its own, although strangely enough many of the most famous Genes were not originally called Eugene: G. Tunney was James, G. Autry was Orvan, and G. Wilder was Jerome.

GEOFFREY. This is the classic British spelling of what we almost universally condense to Jeffrey, except when we're writing a paper on Chaucer.

GEORGE. George was a name that, until recently, seemed eternally fifty-eight-years-old, with thinning gray hair and a Republican Party membership card. Sort of like George Bush, come to think of it. But a new feeling about such traditional names, especially for boys, has breathed some life back into George. It's got a good chance of joining such classics as Henry and Jack, John and Paul—and, not incidentally, Georgia—on the comeback trail. George (which is Greek for "tiller of the soil," or "farmer"), was among the five most popular names in America from 1830 to 1900, and retained its position in the Top 10 until about 1950. It belonged to the king of Great Britain for 116 straight years, as well as to the patron saint of England, St. George, who, by slaying the dragon, became the symbol of good conquering evil. America's most famous George, of course, is Washington. The Italian version is Giorgio, as in Armani.

GERALD, GERARD. We've all known a dozen JERRYs, most of whom are in their fifties at this point, and although they are perfectly nice, we probably won't be naming our babies after them. If by some remote chance you do, you could make the name fresher by using the English pet form, GED.

GERSHOM, GERSHON, GERSON. This biblical Hebrew name was favored by the Puritans and, more recently, by Orthodox Jews. At times it's been Anglicized to GARSON.

GIDEON. An unjustly neglected Old Testament name—Gideon was both a judge and military leader of the Israelites—possibly because of all the jokes made about Gideon Bibles in hotel rooms. It has so few people associations that we think it would make an admirably distinctive and attractive choice.

GILBERT. A name with a sober middle-aged to elderly image, Gilbert once was attached to one of the dashing members of Robin Hood's band, and was considered ultra debonair in the days of silent movies. It has recently come alive via the movie, *What's Eating Gilbert Grape?* Its British nicknames—GIB and GIBBY, have a lot more spunk than the American GIL.

GILES. Pronounced Jiles, this is one of those names that most Americans find too teddibly British to consider, but it has the kind of smooth, almost imperious aura (it was the autocratic Mr. French's name on the old sitcom *A Family Affair*), that might appeal to some upwardly mobile parents. Because its literal meaning is "young goat," it is sometimes used for Capricorn boys. And since it was at one time a Scottish girls' name, that might be a more dramatic way to look at it.

GLENN. Glenn appealed to a lot of post–World War II parents for its cool, leafy image, calling up the sweet sounds of Glenn Miller and the calm, composed impression of Glenn Ford, whose name at birth was the Welsh GWYLLYM (those were the days before ethnic names were in). Now Glenn is gone, no longer fresh, yet not old enough to sound new again—except maybe for a girl. GLYN is a Welsh name with the same meaning and a less familiar, but more conventionally feminine sound.

GODFREY. The down side of this name, which was very popular in the Middle Ages, is that it might be difficult for a boy to handle a name with god as the first syllable, and that has actually been used as a euphemism for Him—one of W. C. Fields's favorite expressions was "Godfrey Daniels!" And the up side? We're still thinking.

GOMER. It may surprise fans of Jim Nabors and the old *Andy Griffith Show* to learn that in the New Testament, Gomer was a grandson of Noah, and that he was never once quoted in the Bible as saying, "Aw-shucks."

GORDON. Gordon is an upstanding Scottish clan name, more substantial than the trendy Jordan, and would make a good conservative but not stodgy choice.

GRADY. Another energetic, friendly Irish family name eminently usable as a first.

GRAHAM. Although this jaunty Scottish clan name has been very popular in England since the fifties, it is just beginning to catch on here, having been used for such enigmatic characters as the James Spader role in *sex, lies and videotape*. The Scots sometimes spell it GRAEME, and the Brits use GRAM as its nickname. Warning: A child with this name might have to endure a couple of years of graham-cracker jokes.

GRANT. This onetime beach-boy name, compadre of Glenn, GREG, and Gary, has ended up in soap opera purgatory, making appearances on such dramas as *As the World Turns* and *General Hospital*, attached to last names like Putnam and Colman.

GRAY, GREY. Gray (the more usual spelling) is the kind of name children come to truly appreciate once they're adults. Strong, subtle, and distinctive, with a slight Southern accent (it probably started as a short form of GRAYSON), its one drawback might be the somber tonality of the color itself. Denzel Washington played a character named Gray in *The Pelican Brief*.

GREGORY. This Greek name that was the second most common papal name (no less than sixteen popes, not to mention at least fifteen saints), has been big in this country since the emergence of Gregory Peck (born Eldred) in the late forties, and has still not worn out its welcome. These days, though, kids with this name are more likely to be called Gregory than the Brady-Bunchish GREG.

GRIFFIN, GRIFFITH. Both these last-name-first names, the first one Irish, the second Welsh, are definitely on the upswing, thanks partly to the general appreciation for all things Celtic, partly to actor Griffin Dunne, and partly to the British artist Griffin Moss, postcard-protagonist of the phenominally successful *Griffin & Sabine* books.

GROVER. Forget the furry little blue Muppet by this name. Forget corpulent President Cleveland (who was born Stephen anyway), and consider this name anew. We think it's spunky and a little funky and well worth a second look.

GUNNAR and **GUNTHER.** These are two exotic Scandinavian names that sound perfectly fine in combination with Anglo-Saxon surnames. Gunnar Nelson, grandson of Ozzie and Harriet and son of Ricky, is half of the rock group called Nelson, and a character named Gunnar has also made an appearance on the soap opera *As the World Turns*.

GUS. Gus is a homey, slightly grizzled grandpa nickname name that's knocking at the gates of style heaven as such former down-to-earth trendies as Max and Sam become overused and, thus, demoted. Most fashionably used on its own these days, Gus can also be short for an unusual number of different names, including GUSTAVE (a royal name in Sweden), Augustus, Augustine, Angus, and, in the case of Gus the Theatre Cat in T. S. Eliot's *Old Possum's Book of Practical Cats*— Asparagus!

GUTHRIE. This attractive Irish name has a particularly romantic windswept aura, with a touch of the buckaroo thrown in.

GUY. Guy Smiley on *Sesame Street* and Guy Lombardo to the contrary, this name still feels upper-crust English to most Americans, and a bit too everyman to be used for their own little guy. Guy is, however, the patron saint of comedians and dancers.

H

∧∧∧∧∧∧∧∧∧∧∧∧∧∧∧∧∧∧∧∧ ◉ ∧∧∧∧∧∧∧∧∧∧∧∧∧∧∧∧∧∧∧∧

HABIB. Habib is a North African name, particularly popular in Tunisia and Syria, meaning "beloved." This Swahili and Muslim name belonged to the first president of Tunisia, Habib Ben Ali Bourguiba.

HADRIAN. Most parents would find this old Roman name pretentious when compared with the more accessible Adrian, but some history buffs might just want to commemorate the enlightened emperor, who was also a scholar, poet, and musician, most famous for building a wall across northern England.

HAKEEM. Increasingly used in America, this Muslim name is also popular in Ethiopia and the Sudan. In Arabic it signifies "wise, all-knowing ruler," one of the ninety-nine qualities of Allah listed in the Koran.

HALE. The name Hale projects a sense of well-being (it does come from the Old English meaning "healthy"), but is also a bit cold. Possibly better as a middle name choice.

HAMILTON. Unless it runs in your family, or Alexander Hamilton is a particular hero of yours, you might want to consider something not quite so imposing, and with a less teasable nickname than HAM. Not that it was a detriment to Hamilton Jordan, chief of staff under President Carter.

HAMISH. This warm, fuzzy Scottish name, pronounced with a long *a*, is a form of the Gaelic Seamus, which in turn is a form of James. While a bit too foreign for most tastes in this country, it does also means "homey, comfortable, and unpretentious" in Yiddish.

HANS. Although this German, Dutch, and Scandinavian form of John (via JOHANNES) is familiar to all of us because of such childhood icons as Hans Brinker, Hans(el) and Gretel, and Hans Christian Andersen, few Americans have chosen it as a name for their children because of its intractably Old Country image.

HARDY. A spirited and durable surname that has been used as a first name abroad since the 1840s, Hardy is starting to be discovered in this country, fitting in with other names in this trendy category, like Harper and Brady. Well-known bearers of the name are designer Hardy Amies and German actor Hardy (born Eberhard) Krüger. Americans may think first of the Hardy Boys or Laurel and Hardy.

HARLAN and HARLEY. Two once highly respectable, Waspy surnames, the latter has now become considerably more renegade because of its association with the motorcycle of the same name. Harlan Ellison is a noted science fiction writer.

HAROLD. This name belongs more to the turn of the last century than this one, having taken on a rather prim, pipe-smoking, bespectacled image. Its sole asset is the relaxed and newly stylish nickname HAL—a compatriot of such fashionable earthy guy names as Sam and Max, Jack and Harry. Over the years, it's been linked with the last Saxon king of England, silent screen star Harold Lloyd, a comic strip character, Harold Teen, two prime ministers of England (Macmillan and Wilson), and the first Black mayor of Chicago, Harold Washington.

HARPER. Harper has a sweet, gentle sound, with Southern overtones, and has of late been used for girls almost equally with boys. The inspiration, in many cases, is female writer Harper Lee, author of *To Kill a Mockingbird*. Singer Paul Simon was ahead of his time when he chose it for his older son.

HARRY. After years of being an all-purpose, regular guy, good-neighbor name, Harry has joined the contingent of fashionable names along with its parent name, Henry. Classic but not pretentious, Harry combines the accessibility of a grandpa with a princely history. Young Prince Harry, formally named Henry and the second son of Charles and Diana, has provided a contemporary role model for the name in this country. In England, Harry is more firmly established among proper, upper-crust name choices, having been the nickname for all eight king Henrys. Other notable Harrys putting a new gloss on the name: singer Harry Connick Jr., actor Harry Hamlin, and from the past, former President Harry S. Truman, and magician Harry Houdini, who was born Erich. Over the years, Harry has been the subject of an inordinate number of song, movie, and TV titles, including "I'm Just Wild about Harry," *The Trouble with Harry*, *Dirty Harry*, *Harry and Tonto*, *Harry and the Hendersons*, and *Harry O*.

HARRIS, HARRISON. These two offshoots of Harry are actually surnames meaning son of Harry. Of the two, the latter is definitely preferable today, having taken on the dashing persona of Indiana Jones himself, Harrison Ford. Some parents who can't quite bring themselves to view Harry as anything other than a potbellied senior citizen are choosing these more modern sounding names instead.

HART. A soap operaish name (*Guiding Light*, *Days of Our Lives*) despite the poetic heritage of Hart Crane, who was born a Harold anyway.

HARVEY. At one time, there were so many dweebs on TV with this name that a league of Harveys (we're not kidding) was formed in protest or maybe self-defense. It's a name that is definitely in baby name purgatory, helped along by its association with the human-size rabbit that could be seen only by Elwood P. Dodd in the play and movie, *Harvey*.

HASKEL, HASKELL. This intellectual-sounding name, not often used now, is, in fact, the Yiddish form of Ezekiel, which we consider preferable, partly because of negative associations to sleazy Cleaver pal Eddie Haskell.

HASSAN. This Arabic name that translates to "handsome" is used by one Nigerian tribe for the first born of a pair of male twins.

HAYDEN. Heard mostly these days as the first name of Coach Fox on the popular TV series *Coach*, Hayden is actually quite a common name in Wales. Among the surname names, then, this one has a good shot at popularity. Musical parents may prefer to give it a different twist with the spelling HAYDN (pronounced hi-den) as in the composer. Others, however, may choose the related Irish name Aidan, made familiar by actor Aidan Quinn.

HECTOR. This heroic ancient Greek name is used primarily by Latino families in this country. Hector was the most noble of all the Trojans in Homer's *Iliad*, incorporating such laudable virtues as compassion, loyalty, and physical strength. The most visible Hector on the scene today is actor Hector Elizondo, and kids may be familiar with one of Maurice Sendak's early books, *Hector Protector*.

HENRY. If you haven't hung out at a playground lately, or checked the "Passages" section of *People*, you may not be aware that Henry is among the hottest names around, chosen for their boy babies by such high-profile parents as Meryl Streep, Julia Louis-Dreyfus and Brad Hall, Amanda Pays and Corbin Bernsen, Dennis Hopper, and Daniel Stern. It's one of the few illustrious, classic male names not overused to the point of cliché in recent years, sounding both more distinctive and more interesting to the contemporary ear than Richard or Robert or John or James. And maybe more fussy, to some: Henry is coming off a long decline that followed its status as sixth most popular boys' name in 1930. It was sixth most popular in 1830, too, and has a distinguished royal (eight British kings, plus the current prince) as well as literary (Longfellow, James, Thoreau, to name a few) tradition. Although most modern parents prefer to use the full and formal version of the name, another of Henry's charms is its range of attractive nicknames: from Harry and HAL to HANK, in honor of baseball great Henry Aaron.

HERBERT. With the exception of Robert, all names ending in "bert," from Norbert to EGBERT to Hubert are now in terminal limbo.

HERMAN. This Old German name, which became associated with certain enemy leaders during World War II, fell into definitive disfavor at that time, and has by no means recovered, not having been helped by the Frankenstein-looking Herman Munster. Strangely enough, a perfectly attractive and young TV character was given the name—in the recent show *Herman's Head*, but we have no hopes for that turning it around either. If you're really thinking about Herman for some personal reason, you might want to consider the French version, ARMAND, or the Spanish ARMANDO.

HERSCHEL. The Hebrew word for "deer," this name takes many forms, including HERZL, HESHEL, and the shortened HERSCH, HIRSCH, HIRSH, and HERSH. Its most prominent bearer is football great Herschel Walker, who may have been among the few tough enough to withstand the inevitable Hershey's bar nicknames.

HILARY. With the advent of Mrs. Clinton, Hilary has lost whatever masculine potency it possessed, despite the fact that the name was 100 percent male until the 1890s. Coming from the Latin *hilarius*, meaning "cheerful," it was the name of one of the most esteemed theologians of his time, St. Hilary of Poitiers.

HILLEL. This popular Israeli name derives from the Hebrew word for "praised"—Hillel the Great was a famous Talmudic scholar of the first-century A.D., who fostered a systematic, liberal interpretation of Hebrew Scripture and was the spiritual and ethical leader of his generation.

HILTON, HYATT. Two surname names to use only if you wish to imply a family connection to the hotel chains.

HIRAM. This is the kind of biblical name that adventurous parents, those who wish to move beyond David and Daniel, are beginning to consider for their sons, in spite of the fact that this one still has large pieces of its old repressed, stiff-collared image clinging to it. Coming from the Hebrew meaning "noble brother," the name belonged to an Old Testament king who helped Solomon plan and build the Temple in Jerusalem, and was a favorite in the eighteenth and nineteenth centuries.

HOGAN. A vibrant Irish surname, sometimes associated with the sixties TV show *Hogan's Heroes*.

HOLDEN. Closely tied to the character of Holden Caulfield in *Catcher in the Rye*, with whom almost every adolescent in America has probably identified at some time, Holden has a correspondingly complex image—preppy, angst-ridden, and rebellious. It's also now starring on the soap opera *As the World Turns*, and was chosen by comedian Dennis Miller for his son.

HOMER. This name has traveled an odyssey from ancient Greece, where it was the name of the composer of the greatest classical epics, to becoming a proper Victorian name given to future politicians and captains of industry, to being classified as *Hee Haw*—type country yokels as well as the name of Bart Simpson's doltish dad. Bill Murray has seen enough potential for its rejuvenation to give it to his son.

HORACE. Horace is probably hopelessly mired in its bespectacled, feeble, elderly image, tied to a prohibitively soft and sissified sound. Its most famous bearer was newspaper publisher Horace Greeley, famous for saying, "Go West, young man, and grow up with the country."

HORATIO. Last heard of as the middle name of Vice President Hubert Humphrey, this name actually has an exotic past, and just could be considered for a comeback. It was the given name of Lord Nelson, one of the most dashing of British heroes, the naval commander who led the British fleet to destroy the French at Trafalgar, and also belonged to Hamlet's loyal friend. HORACIO is the Spanish version (pronounced hor-AH-see-o).

HOSEA. There are many Hebrew prophet names, including Joel, Amos, Daniel, Jonah, Nathan, and Samuel, and Hosea is one of the least used, so this might fit the bill if you feel adventurous and are looking for a distinctive biblical option.

HOUSTON. This lanky, roguish place-name is right in style, with its Texas accent and hip cowboy boots. One well-known bearer of the name is saxophonist Houston Person.

HOWARD. This is a real dad-granddad kind of name, as typified by the Howard Cunningham character in *Happy Days* and numerous others of his ilk. It started life as an aristocratic family name, gradually metamorphosing into a first name in the nineteenth century. It was in the Top 50 list in this country from the 1870s to the early 1950s, but the thought of naming a baby Howard right now seems less likely than using Horatio.

HUBERT. This name may mean "brilliant mind or spirit" in Old German, but it comes as close to being spiritless as any modern name we can think of, and probably did nothing for Hubert Humphrey's image. Variants HOBART and HUBBELL have a bit more style due to their surname sounds; HUBBELL was the first name of Robert Redford's character, Barbra Streisand's hyper-Wasp boyfriend in *The Way We Were*.

HUGH. This name is patrician to the core—you can almost see its hair swept back, its nostrils flaring, wallet bulging: an image personified by the new British leading actor, Hugh Grant—and is definitely on the upswing with upscale Americans. The name, which means "intelligent," has always been particularly prevalent among the Irish—there have been twenty Irish saints by the name, and it's traditionally associated with the O'Donnell clan there. Hugh was an early emigrant to the New World: There were two of them in the first English-speaking settlement in America. Hugh's biggest drawback is its very sound, barely more than an exhaled breath. HEW and HUW are the distinctively (probably too distinctively) spelled Welsh forms. The best known American Hughs are Hugh Hefner and Hugh Downs.

HUGO. The Latin form of Hugh, Hugo has more heft than the original and considerable energy; it's definitely an up and comer among those with high-fashion tastes. It may be the most stylish boy baby name in London today and also holds appeal for Franco- and bibliophiles in its relation to writer Victor Hugo.

HUMPHREY. This name may still have a life beyond Bogart, the icon who was given the maiden name of his successful magazine illustrator mother, Maude Humphrey Bogart (who used baby Bogie as a model for baby food ads). The name, which has a deep resonance, is a royal name in Britain, where it is used far more frequently than here.

HUNTER. Hunter is a front-runner in the family name pack, even beginning to be used for girls as well as boys. It has a semi-bold, semi-conservative, indoor-outdoor image, and is sometimes connected to gonzo journalist Hunter Thompson, as well as the soap opera character on *One Life to Live*. HUNT is the more active, less trendy, version.

HYMAN. Hyman is the Hebrew word for "life," as is Chaim. It, and the pet form HYMIE, were commonly used by first generation Jewish immigrants in New York's Lower East Side and other ghettoes, but it is not a name that appeals to the modern ear, too redolent, in any case, of terms like "heinie" and hymen.

IAGO. This Spanish and Welsh form of James was tied in Shakespeare's play *Othello* to a villain so treacherous that it's never been heard of again.

IAN. This most attractive Scottish form of John was rather late making inroads on our shores—it was already the seventh most popular boys' name in England in 1965. After the emergence of Ian Fleming, creator of James Bond, Americans gradually began warming to the jaunty charm of the name; now it is finally gaining a foothold on some popularity lists, although not yet sufficiently to feel prohibitively overused. IAIN is an alternate, authentic, but needlessly fussy spelling.

ICHABOD. An eccentric Old Testament name that took on a kind of goofy image thanks to the Disney animation of the innocent and shy schoolmaster Ichabod Crane in Washington Irving's *The Legend of Sleepy Hollow.* We can't imagine a parent of today naming a child "icky bod."

IGNATIUS. This was the name of several saints, including the early Christian martyr who was the first to use the word *Catholic,* a Greek churchman who was the patriarch of Constantinople, and also St. Ignatius of Loyola, founder of the Jesuit order in the sixteenth century. As sanctified as it is, therefore, it is more apt to be borne by churches and schools than babies, though very religious parents might disagree and may even enliven the name by shortening it to IGGY, à la Pop.

IGOR. See IVO.

IKE. Freckle-faced and friendly, Ike is rarely used on its own; General/President Dwight Eisenhower and Mr. Tina not withstanding, it's most often a nickname for Isaac.

ILYA. This Russian form of ELIAS is occasionally heard in this country in families of Slavic heritage.

INDIANA. One of the new breed of popular place-names, its image is wedded to that of the dashingly adventurous Raider of the Lost Ark, Indiana Jones. INDIO is the unusual and exotic appellation recently chosen for their son by Deborah Falconer and Robert Downey Jr.

INIGO. Almost unknown in the United States, this name, with its strong beat and creative, evocative sound, is used primarily in England, Spain, and Russia. The only famous Inigo we know of is Inigo Jones, one of England's first great architects and stage designers.

INNIS, INNES. This Scottish place-name turned surname is now, occasionally used as a first name, though it is not one of the most attractive.

IRA. These days Ira is considered more an acronym than a proper name—be it as a retirement account or group of Northern Irish insurgents. Even when it was most widely used as a name, its image was somewhat on the soft side.

IRVING. Surprisingly enough, this name does not come from Israel or the Bronx, but is a Scottish place and surname name (as in Washington Irving). It was a popular name for first- and sometimes second-generation Jewish-American boys, such as best-selling writers Irving Stone and Irving Wallace, although Irving Berlin changed his name from Israel. The sons and nephews of these gentlemen might have been called IRWIN, though their grandsons most definitely would not. IRVIN, is a variation from the Gaelic meaning "handsome," and EARVIN is a basketball immortal.

ISAAC. Isaac is one of the Old Testament names being dusted off by adventurous parents bored with Benjamin and Joshua. A favorite of the Puritans, Isaac went on to assume something of a bearded, rabbinical image. The biblical Isaac was the long-awaited son of the elderly Sarah and the even more elderly (he was one hundred) Abraham. The name means laughter, since that was what it provoked when Sarah was told she would conceive at her advanced age. Baby Isaac lived on to marry Rebecca and to father Esau and Jacob. Other distinguished bearers of the name include Isaacs (and IZAAKS) Newton, Walton, Bashevis Singer, Asimov, Stern, Hayes—and the bartender on *The Love Boat*. It was also the name of Woody Allen's character in his memorable film, *Manhattan*.

ISAIAH. Another biblical name being restored to its former glory, Isaiah was one of the greatest prophets of the Old Testament. Mia Farrow, one of the most creative baby namers in the annals of modern parenthood, has called one of her adopted sons Isaiah. Other parents may be inspired by longtime Detroit basketball superstar star ISIAH Thomas.

ISHMAEL. The first line of the great novel *Moby Dick* is "Call me Ishmael," spoken by the book's young narrator. Although it is a perfectly respectable biblical and literary name, think about some of the more unfortunate nicknames it might invoke if you call your son Ishmael. Ishmael Reed is a noted Black novelist and poet.

ISIDORE. This name has one of the more surprising origins—how many people would be able to identify it as Greek? But it was, indeed, a common ancient Greek name belonging to several saints, including St. Isidore the Ploughman, patron saint of Madrid. It was adopted by Spanish Jews to the point where it became their almost exclusive property. Isidore has been in limbo for a few generations now, but with the growing popularity of Isabel, maybe we'll start seeing some male IZZYs as well.

ISRAEL. With the establishment of the State of Israel in 1948, this name was transformed from a traditional Jewish favorite into an icon of Judaism. In the Bible, Israel was the name given to Jacob after he wrestled with an angel.

IVAN. Whether pronounced with the accent on the first or second syllable, this Russian and Czech (as in tennis star Ivan Lendl) form of John is a bit harsh and heavy-booted. The pet name VANYA does a lot to soften it.

IVO. An interesting, unusual name with the energetic impact of all names ending in *o*. Hardly heard in this country—although Danielle Steel did use it for one of the characters in her novel *Loving*, and some might recognize it at as the name of Noble Prize–winner Ivo Andric, it is used a bit more frequently in England, as is the related IVOR, a favorite of such novelists as P. G. Wodehouse and Evelyn Waugh and the name of the composer of "Keep the Home Fires Burning." A variant spelling is IVAR (a Norse God, popular in Sweden), and if you're looking for a really singular version, you might consider the Welsh IFOR. Yet another variant is IVES, sometimes suggested by astrologers for boys born under the sign of Sagittarius, as the name means "little archer." IGOR, the Russian form of the name, is far more often seen in the cultural sections of the newspaper (Igor Stravinsky, the Borodin opera *Prince Igor*, Dr. Frankenstein's right-hand man), than in the birth announcements.

J

∧∧∧∧∧∧∧∧∧∧∧∧∧∧∧∧∧∧∧ ◎ ∧∧∧∧∧∧∧∧∧∧∧∧∧∧∧∧∧∧∧

JABEZ. A biblical name popular with the Puritans, the rarely used Jabez now has a distinct Southern accent and a sensual, anything but puritanical image.

JACK. Jack is back. This new old name is so durable, dependable, unaffected, and cheery it's being chosen for their sons by trendsetters in Hollywood and beyond, including Meg Ryan and Dennis Quaid, Susan Sarandon and Tim Robbins, Ozzie Osbourne, Ellen Barkin and Gabriel Byrne. Familiar to all of us from earliest childhood, via Jack and Jill, Jack Sprat, Little Jack Horner, Jack Be Nimble, Jack and the Beanstalk, Jack Frost, jack-o'-lantern, and jack-in-the-box, the name Jack was so common in the Middle Ages that it became a generic term for a man. Jack was originally a nickname for John, the name of most of the leading Jacks of our time—Kennedy, Lemmon, Nicholson—were christened. Today's parents might go that conventional route, might choose to use Jack on its own, or might formalize the name to the stylish and presidential JACKSON, now appearing on two soap operas, the choice of rocker-poet Patti Smith for her son and also associated with singer Jackson Browne. In Scotland, JOCK is used as their archetypal nickname.

JACOB, JAKE. One of the most venerable of the Old Testament names, Jacob has leapt up the popularity lists to its current fifth place, actually topping the boys' list in some states. It's easy to see what makes Jacob such an appealing name: It conveys an image of honesty and warmth, and nickname Jake shares a certain unpretentious earthy feeling with equally stylish cousins Max, Sam and, yes, Jack. Jacobs and Jakes abound among the junior celebrity set: Sting, Sinead O'Connor, Dustin Hoffman, Rhea Perlman and Danny DeVito, and Nora Ephron and Carl Bernstein, have all chosen it for their offspring. For you, this means that although Jacob/Jake is a fine name, it's also a very widely used one, threatening to become tomorrow's Jason. In the Bible, Jacob, the youngest son of Isaac and Rebecca, husband of both Leah and Rachel, was one of the central patriarchs in the Book of Genesis, the twelve tribes of Israel evolving from his twelve sons. Name changes: Jacob's name was changed to Israel after a wrestling match with an angel. Centuries later, two show biz notables dropped Jacob and took on new names when they entered the world of entertainment—George Gershwin and Rodney Dangerfield. Literary associations include Scrooge's partner Jacob Marley in A Christmas Carol, and currently Jake is a hunk name on Melrose Place. JAKOB is the spelling used by the Dutch, Scandinavians, and Germans. An interesting alternative nickname is KOBY.

JAEL. This ambisexual Israeli name (pronounced Yah-ehl'), comes from the Hebrew for "mountain goat" and hence is sometimes used for children born under the sign of Capricorn. It is also spelled Yael.

JAGGER. Yes, this really was an authentic English name before Mick and before the appearance on *General Hospital* of Jagger Cates. It swaggers.

JALIL, JALEEL. An Arabic name that reflects majesty, an attribute not particularly identified with Jaleel White in his portrayal of the nerdy Steve Urkel on *Family Matters*.

JAMAL, JAMAAL. Almost as popular in America as it is in the Sudan, this Muslim name means "handsome" in Arabic. It might have been given a push by the popularity of Malcolm Jamal-Warner on *The Cosby Show*. Also the name of a young character on *Another World*, Jamal has been placed by some experts in the Top 50 list of boys' names in America. JAMIL and JAMEEL are also heard.

JAMES. James is one of the classic Anglo-Saxon names. Through the ages it's been biblical (the name of two apostles in the New Testament), royal (kings of both England and Scotland), presidential (there have been more United States presidents named James—6—than any other name), and menial (in the nineteenth century it was used as a generic term for a manservant, as in "Home, James!"). Right now it's upmarket and very popular—James is at the very top of the British list and among the Top 20 in this country. Rapidly disappearing are the nicknames JIM, JIMMY, JIMBO, and JAMIE—baby Jameses tend to be called James, especially those born to such Brits as Mick Jagger and Jerry Hall, and Paul and Linda McCartney. Actually an English form of Jacob, James has some interesting foreign variations: Diego and JAIME (Spanish), JAAKO (Finnish), JACQUES (French), GIACOMO (Italian), Seamus (Irish), Hamish (Scottish), and JAAP (Dutch). The British have been using the catchy Cornish form, JAGO. Usable last name offshoots are JAMISON and JAMESON. The once-Scottish Jamie blazed through the entire English-speaking world in the sixties, but its star has now dimmed.

Jamie,
Jay

JAPHETH. This is the name of the youngest son of Noah, whose descendants were supposed to have populated Europe. It was well used by the seventeenth-century Puritans, but pronunciation difficulties would surely hinder its popularity in our day.

JARED. Jared has been steadily used since the mid-sixties, and is a sturdy, attractive, current, but not unduly trendy name that could be an inspiration to late-blooming parents. In the Bible, Jared was a descendant of Adam who became the father of Enoch at the age of 162. But lest you feel sorry for poor little Enoch, his father lived on for another eight hundred years. *This Morning*'s Paula Zahn chose the name for her son. There are several variations on the name: JARROD, JARRED, JAROD, JARRETT and even the surname JARVIS.

JASON. It was one of the buzz names of the seventies, riding in with the posse of sensitive, new-manly monikers that resurfaced in the westerns of the period (*Wanted Dead or Alive, Here Come the Brides*), following a century-long siesta. After years of JOHNNY and JIMMY, Jason sounded cool and fresh and in fact reached number two on some popularity lists in the early seventies. But Jason's long run of popularity eventually reached an overrun and the name came to be seen as a cliché of trendiness, as in the title of our other baby naming book, *Beyond Jennifer & Jason*. It has had considerable exposure recently via *Beverly Hills 90210*'s teen idol Jason Priestley.

JASPER, JASPAR. A hip name in England, Jasper is still kind of a grizzled grandpa name over here. Unfortunate, we think, because it has a good deal of intrinsic charm. Although it doesn't appear in the Bible, Jasper is the usual English form for one of the three Wise Men who brought gifts to the infant Christ according to medieval tradition, and it is also the name of a reddish semiprecious stone, one of the few such names for boys. One celebrated bearer of the name is artist Jasper Johns.

JAY. At one time a few decades ago, Jay sounded more dapper than James, but certainly does no longer. Besides, most of the most notable Jays (Gatsby, Leno) started life as James anyway.

JEB, JED, and JEDIDIAH. Jeb and Jed, shortened forms of such mouthfuls as Jedidiah, were used almost interchangeably in such early TV westerns as *Wells Fargo*, *Rawhide*, and *How the West Was Won*, not to mention *The Beverly Hillbillies*. Although they still sound attractive, they don't feel quite substantial enough to face the coming rigors of the twenty-first century. Jedediah, on the other hand, might be a bit too overpowering. It was the name given by the prophet Nathan to Solomon in the Old Testament, and some of us associate it with the Joseph Cotten character in the immortal *Citizen Kane*.

JEFFERSON. Presidential names—Tyler, Taylor, Madison, Carter— are decidedly in these days and Jefferson counts as a charter member of this stylish club. Used as a first name long before our surname-crazed era, Jefferson was most famously the name of President of the Confederacy Jefferson Davis. Even if you have no wish to honor these nineteenth-century political Jeffersons, the name may be of interest as a much fresher alternative to the outmoded Jeffrey.

JEFFREY. One of the peak names of our youth (it was the sixth most popular boys' name in the country in 1970), Jeffrey and JEFF have become the property of today's dads, just as Karen and Susan and PATTI are the names of mothers rather than babies.

JELANI. An energetic name that has been used by some African-American parents, including actor Wesley Snipes.

JEREMIAH, JEREMY. Jeremiah, the name of one of the chief Prophets of the Old Testament, is regularly used in Ireland, and was reintroduced to Americans with the 1972 Robert Redford-starring western, *Jeremiah Johnson*. It sounds quite a bit fresher than the overused Jeremy, which has been current for twenty years, but lives on in the popularity of Jeremy Irons and, for kids, in Beatrix Potter's *The Tale of Jeremy Fisher*. Another interesting possibility is JEREMIAS. The big drawback of all these names is the lack of viable nicknames, the British JEM sounding too feminine and JERRY being the name of the family dentist.

JERMAINE. Jermaine is as much a Jackson Family name as TITO and LaToya. A spelling twist on Germain, which originally indicated someone who came from Germany, the female version is the identical-sounding *GERMAINE*, as in writer Greer.

JEROME. This name has a bespectacled, serious, studious image, as well it might, since St. Jerome was the brilliant scholar who translated the Bible from Greek and Hebrew into Latin and is now the patron saint of students, librarians, and archaeologists. But despite such accomplished namesakes as Kern, Robbins, and Salinger, Jerome is definitely unstylish right now.

JERSEY. A place-name with a lot of diverse associations: the east coast state, the island in the English Channel, the flexible fabric, even a phonetic version of JERZY (as in Kosinski). Still, among the place-names it is now more often used for girls.

JESSE. The laid-back, easygoing cowboyish image of this name somewhat belies its biblical roots—Jesse was in fact the father of King David in the Old Testament. It came to the fore in the seventies, as one of the fashionable ambigender, back-to-basics band, peaking in 1988, when it reached number eight on the hit parade, and has long been associated with Rev. Jesse Jackson. These days, especially because of the long-term popularity of the female Jessica and JESSIE, the name's energy is flagging and we feel it deserves a respite. Besides, its use for the uncle character on the long-running *Full House* series definitely stamped it FOR ADULTS ONLY. The shortened form JESS is sometimes used independently, but feels a little flimsy.

JESUS. Used almost solely by Latino families, Jesus (pronounced Hay-zuse) is currently the number four most popular name for Hispanic boys in the state of Texas.

JETHRO. Jethro may mean wealth and abundance, he may be the Old Testament father-in-law of Moses, but his popular image is pure hillbilly—partly thanks to Beverly Hillbillies son Jethro. The seventies English rock group Jethro Tull was named after an eighteenth-century agricultural reformer who invented a new kind of drill for sowing seeds. Some really adventurous parents might consider updating and urbanizing its image.

JETT. This was the name of the character James Dean played in his last movie, *Giant*. John Travolta passed it on to his son to commemorate his love for planes.

JEX. A decidedly offbeat name—we've run into only one of them— that combines jauntiness with sex appeal and would certainly set your son up for life outside the bourgeois mainstream.

JODY. A quintessentially sweet and wide-eyed unisex-epidemic name of the sixties and seventies, with none of the strength today's parents demand of a name. President Carter's press secretary, Jody (born Joseph) Powell got his nickname from the wistful young boy in *The Yearling*, whom he resembled.

JOEL. Parents of the forties and fifties who were trying to jazz up or formalize the old standby JOE turned back to the biblical name Joel, borne by one of the minor Old Testament prophets and the angel who suggested to Adam that he name all things. It now belongs to the cynical Dr. Joel Fleischman on *Northern Exposure* and once was attached to, of all people, Peter Lorre playing Joel Cairo in the immortal *Casablanca*.

JOHN. Without doubt the most timeless, perennially popular of all Christian names, John led the pack for four hundred years, from the time the first Crusaders carried it back to Britain until the 1950s. At that point, American baby namers finally seemed to be tiring of this most straight-arrow, almost anonymous John Doe, John Q. Public of names and started to replace it with fancier forms—Jonathan, JON, the imported Sean and Ian. But now the pendulum appears to be swinging back. As Jonathan and Sean recede, John is once more proudly embossed on the blankets in Park Avenue prams, and someone like Tracey Ullman, who named her first child Mable, calls her second one John.

In the second half of the seventeenth century, one fourth to one half of all baptized boys in the English-speaking world were called John. The English form of the Latin JOHANNES, John was a key name in early Christianity: It was borne by John the Baptist, the herald of Christ, who baptized sinners in the river Jordan; by one of Christ's disciples, John the Apostle; and by the author of the fourth gospel, John the Evangelist, as well as by eighty-four saints (including St. John the Divine, the fisherman whom tradition made the favorite apostle when Jesus asked him to take care of his mother Mary after his death) plus twenty-three popes.

Forms of John are often among the top choices of their own countries and have sometimes been imported here—Ian or IAIN in Scotland, Evan in Wales, Sean in Ireland, JEAN in France, JUAN in Spain, JOHANN, Johannes, and Hans in Germany, JENS in Scandinavia, Ivan in Russia, JAN in Holland. That hottest of hot names, Jack, is sometimes short for John, replacing the previously ubiquitous JOHNNY. This probably means the end of a whole genre of Johnny movies: *Johnny Allegro*, *Johnny Angel*, *Johnny Apollo*, *Johnny Concho*, *Johnny Cool*, *Johnny Dark*, *Johnny Eager*, *Johnny Guitar*, *Johnny O'Clock*, *Johnny Trouble*.

JONAH. This would be an excellent choice for parents who are seeking a biblical name that is neither too popular (e.g., Jacob and Joshua) nor too obscure (like OZNI or UZI). In the familiar Old Testament story, Jonah was the prophet who disobeyed God, precipitating a storm at sea during which he was thrown overboard, swallowed by a whale, and then disgorged three days later, unharmed, assuring that modern Jonahs would come with a ready-made room decorating motif. Jonah was also the name of the appealing young boy in *Sleepless in Seattle*. JONAS is the Greek form of the name, and is somewhat more earthy. It has been associated with Jonas Salk, developer of the polio vaccine. JOAH is an unrelated and very rare biblical name that is nevertheless close in sound and might provide an alternative for parents who want something less familiar.

JONATHAN. This is the name that started to replace the stalwart John in the late fifties, sounding at once more suave, sensitive, and playful, as well as being both biblical and modern. According to the statistical research of a Harvard sociologist, Jonathan is one of the boys' names most favored by highly educated mothers. Now, as John is making a comeback, Jonathan will inevitably take a back seat. In the Old Testament, Jonathan was the valiant eldest son of King Saul, and it was his loyal friendship with brother-in-law David that gave rise to the expression "Jonathan and David" to describe devoted, steadfast friends. Notable Jonathans, both real and invented: Jonathan Swift, author of *Gulliver's Travels*; comedian Jonathan Winters; Jonathan Steed, the wily secret agent on *The Avengers*; and Jonathan Hart, the debonair mystery solver of *Hart to Hart*. Jonathan is one name that's frequently misspelled—so frequently that JONATHON and JOHNA-THAN have come to be accepted as viable forms.

JORDAN. A name that has popped into favor in the last few years with extraordinary speed, nestling not far below the other big *J* names, Justin and Joshua (it must mean something that eight of the current Top 25 favorites start with the same letter). Now used almost as frequently for girls, Jordan in fact was originally a name given to a child of either sex baptized in holy water brought back from the River Jordan, the only river in Palestine. As attractive as it is, though, Jordan is already beginning to feel dated, even as it continues to ascend.

JOSEPH. This is a name that has never left the New York City Top 10 since the list of most popular names was initiated in 1898, a statistic that's applicable to much of the rest of the country as well. Through the forties, and beginning again recently, Joseph has had some style power but even when its fashion status was at its lowest ebb, the name had dual-religious appeal. In the Old Testament, Joseph was the favorite son of Jacob and Rachel, whose brothers were jealous of him and sold him into slavery in Egypt; in the New Testament it is the name of the upright carpenter husband of Mary, mother of Christ, and then there's St. Joseph, the protector of working men. The nickname JOE is the all-time regular guy name (as in Good Joe, Cowboy Joe, GI Joe, Joe Blow, etc.), and several celebrities including Kevin Costner, Christine Lahti, and Sting, have recently chosen it as the full name for their sons—much hipper, in any case, than JOEY, which we always hear as a mother's shout from a Brooklyn window. Some foreign variations of interest: JOSEF (Scandinavia and Germany), GIUSEPPE (Italy), JOSE, PEPE, and CHE (Spain), XOSE (Galician), JOSEBA (Basque), JOSEEF (Russian), and YUSSUF (Arabic).

JOSHUA. Even though it has been used by so many parents—it has been one of the Top 10 boy baby names in the country since 1983 and is currently number two (number one in the state of Hawaii)—Joshua retains a relaxed, attractive image, with a bit of the old West mixed in with its biblical persona. In the Old Testament, Joshua was the successor to Moses who finally led the Israelites, after many battles, into the promised land, thus inspiring the rousing hymn, "Joshua Fit the Battle of Jericho." And if you're tired of hearing the nickname JOSH, a fresher substitute to consider is JOSS.

JOSIAH. A biblical name with a quaint, old-fashioned charm, Josiah is certain to become more popular as parents seek worthy substitutes for such long-time favorites as Joshua and Joseph, that might be agreeably abbreviated to JOE. Josiah was the son of Jedidiah who succeeded his father as king of Judah when he was only eight years old.

JUBAL. A possible choice for musical families: Jubal was the descendant of Cain who is credited in Genesis with the invention of the lyre, harp, organ, and other musical instruments.

JUDAH. This strong, resonant Old Testament name belonged to the fourth son of Jacob and Leah, founder of one of the twelve tribes of Israel. Though Judah is getting some attention along with the emerging wave of less common Bible names, it may be too reminiscent of the unpleasant JUDAS to become widely popular. JUDE is similarly encumbered, though John Lennon's poignant song, "Hey Jude" improved its image. St. Jude is the patron saint of those in hopeless situations; Jude Fawley was the unhappy hero of Thomas Hardy's *Jude the Obscure*. The more appealing short form, JUD or JUDD, has been used by actors Hirsch and Nelson; JUDSON is the patronymic. In Hebrew the name is YEHUDA, source of the words *Judaism*, *Jew*, and *Jewish*.

JULIAN. Because of the ways it's been used in literature, this beautiful name projects a somewhat pale, sensitive image, and it does, indeed, come from the Greek word meaning "soft and fair-complexioned." More common in Britain, where it is definitely upper crust, Julian is starting to be appreciated here. It was, for many centuries, used for women as well as men. St. Julian the Hospitaler is the patron saint of innkeepers, travelers, and boatmen. Other links to recognition: singer Julian (actually John Charles Julian) Lennon, actor Julian Sands, Black activist and politician Julian Bond, the great jazz alto saxophonist Julian "Cannonball" Adderley, the hero of Stendhal's *The Red and the Black*, and the lost soul character in *Less Than Zero*. The French spelling is JULIEN.

JULIUS. Far less fashionable than its derivative Julian, Julius seems much fustier and fogyish. It was the name of the Roman clan to which Caius Julius Caesar belonged, the real name of Groucho Marx, and is now very much associated with basketball great Dr. J, Julius Winfield Erving II. The French version, JULES, has more sparkle, as does the Spanish JULIO.

JUSTIN. This crisp, British-inflected name has been fully embraced in this country, to the point where it is now consistently on the list of most popular boys' name in America. Often chosen by parents who want a less conventional name for their sons, this choice—like such other *J* favorites as Jason and Joshua and Jeremy—can backfire because its widespread appeal makes it conventional in a more contemporary way. It stems from the Latin meaning "upright," "righteous," and "true"—in other words, just. St. Justin was the first great Christian philosopher, thereby becoming the patron saint of philosophers. All of which may have led Andie MacDowell to choose it for her son.

K

∧∧∧∧∧∧∧∧∧∧∧∧∧∧∧∧ ◉ ∧∧∧∧∧∧∧∧∧∧∧∧∧∧∧∧∧∧

KADEEM. An African-American name made familiar by the TV actor Kadeem Hardison, who became known as Dwayne Wayne in the sitcom *A Different World*, this could provide a fresh alternative to Kareem.

KAI. This exotic name (it rhymes with *eye*) is found in several languages: in Hawaiian it means "ocean" and in Welsh "keeper of the keys." But Kai is perhaps most famous as the name of the boy enchanted by the Snow Queen in the fairy tale. Kai's problem: It has a somewhat feminine sound, especially if mispronounced (as people will) as Kay.

KALIL, KAHIL, KHALIL, KAHLIL, KALEEL. In their sundry spellings, these names, first brought into the American consciousness by the inspirational Lebanese poet, Kahlil Gibran, in the twenties and thirties, have various meanings (all of them pleasant) in various cultures: in Arabic it is "good friend," in Hebrew "complete, perfect," and in Greek, Kalil means "beautiful."

KAMAL, KAMIL. Both these African names mean perfect, one of the ninety-nine qualities of God listed in the Koran.

KANE. This soap operaish single-syllable name is a take-off on both the Irish surname and the name of the world's first murderer, the biblical Cain. The Irish surname may also be spelled KEAN or even KEANE, but then most people will be tempted to pronounce it as keen. When found in Japan and Hawaii, Kane expands to KA-neh. Keanu Reeves introduced a more exotic form into the mix.

KAREEM, KARIM. A favorite in Muslim countries, particularly in the Sudan, this Arabic name means "generous, noble, and exalted," generosity being one of the ninety-nine qualities of God listed in the Koran. Seven-foot-three-inch basketball star Kareem Abdul-Jabbar was born Lewis Ferdinand Alcindor, but changed his name to Kareem when he converted from the Catholic religion to the Black orthodox Hanafi sect.

KARL. The somewhat severe German and Scandinavian form of Charles, Karl, quite appropriately, means strong and manly. Translating it into other languages can have a softening (and feminizing) effect: KAREL in Czech, CHARLOT in French, KALMAN in Hungarian, KALLE in some parts of Scandinavia, KAROL in Poland. A current sports hero Karl is Karl Malone, superstar Utah Jazz basketball player who was a member of the 1992 Olympics "Dream Team;" Karl Lagerfeld is its fashion rep.

KEENAN. This cheerful Gaelic name (the Irish spell it CIANAN), which was the name of three Irish saints, is a very feasible choice. The older generation will associate it with actor Keenan Wynn (born Francis), younger people with Keenen Ivory Wayans, creative force behind *In Living Color*.

KEITH. Strong but gentle, Keith is one of the Scottish surnames (like Douglas and Bruce) that was considered the epitome of cool in the sixties and early seventies, just when heartthrob David Cassidy was playing a Partridge named Keith. Since then Rolling Stone Keith Richards and baseball great Keith Hernandez have kept the name in the headlines.

KELLY. When Bill Cosby's costar Robert Culp's character was given this Irish surname name in the sixties series, *I Spy*, it was a perfectly acceptable male name. By the time of *Charlie's Angels*, a decade later, though, it had become almost exclusively female, and so it remains.

KELSEY. Just as this name was becoming terminally female, Kelsey Grammer's character Dr. Frasier Crane was spun off from *Cheers* into its own hit sitcom, bringing the name a lot of much-needed masculine press coverage. Still and all, be aware that Kelsey is now firmly ensconced on the most-popular-girls'-name list.

KELVIN. An unfortunate cross between Kevin and Melvin.

KENNEDY. A family name long used as a first in Ireland—King Kennedy of Munster was the father of the famous medieval high King, Brian Boru—Kennedy translates from the Gaelic as "ugly head," a meaning certainly less attractive than its once-shining image as the name of America's Camelot family. Still linked to the Kennedy clan, the name will connect that association to your child if you choose this strong-sounding name.

KENNETH. It may sound lackluster now, but in ancient Scotland, Kenneth, which comes from the Gaelic meaning "handsome," was as dashing as a name could be. The first king of Scotland was Kenneth, and in Sir Walter Scott's novel, *The Talisman*, the hero is Sir Kenneth, a Christian Crusader known as Knight of the Leopard. Kenneth had its moment of glory in this country as well—it was among the Top 20 boys' names in 1925, and was still there in 1950, lasting even longer for nonwhite boys. And for many girls growing up, KEN was the name of Barbie's boyfriend, the ultimate dream date. These days, jazz saxophonist Kenny G. (for Gorelick) gives the name what sex appeal it has left. Then there is KENN, an occult name for babies born under water signs—Pisces, Cancer, and Scorpio. Other Ken names include KENDALL, KENDRICK, KENELM and the Irish Gaelic KENYON—the most attractive and stylish of the lot.

KENT. One of several no-nonsense, brief, brisk, one-syllable *K* names, Kent has both a noble old image (via the devoted earl who risked his life to save King Lear) and a more modern daytime-drama one (there have been Kents on both *All My Children* and *As the World Turns*). It can also be considered as a place-name, when one thinks of the lush English county of that name.

KERMIT. The question here is, can anyone forget the frog? This otherwise very appealing variation on the Irish name DERMOT would, except for that powerful Muppet connection, be an ideal choice. It isn't easy being green.

KERR. A Scottish place-name/surname without much spine. The variant KEIR, publicized by actor Keir Dullea, has a good deal more force, plus the hint of a Scottish burr.

KERRY. An Irish county but, more important, now a well-established girls' name that is sometimes used for boys, but shouldn't be.

KEVIN. No longer a baby name—it belongs to the past generation of popular Irish names such as Kathleen and Shannon and Sean—Kevin now seems to be the one script writers inevitably assign to cute young boys, such as Fred Savage in *The Wonder Years* and Macauley Culkin in the *Home Alone* movies. Irish Gaelic for "handsome," it was first made popular by the seventh-century St. Kevin, who founded a monastery near Dublin distinguished by its scholarship, and who was rewarded by becoming one of that city's patron saints. In contemporary America, Kevin has had a long run of popularity—well over thirty years, and we are still reminded of its charm via such leading men as Kevins Costner, Kline, and Bacon.

KIERAN. This Gaelic name, which is widely used in both England and Australia, is a stranger to these shores, though one rising-star brother of child actor Macauley Culkin is named Kieran. An Anglicized form of the Irish name CIARAN, which means "dark-haired, dark-complexioned one," it was the name of many Irish saints, including the Kieran considered Ireland's firstborn saint. A name with a strong, attractive sound, Kieran may nevertheless prove too close to such feminine choices as Karen and Kyra to win widespread favor among American parents.

KILLIAN. A sprightly yet resonant Gaelic surname that was borne by several Irish saints and could make a distinctive replacement for Kelly. Killian's Red is a trendy beer.

KIMBALL, KIM. If this old Welsh surname has never been heard very much, its short form surely has, albeit more for girls than for boys. It gained prominence through Kipling's 1901 novel, *Kim*, which related the adventures of a clever, orphaned Irish boy named Kimball

O'Hara growing up in India. These days, the full name Kimball would be preferable to the outmoded, feminized Kim.

KING. While some might relate to King as a canine choice, others see it as a strong name with lots of offbeat style and a full court of rich associations, from Elvis to Sky King to jazz great King Oliver to Martin Luther King Jr. Originally a last name evolving from the nickname for someone employed in a royal household, King later began to be used as a given name by plantation owners for their slaves. Today, King might be used on its own or as a short form of KINGSTON, as in Jamaica, or KINGSLEY, as in Amis.

KIP and **KIT.** These are two nickname names, usually for Christopher, that are more prevalent in England and rarely used on their own even there.

KIRBY. An attractive English place-name with a sense of humor. Kirby Yorke is the name of the character John Wayne played in John Ford's 1950 epic, *Fort Apache*, and Kirby Puckett is a sure future baseball Hall of Famer.

KIRK. For years this name was associated with one person: Kirk Douglas (whose given name was Issur). Its use has since become more widespread—it's far friendlier and more open than such similar names as Kent and Kurt. Kirk has also made several media appearances—although not always attached to the most likable characters—on soaps *As the World Turns* and *Santa Barbara* and the sitcom *Dear John*. Kirk Gibson is a world series hero.

KLAUS. This German pet form of NICOLAUS has some unpleasant associations—the Nazi Gestapo chief, Klaus Barbie, for example. And while Santa CLAUS certainly projects a much more jolly persona, we don't think a modern American child would appreciate the inevitable teasing.

KNUT, KNUTE. The *K* is silent in this rarely used Scandinavian name that is, in this country, linked with a single figure—the iconic

Notre Dame football coach Knute Rockne, further immortalized in the film, *Knute Rockne, All American*, in which Ronald Reagan co-starred as the Gipper. Long before that, the mighty Danish king, Knute II, also called CANUTE, ruled over England, Norway, and Denmark.

KOREN. An unusual and attractive Hebrew name meaning shining or beaming.

KRISTOFER, KRISTOFFER. This Scandinavian spin on Christopher gives that old classic a lighter, more individual twist but may ultimately make it seem too airy. Despite singer Kris Kristofferson, Kris is almost always the girls' spelling.

KURT. It's difficult to separate this German name from the meaning of the adjective, although some celebrity bearers, including Kurt Vonnegut and Kurt Russell, have done their share to soften it. Kurt is actually a German diminutive not of Curtis but of KONRAD, a name we prefer.

KWAME, KWAMI. This is a popular name among the Akan of Ghana for boys born on Saturday. Kwame Nkrumah was the first president of independent Ghana in 1960.

KYLE. Kyle is a name that's claimed a place within the boys' Top 20 in the past couple of years, secure alongside Tyler and Taylor as a newmanly choice, both sensitive and strong. Some parents are beginning to use this Scottish name for girls as well, joining (and perhaps replacing) other trendy androgynous *K*-initial names such as Kendall and Kelsey. Whether this encroachment from the girls' camp will cause the name to fade among boys—as it did for Lindsay and Ashley, for example—remains to be seen. *Twin Peaks* alumnus Kyle MacLachlan bolsters the masculine end of the name's stylish image.

I

〜〜〜〜〜〜〜〜〜〜〜〜〜〜 ◉ 〜〜〜〜〜〜〜〜〜〜〜〜〜〜

LABAN. Less well-known than his female biblical relations—sister Rebecca, daughters Rachel and Leah—and certainly less frequently used as a name, Laban, and its diminutive **LAEB**, are occasionally found in Jewish families. **LABAAN** is a Somali boys' name.

LACHLAN. A name as Scottish as haggis and tartan plaid kilts, Lachlan has hardly been heard here in the past, but could blend in well with such Irish classmates as Liam and Lorcan—and the more closely related **LAUGHLIN**. And since it derives from the Gaelic word referring to a "migrant from Norway," it would be perfect for a family that contains both Scottish and Scandinavian roots.

LAIRD. A Scottish name for wealthy landowners—lairds of the manor—this name projects an aristocratic image, with a pleasant Highland burr.

LAMAR and **LAMONT.** Two once-toney surnames that have lost their upper-class edge. Lamar Hoyt is a well-known pitcher, and Lamont Cranston will be remembered as the affluent young alter ego of *The Shadow* on the vintage radio series that was made into a movie in 1994.

LANCELOT. One of those probably-too-loaded names to impose on a baby, in spite of—or because of—its rich legacy. In Arthurian legend, Sir Lancelot was one of the most dashing and romantic of the Knights of the Round Table, who eventually betrayed King Arthur's trust by having an affair with Queen Guinevere, which led to war. **LANCE** is more manageable, but at this point in time has an image that verges on the caricaturish.

LANFORD, LANDON, LANDAN, LANGDON, LANGLEY, LANGSTON. A group of family names best reserved for those with a legitimate ancestral connection, or who want to honor playwright Lanford Wilson or poet Langston (born James) Hughes.

LANE. An attractive single-syllable name, unusual and appealing for both boys and girls, bringing up associations with leafy country lanes. Lane Frost was the rodeo star recently portrayed on film by Luke Perry.

LATEEF. A Muslim male name that is popular in North Africa and whose meaning—"pleasant, gentle"—is reflected in its sound.

LAWRENCE, LAURENCE. A solid, sturdy name poised in that netherworld between stodginess and style, Lawrence had a long run of popularity, covering the first seventy years of this century—a fact to which the large numbers of balding, forty-five-year-old Larrys will attest. Going back further in history, it was a favorite in the Middle Ages, largely resulting from the fame of a third-century saint, and was revived in the Tudor period after Shakespeare bestowed it on the benevolent friar who married the young lovers in *Romeo and Juliet*. Lawrence of Arabia (Lawrence was his surname) added further dash. It reached as high as fifteenth most popular names for boys in America in 1940 (when Larry, on its own, was number twenty-four), but of late the only fashionable young Laurence we've heard of was a *girl*. LOREN and LORNE are two more up-to-date variations, Lorne being especially popular in Canada (the two most well-known bearers, *Bonanza*'s Lorne Greene and *Saturday Night Live's* Lorne Michaels were both born there). Some foreign variations with a bit more bite: LO-RENZO (Italian and Spanish), LARS (Scandinavian), LAURENT (French), and LORENZ (German). And the Scots have a nickname with more life than Larry: LAURO.

LAZARUS. This is one name that most people would agree has too much heavy biblical baggage to be considered feasible for a modern baby. It belonged to two New Testament characters: the brother of Mary and Martha, who was raised from the dead by Jesus, and a beggar who appears in the parables. In the Middle Ages, the name was used as a generic term for a leper.

LEANDER. This is an almost unknown name that we think is worthy of consideration, perhaps as a substitute for the overused Alexander. In Greek legend, Leander was the powerful figure who swam across the Hellespont every night to visit his beloved Hero, a priestess of Venus.

LEE. A name with a fairly feeble shouldn't-I-be-a-middle-name image, despite its attachment to such macho men as Lee Marvin and Lee Majors (who was actually born Harvey Lee). Another famous Lee, Iacocca, was christened Lido. The name was also somewhat tainted by the image of Lee Harvey Oswald. All in all, nineties parents would probably prefer a more substantial name like Liam.

LEIF, LEAF. Two names with the same pronunciation but very different job descriptions. Leif, the name of the Norse navigator credited with discovering the New World, has an exotic Scandinavian feel, while Leaf, the name of one of the members of the Phoenix acting clan, has a distinctly New Age nature-boy aspect.

LELAND. A rather distinguished, middle-aged surname, as personified by the buttoned-down character of Leland McKenzie on *L.A. Law*.

LEMUEL. This unjustly neglected biblical name is much more strongly associated with the hero of Jonathan Swift's satirical *Gulliver's Travels*, Lemuel Gulliver, than with the obscure Old Testament king of that name. If you're tired of the ubiquitous Samuel/Sam combo, you might want to consider the fresher Lemuel/LEM.

LENNOX. This aristocratic Scottish surname and place-name has a lot of brute power, perhaps due to Lennox Lewis, the Canadian super heavyweight boxer who won the 1988 Olympic gold medal. A more fine-china-shop image results when you spell it LENOX.

LEO. Leo is making a surprise comeback, which turns out to be not so surprising after all if you consider the many elements it has going for it. Its leonine associations suggest strength of character and physique. Its zodiacal reference appeals to New Agers and its *o*-ending gives it some added energy. It is a name that looms large in religious history—having belonged to a large number of early Christian saints, including Pope Leo the Great, a noble figure who twice saved Rome from attack, plus twelve other popes. It's even appeared in a soap opera—*Loving*. And shortly before *thirtysomething* went off the air in 1990, the Steadmans named their new baby Leo, a sure sign of impending trendiness. Famous Leos of the past have ranged from Tolstoy to Leo ("the Lip") Durocher, the irascible manager of the Brooklyn Dodgers. LEV is the Russian form of the name—it also means "heart" in Hebrew. LEOPOLD is a more formal and forbidding Germanic variation. LEON, the Greek form of Leo, shows no sign of a similar rejuvenation, not having been really popular here for almost a century. It last made the headlines when Leon Spinks defeated Mohammed Ali in 1978.

LEONARD, LEONARDO. Another lion-related name, Leonard comes from the German meaning lionhearted, and has been out of fashion for several decades, even though one of several St. Leonards is the patron saint of childbirth. It is perhaps more famous for those who dropped the name when they entered show business than for those who kept it: former Leonards include Roy Rogers, Tony Randall, and Buddy Hackett. Much more au courant these days is Leonardo, partly because of the versatile young actor, Leonardo di Caprio, and partly, we're afraid, because Leonardo is one of the Renaissance artist-inspired names of a Teenage Mutant Ninja Turtle.

LEROY. From a French nickname meaning "the king," LeRoy/Leroy was considered a typical Black American given name of the last generation. In fact, Arsenio Hall used to open his act by introducing himself as "Hi, I'm Arsenio. A very unique name for a Black man. In Greek, it means LeRoy."

LESLEY, LESLIE. This ancient Scottish clan name is almost exclusively female at this point, with Leslie (*Naked Gun*) Nielsen being one of the last male holdouts.

LESTER. This British place-name (it's the phonetic form of LEICESTER) and surname has gone the way of Hester, Esther, and Sylvester. They all share a sound that is not pleasing to the modern ear.

LEVI. We predict that this name will be in the forefront of the next wave of biblical names. It has a unique combination of Old Testament profundity (Levi was the name given by Jacob's wife Leah to her third son), with the casual flair associated with Levi Strauss jeans. It was used as a middle name for Emilio Estevez's son Taylor.

LEWIS, LOUIS. Lewis is the common English form of the French Louis and yes, the latter can be pronounced either like the former or as LOUIE. Both versions have been in the Top 25 in this country at various times—Louis (the name of sixteen French kings) peaked around the turn of the last century and Lewis was most popular around 1930. Modern parents in search of interesting names from their family trees have been holding Lewis and Louis up to the light these days to see if it has any life left. The verdict? Maybe: if you've got an adventurous sense of style, if you're confident your child will have other entrees to the mainstream, if you really love Louis Armstrong. Trendy Brits, including Princess Di's brother, have already rediscovered it. For a completely different spin on the name, you might consider the other French form, CLOVIS. You might *not* want to consider the Latinized form, ALOYSIUS.

LEX. It started as a short form of Alex or Alexander (its most famous bearer, onetime Tarzan Lex Barker, was born Alexander), but is now sometimes used on its own. And like all the other names that rhyme with sex, it does have a seductive edge. One bad-guy Lex was Superman villain, Lex Luthor.

LIAM. One of the hottest of the recently imported Irish names, Liam was originally a pet Gaelic form of William (or UILLIAM) in the Emerald Isle, and is currently among the Top 25 in England as well. It is both jaunty and richly textured, and has recently been brought to prominence by Academy Award–nominee Liam Neeson. Faye Dunaway chose it for her son, as did Rachel Hunter and Rod Stewart for their baby, Liam McAllister.

LINCOLN. Like Taylor, Tyler, Madison, and Jefferson, Lincoln is a presidential possibility. Reflecting its namesake, it has a tall, rangy, honest image. And LINC is a cool nickname, as reflected in such TV characters as Linc Lafferty on *As the World Turns* and Linc Hayes, played by Clarence Williams III on the old *Mod Squad*.

LINUS. If you can separate the name from the little boy clinging to his security blanket in *Peanuts*—not, admittedly, a simple feat—you could discover a name with a great deal of charm and other kinds of associations. In Greek mythology Linus is both a musician and poet, the inventor of rhythm and melody who taught music to Hercules. In the Christian era, Linus was the name of the second pope, St. Peter's successor. More recently, Linus Pauling won two Nobel prizes, in chemistry and peace. And it may be hard to picture, but Humphrey Bogart played a Linus in the film *Sabrina*.

LIONEL. A name that has been fairly well used over the years (there were Lionels Barrymore, Trilling, Richie, and Hampton, a Knight of King Arthur's Round Table, and characters on *The Jeffersons* and *Santa Barbara*, to name a few), but has never become trendy or dated. We think it would make an interesting, multidimensional choice.

LLEWELYN. One of the commonest Christian names in Wales would make a distinctively offbeat American alternative for a child with Welsh roots. Llewelyn has some appealing, if quirky, short forms as well— LLEW (a lot cuter, if more confusing, than LEW), and LLELO.

LLOYD. Originally a nickname for a gray-haired man, Lloyd is a sleek, middle-aged Welsh name, which had some degree of popularity in the forties but is rarely used for children today. That *oy* sound in the middle, as in Floyd or Boyd, is hard to transcend. The name's best-known bearers are Lloyd Bridges and Lloyd Bentsen, both of whom were born before 1922.

LOGAN. Logan is a bright and cheerful Scottish surname that is making rapid strides in this country, actually approaching the lower rungs of the popularity ladder. It was chosen for his son by Led Zeppelin's Robert Plant and a character named Logan Staffiord has been featured on the soap opera *The Guiding Light*.

LORCAN. A name rich in Irish history, just waiting to be invited over to this country, Lorcan was the name of several Irish kings, including the grandfather of the most famous high king of Ireland, Brian Boru. In the old country it has been associated with the O'Toole family, and sure enough, actor Peter O'Toole used it for his son.

LORENZO. Like Leonardo, this attractive Latin version of Lawrence has been somewhat integrated into the American stockpot of names. In addition to the contemporary hunk Lorenzo Lamas, other associations are with Lorenzo de'Medici, the merchant prince ruler of the Florentine city-state and Renaissance patron of the arts, and the upstanding young man who married Shylock's daughter Jessica in Shakespeare's *The Merchant of Venice*.

LOUIS. See LEWIS.

LOWELL. Stalwart and somewhat conservative, Lowell calls to mind the genteel, patrician families of nineteenth-century New England, like the one poet Robert Lowell came from. An interesting upper-class British version is LOEL.

LUCAS. An amplified, Latinate version of Luke, Lucas has proved to be a favorite of scriptwriters, from the days of *The Rifleman* (Chuck Connors as Lucas McCain) to the schoolteacher series, *Lucas Tanner*, to recent soap operas *Days of Our Lives*, *Another World*, and *All My Children*, to the 1986 teen flic, *Lucas*. Country singer Willie Nelson named his baby boy Lucas Autry, but the young actor spells his name LUKAS Haas. Parents who find Luke too casual may want to upgrade to Lucas.

LUCIUS. This exotic old Roman given name has lots of religious and other resonances. It was the name of three popes, appears in several Shakespeare plays, and in Ireland is associated with the O'Brien family. LUCIAN and LUCIEN are the smoother French versions, while LUCIANO is the form you would hear in Italia.

LUKE. One of the quintessential kicked-back cowboy names of the seventies and eighties, Luke is finally beginning to fade in this more formal decade, although Beverly Hills heartthrob Luke Perry has given it a bit of a reprieve. The most famous Luke of all is the first-century Greek physician, evangelist, friend and convert of St. Paul, and author of the third Gospel, who became patron saint of doctors, artists, and butchers. Other Lukes of lesser note have been Luke Skywalker of *Star Wars* fame, Luke Macahan in the seminal TV western *How the West Was Won*, Luke Duke, one of The Dukes of Hazzard, *Cool Hand Luke*, and half of the most famous couple in soap opera history, Luke and Laura of *General Hospital*. Bill Murray named one of his sons Luke. Foreign versions include LUC (French) and LUCA (Italian).

LUTHER. In the past, this German surname was pretty much restricted to evangelical Protestants honoring the ecclesiastical reformer and theologian Martin Luther, leader of the Protestant revolution. In more recent times it has been heavily used by African-Americans to honor civil rights hero Martin Luther King Jr. A current bearer of the name is singer Luther Vandross. LOTHAR is another German form.

LYLE. This English and Scottish surname, currently identified with singer/actor/star husband Lyle Lovett, is a perfectly respectable, straightforward, single-syllable name, but be warned that by the time he's four, any child with this name will be sick of hearing the chant, "Lyle, Lyle, crocodile," from the popular children's book.

M

MMMMMMMMMMMMMMMMMMMMMM ◉ MMMMMMMMMMMMMMMMMMMMMM

MACK, MAC. In Ireland and Scotland Mac is the part of a name that means "son of," but here, with or without the final *k*, it's sometimes used on its own and makes an appealingly congenial choice. It is also suggestive of Mack the Knife and a whole family of computers. Then there is an extended clan of appealing Mac last-name-first names, most prominent of which are MACKENZIE (climbing girls' charts),

MACDONALD (as in the late actor MacDonald Carey, who was given his mother's maiden name), **MACAULAY** (most noted now for young Culkin, it was also the Jimmy Stewart character's first name in *The Philadelphia Story*), **MACALLISTER, MACDOUGAL, MACKINLAY, MACLEAN,** and **MACGEORGE.** In the same family is the nonchalant, loose, and lanky **MAGEE.** Trivia note: McKinley was the given name of blues legend Muddy Waters.

MACON. An attractive place-name, with a thick Georgia accent. The protagonist of Anne Tyler's *The Accidental Tourist* was called Macon Leary.

MADISON. This is both a place- and a presidential name—two categories that are becoming increasingly fashionable. But although it means "son of a mighty warrior" in Old English, Madison is used more frequently for girls these days.

MAGNUS. A name with a somewhat weighty, magisterial quality, Magnus comes from the Latin meaning "great one." It belonged to several important early Norwegian kings, but its spread was due almost entirely to Emperor Charlemagne, who was called Carolus Magnus, meaning Charles the Great. Some unknowing followers of his picked up on the Magnus part and started using it as a first name. During the Middle Ages, the name traveled from Scandinavia to Ireland and Scotland, where it became very popular and remains well used to this day.

MALACHI, MALACHY. This Old Testament name, which is a great favorite in Ireland, has an expansive, bouncing, boisterous image. In the Bible, Malachi was the last of the twelve Hebrew prophets, who prophesied the coming of Christ. Malachy was the name of two famous high kings of Ireland, one of whom defeated the Norse invaders in an important battle. In Eire, it has been associated with the O'Kelly, O'Morgan, O'Flanagan, and MacCann clans, and would be especially appropriate for a child with one of those surnames. The pronunciation distinction between the two: Malachi is pronounced with the final syllable as *eye* while Malachy ends with an *ee* sound.

MALCOLM. A warm, friendly Scottish appellation that fits into our golden circle of names that are highly distinctive without verging on the bizarre. Malcolm was the name of four Scottish kings—including the son of Duncan who became king after Macbeth murdered his father—and it has always been one of the most popular names in that country. A modern hero for many in this country is radical civil rights activist Malcolm X, whose name was even more strongly imprinted on the American consciousness by the recent Spike Lee biopic. The star of that movie, Denzel Washington, named one of his sons Malcolm; Harrison Ford is another celebrity parent of a Malcolm. Other Malcolms in the public eye: the late high-living millionaire publisher, Malcolm Forbes, and the only male Cosby kid, Malcolm-Jamal Warner.

MANFRED. A rather dated Old German name meaning "man of peace" that got some attention in this country via the pop singer Manfred ("Doo Wah Diddy Diddy") Mann. Parents seeking a "Fred" name would be better advised to stick to the classic Frederick.

MAOZ. Pronounced MAH-ohz, it means "strength" or "force" in Hebrew and is a symbolic name given to boys born on Chanukah, because of the song "Maoz Tzur" ("Rock of Ages") sung at that time.

MARCUS. This is the original Latin form of Mark, and has a bit more verbal and secular substance. It was commonplace in classical Rome—not surprising as it was one of only about a dozen given names in general use then—and a renowned bearer during that period was the emperor and philosopher Marcus Aurelius. African-American parents might find it appealing as a hero name (it was actually among the dozen most popular names for nonwhite boy babies born in America in 1993), honoring Marcus Moziah Garvey, the Jamaican political leader who led the Back to Africa movement in this country at the beginning of the century. On TV we've seen Marcus Welby, the kindly physician on the popular medical show of the seventies, and the soap opera character Marcus Hunter on *Days of Our Lives*; in sports, football player Marcus Allen won the Heisman Trophy in 1981. And Brigitte Nielsen and Mark (born Marcus) Gastineau (remember them?) chose it as their son's name.

MARIO. Like Emilio and Leonardo, Mario is a Latin name that has become integrated into the North American mainstream, adding a lot of punch to any compatible Anglo surname. Marios in the public eye include longtime New York Governor Mario Cuomo, auto racer Mario Andretti, and actor-director Mario van Peebles. MARIUS is the more formal Latin version.

MARK, MARC. After a long history of lagging behind many of the other apostolic names, Mark leaped into massive popularity around 1950, suddenly sounding a good deal fresher and more modern than Peter or Paul. By 1960, Mark had become the sixth most popular boys' name in America. Deriving from the Latin name Marcus, in turn derived from Mars, the Roman god of war, it was borne by numerous great Romans, including Mark Antony, and by St. Mark the Evangelist, the author of the second Gospel of the New Testament and the patron saint of secretaries, notaries, and the city of Venice. The most noted Mark in this country was the great humorous writer Mark Twain, born Samuel Clemens, a Mississippi River steamboat pilot who took his pen name from the nautical term meaning mark two fathoms. But although Mark made its mark on baby naming in time to impress itself on many baby boomers, it has very little life left for their offspring. MARCEL is the French version, MARCELLO and MARCO, the Italian, and MARCOS the Spanish.

MARLON. For forty years, this name has been identified with Marlon Brando, who inherited the French-inflected name from his father. More recently there have been Jackson and Wayans family Marlons and a press secretary named MARLIN Fitzwater. Your own little Marlon? Iconoclast Dennis Miller has one, but most modern parents would consider it beyond the pale.

MARSHALL. This rarely used name has subliminal ties to the military (martial, Field Marshal), and the old West (Marshals Matt Dillon, et al.) It had some play during the heyday of communications maven Marshall McLuhan, but would probably be seen as outdated and slightly pretentious today.

MARTIN. Suddenly an "in" name in upper-class England, Martin still has a long and winding road to travel before it arrives back in style here, though the newfound cool of such former musties as Henry and Homer leads us to believe Martin's revival could conceivably be just around the corner. It has definite potential as a hero name, honoring the Reverend Martin Luther King Jr. (interestingly enough, both Martin Sr. and Jr. were originally named Michael Luther King, which was changed in honor of religious leader Martin Luther). Another boost may come from the TV show, *Martin*, and the fresh appeal of its star, Martin Lawrence. MARTY was a popular guy from the thirties to the fifties, until the Academy Award—winning film of that name linked it with a sad, sweet loser of a Bronx butcher. A name borne by five popes, Martin was also the appellation of Mel Gibson's character in *Lethal Weapon*.

MARVIN. Talk about unexpected origins! Would you believe that this now (let's face it) schleppyish name hails from Wales? The real first name of playwright Neil Simon and of the singer known as Meatloaf, it did take on a little of the charisma of Marvin Gaye in the sixties and seventies. But not much.

MASON. This occupational family name, originally applied to workers in stone, has long been used as a first name. But today Macon might make a more dynamic choice.

MATTHEW. The epitome of the fashionable classic, Matthew, after having been very lightly used in the first half of this century, has been in the Top 10 for more than twenty years now, rising as high as the third most popular boys' name in the country for several years, and still sitting comfortably at number four. Why? Because it's safe and sturdy, yet has a more engaging personality than, say, John or James, which can be perceived as being common to the point of anonymity. The biblical Matthew was the apostle who wrote the first Gospel of the New Testament, and a modern fictional hero who promoted the name was Marshall MATT Dillon on the phenomenally successful vintage TV Western, *Gunsmoke*, to be followed by other video heroes like Matt Helm and Matt Houston, not to mention such real-life leading men as Matthews Broderick and Modine and Matt Dillon. Some celebrities who have made this semiconservative choice for their sons are Christopher Reeve, Rob Lowe, Alex Trebeck, and Mia Farrow. MATTHIAS was the form used by the Puritans and would make an interesting alternative today.

MAX. It seems like only yesterday that Max was an unthinkably fusty, cigar-smelling old grandpa name, completely out of the question as a baby naming choice. But then Max—like his pinochle-playing partners Sam and JAKE—suddenly became hip, influenced, perhaps, by the Mad Max character Mel Gibson played in the early eighties. Max became one of the star baby names of the decade—chosen by such highly visible parents as Amy Irving and Steven Spielberg, Henry Winkler, Jill Eikenberry and Michael Tucker, Nora Ephron and Carl Bernstein, and Theresa Russell and Nick Roeg, to name a few. And, sure sign of its success, it made it onto a soap opera—*One Life to Live*. Its popularity has begun to fade among the avant garde, to be replaced by less ethnic classics such as Jack and Henry. But there is one arena where it's still on top—Max is one of the hottest names for dogs in both New York City and Los Angeles. A pair of more ostentatious forms are MAXWELL (chosen for his son by Andrew Dice Clay) and MAXIMILIAN (used by Mel Brooks and Anne Bancroft for theirs). MAXIM/MAXIME is the restaurantish French version.

MAYNARD. An offbeat German name sometimes still associated with beatnik Maynard G. Krebs on the old *The Many Loves of Dobie Gillis* TV show, or with Canadian jazz trumpeter Maynard Ferguson.

MELVIN. This once perfectly respectable Scottish surname has been irretrievably demeaned over the past few decades, not least of all by Jerry Lewis turning it into a near-demented, spastic character in the fifties. MELVILLE is equally out of the question, as are most names ending in *ville*. MEL is sometimes used on its own, more in other countries than here, as handsome hero Mel Gibson protests to people who assume his full name must be Melvin. Mel is, in fact, the full name of an Irish saint.

MENACHEM. This rarely used biblical name, now associated with onetime Israeli Prime Minister Begin, is a symbolic appellation used for boys born on the Jewish holiday of Tishah-b'Av, a day of fasting and mourning for the destruction of the Temple. The Yiddish version is MENDEL.

MERCER, MERCE. Two names with artistic images, thanks to their associations with musician-bandleader Mercer Ellington and dancer-choreographer Merce Cunningham.

MEREDITH. This Welsh name related to the sea is still used for boys in Wales, but is far more common for girls in America, having come to sound somewhat soft and wispy as a male name.

MERLIN, MERTON, MERVYN. A trio of completely antiquated names almost unheard of for decades. Of the three, Merlin has the most interesting history, being the name of the famous fifth-century sorcerer and mentor of King Arthur, who helped him rise to power. In recent times, football player turned sportscaster turned actor Merlin Olsen has single-handedly kept the name alive. MERLE (which means "blackbird" in Latin and was originally given as a nickname to someone who loved to sing or whistle), associated with country singer Merle Haggard, and MERRILL have similarly lost virtually all their masculine punch.

MESHACH. This Old Testament name of the companion of Daniel, SHADRACH, and ABEDNEGO has a rousing, gospel feel. It has been rescued from complete obscurity by the genial actor Meshach Taylor, who made his mark in *Designing Women*.

MEYER. An obsolete German name that was favored by first-generation Jewish families, including the affluent Guggenheims and Lehmans. Now pretty much relegated to poolside gin games in Miami and Fort Lauderdale.

MICAH. An interesting alternative to the all-pervasive Michael, with a shinier, more lively image. Micah is the name of a biblical prophet and was used fairly frequently by the seventeenth-century Puritans.

MICHAEL. Michael has been the number one name for boy babies born in this country—at times twice as well used as the next name on the list—for forty years now. One reason for this phenomenal record is that Michael has been embraced by parents from an exceptional range of religious and ethnic groups and ways of life. In fact, another reason for the length and breadth of Michael's popularity is its eminent usefulness as a compromise name. If one of you is Catholic and the other Jewish or you're trying to meld wildly disparate ethnic considerations; if you want a name that's contemporary and your partner favors something classic; if you're after a name with music and your mate's looking for one with muscle; then Michael is sure to be on the short list of names that satisfies both of your tastes and requirements. The biblical Michael is one of only two archangels (the other is Gabriel) recognized by Jews, Christians, and Muslims alike. St. Michael is the patron of bankers, radiologists, and policemen, and Michael also excels at rowing boats ashore. Superstar Michaels range from Jackson to Jordan to Douglas to J. Fox. With an image that diverse, it's not surprising that it has also become enervated and diluted, even though Michael still projects a genuine sweetness and honesty. Several of its foreign versions are sometimes used in this country, including MICHEL (French), MIGUEL (Spanish), and MIKHAIL (Russian). The pugnacious nickname MICKEY was used on its own a lot more often fifty years ago than it is today, although we're still very much aware of Mickey Mouse, Mickey Mantle (who credited his catchy name with contributing to his fame), Mickey Rooney, and Mickey Rourke. MICK, most often associated with Rolling Stone Jagger, is also used as a generic, often derogatory, term for an Irishman.

MILES, MYLES. Miles has suddenly zoomed into popularity with the movers and shakers, largely due to its polished, cool, confident image, inspired by jazz great Miles Davis. Celebrities who have recently chosen it for their offspring include Susan Sarandon and Tim Robbins, the Eddie Murphys, and actress Sherilyn Fenn and musician Toulouse Holliday. It was, of course, also the name of the Pilgrim leader Miles Standish and, in a very different realm, is the producer character, Miles Silverberg, on *Murphy Brown*.

MILO. With its German, Greek, and jaunty British input, Milo is, in our opinion, a real winner. Its image combines the strength of the great ancient Greek wrestler of that name—a six-time winner of the Olympic games—with the debonair charm of an RAF pilot.

MILTON. Long before the outrageous antics of Uncle Milty (born Uncle Mendel) invaded videoland, Milton was an upper-class British surname, conjuring up etched impressions of rustic mills and placid streams or the epic poetry of John Milton. Nowadays, Milton is about as far out of step as a name can be, and we don't see it coming back in any of our lifetimes.

MITCHELL. A name that had quite a bit of panache in the forties and fifties, seen then as a sharper alternative to Michael, Mitchell is rarely used for babies today. The nickname MITCH retains some semblance of the old flair and is still used by scriptwriters of shows like *Baywatch* and *General Hospital*.

MOE. This could be the Max of tomorrow, although we haven't seen any signs of it taking off yet. Perhaps it won't as long as *The Three Stooges* are in reruns. It was originally a diminutive of Moses and might still make a cute nickname for that weighty appelation.

MOHAMMED, MUHAMMED, MUHAMMAD. These are only three versions of the over five hundred names for the Arab prophet who founded the Moslem religion. Others include MAHMUD, MEHMET, AHMAD, and HAMMAD. In fact, there is a Muslim saying, "If you have a hundred sons, name them all Muhammed," and as a consequence it is generally considered the most common boys' name in the world. The most famous bearer on this continent is champion fighter Muhammed Ali, who changed his name when he joined the Nation of Islam in 1964, dropping his "slave name" of Cassius Clay. Muhammed Ali's great-great-grandfather was indeed a slave, owned by Cassius Marcellus Clay, the United States ambassador to Russia in the 1860s.

MONTEL. Is this strictly a one-person name or will enough people admire the shiny-domed talk show host to bring it into the mainstream of names? We'd vote for the former—although there were several baby Montels born in Pennsylvania in 1993.

MONTGOMERY. This is not the kind of surname name that is in favor right now, feeling far too fussy and formal.

MORDECAI. Although it has a noble heritage, this name has never caught on in this country and we see virtually no possibility of it ever doing so. It is a symbolic name for boys born on the holiday of Purim, because this cousin of Queen Esther helped her save the Jews from destruction at the hands of Haman.

MORGAN. Now used more for girls than boys, Morgan is an attractive Welsh name that means "born in the sea" and has in the past been used for babies born under water signs—Pisces, Cancer, and Scorpio. Actress Rae Dawn Chong chose it for her son.

MORLEY. A soft pleasant English surname primarily associated in this country with Canadian-born 60-Minuteman Morley Safer.

MORRIS, MAURICE. These names, which have identical pronunciations in England, have very different images in this country, Morris being much more quiet, as comfortable as a Morris chair, while Maurice—Frenchified in the U.S. to Maur-EES—is far more flamboyant. They both spring from the Latin meaning a "moor," and spread as a result of the fame of St. Maurice, a third-century Swiss martyr. The name came to Britain as MEURISSE, which was then Anglicized to Morris. Children at a young age are sure to become familiar with the engaging tales and illustrations of Maurice Sendak, older folks with the ex-astronaut on *Northern Exposure*. Common pet names are MOREY and MAURY and a more contemporary surname variation is MORRISON.

MORTIMER, MORTON. Two English family names used a generation or so ago as Anglicizations of Moses, but lately more famous as posh restaurant names than as baby name possibilities. Mortimer was

Walt Disney's original choice for the name of his Mouse, until his wife talked him out of it.

MOSES. Some people may find this name just too overwhelmingly biblical—conjuring up images of white beards and the sacred Ten Commandments—but we see it as a definite candidate for rejuvenation in the modern world. In the Old Testament, of course, Moses, the brother of Aaron and Miriam, led the Israelites out of Egyptian bondage and into the Promised Land, and brought down God's commandments from Mt. Sinai. In contemporary life, Moses was the name chosen for one of her children by Mia Farrow, and Moses Malone is a basketball superstar. MOSHE is the Hebrew version, MOSS is a secularized English variant, and MOSE is a frequently used nickname.

MUNGO. This is a Scottish name meaning "beloved," which was originally used as a term of endearment, while MONGO means "famous" in Yoruba. And although these names may be widely used in those disparate cultures, we're afraid they might be too close to the word *mongrel* to have much success in this country.

MURRAY. At this point, this venerable Scottish name meaning "sea warrior" has become a Hollywood joke name, as manifested in the name of the dog on *Mad About You*. In the sixties it was associated with New York radio disk jockey Murray the K, self-proclaimed "Fifth Beatle."

MYRON. This name has not retained much of its original essence—Myron means "sweet and fragrant" in Greek. It belonged to the famous ancient Greek sculptor whose best known work is *The Discus Thrower*. The real first name of TV newsman Mike Wallace, it was one of many M names (among them Murray, Marvin, Morton, Milton, Melvin) given to first-generation Jewish immigrants in place of Moses. Today, if you want to honor Grandpa Myron, the best choice might be the original Moses.

N

〰〰〰〰〰〰〰〰〰〰〰〰〰〰 ◉ 〰〰〰〰〰〰〰〰〰〰〰〰〰〰

NATHAN. A rather serious, industrious name, Nathan is an Old Testament option that one wouldn't think of as trendy in the sense that, say, Joshua is trendy, yet in its own quiet way Nathan has been climbing the popularity charts. (Curiously enough, it was number forty-one on the most popular list of 1900 and number forty-one again in 1990.) The real name of comedian George Burns, it has appeared on the daytime drama *The Young and the Restless* (funny, you don't sound like a soap opera name) and has been chosen for their sons by John Lithgow and Mark Hamill. And every school child knows the name, of course, through Nathan Hale, the revolutionary war spy. NAT and NATE are modern, though slightly old-mannish, nicknames.

NATHANIEL. Nathaniel has a slight edge on big brother Nathan in terms of style, though its popularity is rising so rapidly that, much as we essentially like the name, it would not be a great choice for parents in search of a name that will stand apart. In the New Testament, Nathaniel was the apostle who was also called Bartholomew. And no matter what its fashion standing, Nathaniel does have some worthy namesakes: writer Nathaniel Hawthorne, slave rebel NAT Turner and singer Nat "King" Cole. Another singer, Barbara Mandrell, chose it for her son.

NED. This Nancy Drew—era nickname for Edward has been neglected all through the long epoch of EDDIEs, EDs, and TEDs, during which, if Ned existed at all, it was as a kind of nerdy country bumpkin. We would like to put in our vote for the return of Ned, not only as a short form for Edward (which, we know, is usually used in full these days), but also as a nostalgic, clean-cut name on its own.

NEHEMIAH. A bearded, Old Testament/Puritan name that's lain near extinction for a few hundred years but conceivably could (it's a stretch) be revived, à la Jeremiah, in the new wave of interest in biblical names. Nehemiah was a Jewish leader given a mandate to rebuild Jerusalem, which might make it a good name for the child of an architect.

NEIL. Neil is an affable, neutral, safe kind of name that has moved a long distance from its Irish roots, being now more associated with people like Neil Simon and Neil Sedaka than the dauntless NIALL of the Nine Hostages, one of Ireland's most famous kings. Popular, particularly in Scotland, since the Middle Ages, Neil—also frequently spelled NEAL—was a favorite in the United States in the forties, but hasn't been heard from much in the intervening decades, and shows no signs of resuscitation. Parents of Irish descent with any interest in reviving it should consider returning to the original Gaelic spelling, Niall.

NELSON. This name, which literally means Neil's son, is miles away from the father name in image. There is a bit of formality still remaining from associations with Lord Nelson, New York Governor Nelson Rockefeller, and that stiffest of singers, Nelson Eddy. On the other hand it could be a heroic choice for parents who admire South African activist Nelson Mandela.

NEVADA. This is a western place-name that's been lounging at the periphery of the name map for a long time (first Alan Ladd, then Steve McQueen played a character called Nevada Smith in sixties films), yet it still sounds as if it might become prohibitively dated, a name—like fellow trendies Dakota and SIERRA—destined to be permanently tagged to the nineties.

NEVILLE. Most names ending in *ville* fall into the unthinkable class, but this one, perhaps because of more laid-back associations with singer Aaron Neville and The Neville Brothers, has become almost rethinkable.

NEVIN. An Irish Gaelic name that's fresher than Kevin and more familiar than Neville.

NICHOLAS. Nicholas has an unusually genial and robust image for a classic Christian name—could it be because of our collective warm childhood connection to jolly St. Nick? Unfortunately, this feeling has been shared by so many parents of all backgrounds that Nicholas is right up there in the nationwide Top 10 list of boys' names. A Greek name stemming from Nike, the goddess of victory, it is a New Testament name that's been well accepted by many Western cultures over the centuries. And St. Nicholas has a lot more to do than take a sleigh ride through the sky once a year—he is also the patron of schoolchildren, merchants, sailors, scholars, brides, bakers, travelers—and Russia, where the name was a star of the czarist dynasty. NICHOLSON, a surname name recently brought to wider attention by bestselling author Nicholson Baker, may be a fresher, if less classic and friendly alternative, that still gets you to nicknames NICKY and NICK. Nick, like TONY, has long been a favorite of novelists and screenwriters, for rich boys, Romeos, thugs, and detectives (Nick Carter, Nick Charles) in particular. The British form NICOL may remind Americans too much of the female Nicole. The name has had many international variants and offshoots, including NIKOLAS, NIKOLAI, and NIKITA (Russian), NICOLAS (French and Spanish), MIKLOS (Hungary), NIKLAS, NILS, NELS, NIELS, and Klaus (Scandinavia), CLAUS (German), NIC(C)OLO (Italian), NIILO and LASSE (Finnish), plus NICO, Cole, and Colin.

NIGEL. For most Americans, Nigel is just too steeped in tea and crumpets to be considered, but, combined with the right last name, it does have a measure of Sherlock Holmes—era dash that could appeal to devout Anglophiles. Nigel is the given name of *Jurassic Park*'s Sam Neill.

NILES. The perfect name for Frasier's persnickety brother, Niles is mega-miles away from the trendy Miles.

NOAH. Although it hasn't ever quite reached the best-seller lists, this appealing biblical name has achieved official fashion status along with Old Testament companions Nathan and Nathaniel. Parents in search of a truly distinctive O.T. name will have to consider other patriarchs: Moses or Abraham, perhaps? As every Sunday school alumnus knows, Noah was deemed the only righteous man of his time, singled out by God to survive the great flood sent to punish an evil world.

NOAM. This is a modern Jewish name that doesn't have the traditional weight of the above, but could make a distinctive alternate. It comes from a Hebrew word meaning "delight" and was made famous by the noted linguist Noam Chomsky.

NOEL. British, fey, slender, and sophisticated—à la playwright Noel Coward—this is not for you if you're seeking a macho kind of name. On the other hand, it also connotes wit and creativity. It was once reserved for children of both sexes born at Christmastime, but that exclusivity no longer holds.

NOLAN. A spirited Irish surname that actually has been used as a first name since the end of the nineteenth century, but has really only come to the fore since the recent renown of star pitcher Nolan (born Lynn) Ryan and designer Nolan Miller.

NORBERT. Even a hipster in search of a name so clunky it's cool—like Bill Murray's Homer or Jack Nicholson's Raymond—would bypass Norbert . . . or so we hope. The same is true of NORVILLE, whose one claim to fame is being the real name of Oliver Hardy.

NORMAN. Maybe it's because it sounds so much like the word *normal*, but the name Norman has a serious image problem, conjuring up the picture of a normal-looking guy, with a normal kind of job, living in a Norman Rockwell kind of town—unless of course he's Norman Mailer or a twisted Mama's boy like Norman Bates. Either way, probably not the kind of image you would want for your son.

NORRIS. Seen as a contemporary last-name-first name, Norris has a certain offbeat appeal, never having been as well used as Morris and so not saddled with that name's scruffed-up baggage.

O

〰〰〰〰〰〰〰〰〰〰〰〰〰 ◉ 〰〰〰〰〰〰〰〰〰〰〰〰〰

OBADIAH. Only for the audacious, this near-extinct Old Testament name (he was one of the twelve minor prophets) has, like Jedidiah and Zebedy, its own measure of old-fangled charm. Popular from the seventeenth to the nineteenth century, it was used by Anthony Trollope for the character of a hypocritical chaplain, Obadiah Slope, in his novel *Barchester Towers*.

OLAF. Olaf is one of those ethnic names that's become completely familiar without ever being assimilated—the German Hans and the Spanish JOSÉ are other examples—so that a child named Olaf will still be perceived as somehow un-American.

OLIVER. Since the sixties and seventies, when new productions of Dickens's *Oliver Twist* and a general taste for things British brought the name to wide attention, Oliver has been a fashionable favorite. Perhaps the biggest boost for the name came from the hit book and then movie *Love Story*, which also catapulted the name Jennifer to stardom. Since then there have been several high-profile Olivers on the scene, from Oliver North to director Oliver (born William) Stone, adding some yankee bravado to its image. Oliver has been chosen for their children by such celeb parents as Goldie Hawn, Corbin Bernsen and Amanda Pays, and Martin Short—not to mention its long-term connection to nostalgic favorite Oliver Hardy. Where does it stand today? It is still an attractive and stylish name that doesn't quite tip over the edge into trendiness, retaining the flavor of Britain (where it remains among the Top 10 boys' names) without seeming at all twee.

OMAR. An Arabic and Muslim name poised for appeal to a wider audience, Omar's got the perfect mix of exoticism and familiarity, plus that strong, appealing initial O. Deriving from the Arabic meaning "long life," the name has been tied for centuries to the Persian mathematician and poet Omar Khayyám (author of the *Rubáiyát*: "A loaf of bread, a jug of wine, and thou"), and later to General Omar Bradley and actor Omar Sharif (who was born Michael).

OREN. This Hebrew nature name—it symbolizes the pine tree—is quite popular in Israel, and has become familiar to some Americans via Senator ORRIN Hatch. ORIN is an alternate spelling.

ORLANDO. An ornate Italianate twist on the name Roland, Orlando has an impressive literary resumé, including Shakespeare's *As You Like It* and Virginia Woolf's enigmatic eponymous novel. We like Orlando's bookended *os* and exotic feel, and recommend it to the intrepid baby namer. A current champion athlete bearing the name is Orlando Woolridge, one of basketball's star power forwards; another is baseball player Orlando Cepeda.

ORSON. For a long time (and despite the fleeting fame of Orson Bean), Orson was considered a quintessential one-person name. A Norman French nickname meaning "bear cub," it seemed a perfect fit for the onetime boy wonder Welles (who early on dropped his more ordinary given name of George in favor of his more distinctive middle one) as he grew more bearlike with time. But now the creator of *Citizen Kane* is gone and Orson is back in the public domain, available to any parent looking for a distinctive yet solid name.

ORVILLE. We consider this a middle-name-only choice that should be confined to the babies of parents either deeply interested in aviation, or heavily addicted to popcorn.

OSBERT. Names that begin with the Anglo-Saxon *Os-* may have been a minor rage a hundred years ago, but they rate less than zero today. Poor Osbert suffers from the double whammy of the soft *Os*-beginning and the wimpy *-bert* ending. OSMOND relates to aging teens Donny and Marie and OSWALD (despite Oswald the Lucky Rabbit, Walt Disney's first successful cartoon character), is one of the biggest joke names of our time. OSGOOD has some offbeat surname name charm, but only OSBORNE—or OSBORN or OSBOURNE—has any real class or style or masculine punch, perhaps because rock star Ozzy Osbourne has lent it some modern pizzazz. Nickname OZZY or OSSIE or OZZIE (as in *Ozzie and Harriet*; his real name was Oswald) is infinitely livelier than any of the more formal versions.

OSCAR. Round and jovial and cuddly, Oscar is a real grandpa name, which, with the newfound fashionability of others like Max and Harry and Gus, finds itself sticking a toe into the limelight again. True, most parents will still consider it far too fuddy-duddy for a baby, but some style-conscious souls who know that Max isn't Max anymore may opt for this alternative. Popular with Latino families, Oscar is in the 1993 Top 25 list for Hispanics in California. Famous Oscars include Wilde (whose given name was the Irish Fingal), Schindler, Madison, Hammerstein, de la Renta, the Academy Award, and The Grouch.

OTIS. Otis has had something of a split-screen image over the years. On the one hand it's been associated with the seductive, bluesy tones of Otis Redding (coincidentally, its Greek meaning implies someone with a good ear for music), on the other with the upscale activities of such society figures as Otis Chandler, publisher of the *Los Angeles Times*. The two images seem to be merging now as Otis becomes more and more upwardly mobile and fashionable, with parents attracted to its catchy *O* initial and combination of strength and spunk. A contemporary athlete who heaps further honors on the name is the spectacular Otis Anderson, New York Giant MVP of 1991.

OTTO. Truly cutting edge parents may consider the old German name Otto outlandish enough to be cool. Our advice: Unless you're a rock star, a major movie star, or a billionaire (it does mean prosperous), let Otto lie. Trivia tidbit: How many people remember (or care) that Don Rickles's first name on the old *CPO Sharkey* series was Otto?

OWEN. Owen is the wonderfully resonant Celtic name that is picking up where the over-fashionable Ian left off. Kevin Kline and Phoebe Cates have a little Owen; so does Christopher Reeve; and so, truth be told, does one of us. Owen (or EOGHAN or EOIN in its impossible Irish Gaelic spellings; Owen is the phonetic Welsh version) was an ancient and legendary Irish saint who was kidnapped and sold into slavery, but released after the slave master found him reading while an angel did his chores. Smart boy. Through the years, Owens have appeared in Shakespeare's plays (*Henry IV*, *Part 1*), Irish plays (*Deirdre of the Sorrows*), and on TV (*Owen Marshall, Counselor at Law*).

P

PALMER and **PARKER.** Two Waspy surname names that would tend to put an instant upper-class gloss on a boy, and have a certain snob appeal. Palmer Cortlandt is a character on *All My Children*, Parker Stevenson is the onetime Hardy Boy who grew up and married Kirstie Alley.

PATRICK. Patrick has never quite transcended its hyper-Irish image in the United States, not having achieved the mainstream acceptability and style cachet here that it has in, ironically, England, where Patrick is one of the most fashionable names for young gentlemen. One problem with Patrick's American image may be our tendency to abbreviate names: Where the formal Patrick seems masculine and distinguished, the almost-inevitable PAT feels weak and unattractively androgynous (especially if you've watched *Saturday Night Live* in the past couple of years). And the tendency is to lump Patrick with those Irish-y names— Colleen, say, or Sheila—mildly popular in the forties and fifties but now faded, although some oomph was injected into the name by Dirty Dancer Patrick Swayze and basketball superstar Patrick Ewing. Parents who are drawn to Patrick's strongly nationalistic Irish flavor may want to look beyond the name's usual American form to its native versions, most notably PADRAIG (pronounced Parrig and used for his son by Patrick Ewing) and PADRAIC (somewhat confusingly pronounced Parrick). There are, in fact, a few dozen Irish variations of Patrick, among the most usable of which are PATRIC, PAXTON, and FITZ-PATRICK.

PAUL. To the thousands of girls who screamed the name of their favorite Beatle in the sixties, Paul had a thrillingly unique image, but to the rest of the world, then and now, it's a name that's so simple and yet so widely diffuse that it could belong to almost anyone. One of the traditional masculine names, Paul has been out of favor for so long, that it's starting to sound fresher than, say, John or William to the most recent generation of parents, who are beginning to reappraise its classic strength. It also has a rich religious background: St. Paul (originally named Saul but who, after seeing a vision, converted from Judaism and was baptized Paul) was a cofounder with Peter of the Christian church, and there have been six popes with the name. There are scores of famous Pauls whose individual personas have colorized the name: from Paul Bunyan to Paul Revere, from Paul Newman to painters Cézanne and Gauguin. Two creative foreign variations: PABLO, the lively Spanish version and PAOLO, the sensual Italian one.

PERCY. Percy is one of those unfortunate names that's been consumed by a negative image: Despite the poet Lord Shelley's dashing image, Percy is, with the possible exception of singer Percy Sledge, a wimp. Its more formal version, PERCIVAL, coined by a twelfth-century poet for King Arthur's most perfectly pure and innocent knight, is similarly damned.

PEREGRINE. Most people will skip right by this entry, and we really wouldn't blame them. But if there is anyone out there looking for an outrageously eccentric British name to set a child apart from all others, this one's for you. In England it is a name heard at hunting parties (a peregrine is, after all, a kind of falcon that can be trained to hunt birds) and borne by trainees at Sotheby's, and it has literary and historical points as well: Peregrine was the name of the first child of British parents born on the *Mayflower*; it was the name of Smollett's swashbuckling scoundrel, Peregrine Pickle; and PEREGRIN was a lively Hobbit in *The Lord of the Rings*.

PERRY. Perry, which came into being as a pet form of Peregrine, has recently acquired a measure of style and charm for girls, but for boys it's a pipe-smoking, cardigan-sweatered remnant of the Perry

Como-Perry Mason-Perry White era that we don't expect to see getting up out of its easy chair.

PETER. For generations, there have been pleasant childhood associations with this name—what with Peter Rabbit; Peter Piper; Peter, Peter, Pumpkin Eater; and, especially, Peter Pan. But as user-friendly as this makes the name, it has a solid, traditional side as well. One of the most important figures in the Christian hagiography is St. Peter, keeper of the Gates of Heaven. Born Simon bar Jonah, he was given the nickname Peter (which means rock) by Jesus, to signify that he would be the rock on which Christ would build Christianity. Centuries later, there was Peter the Great, the czar who developed Russia as a major European power. Never as widely used as some of the more traditional Anglo-Saxon stalwarts, Peter has an enduring appeal to parents seeking a name that is outside questions of style and trendiness, familiar but not faddish. Peter also has some interesting derivatives: The Brits like PIERS and (more American-sounding) PIERCE (as in Irish-born actor Pierce Brosnan), both of which were introduced to England by the Normans. Other versions around the world include PEARSE (Irish), PIETRO (Italian), PIET (Dutch), PEDRO (Spanish), and FERRIS (Celtic).

PHILIP, PHILLIP. Philip has a certain built-in reserve, as straight and staid as the public image of the Duke of Edinburgh, qualities that gained a measure of favor during the upwardly mobile eighties. St. Philip was one of the twelve Apostles, King Philip the Great was the father of Alexander the Great, and there have been numerous other French and Spanish rulers bearing the name. Nicknames include PHIL (as in Donahue), FLIP (as in Wilson, who was actually born CLEROW), and PIP (as in the Dickens's *Great Expectations* character).

PHILO. A dynamic and distinctive Greek name (it means "friendly"), Philo has been used in literature—as a minor character in Shakespeare's *Antony and Cleopatra*, and the S. S. Van Dine detective, Philo Vance, but rarely in real life. Possible drawbacks: 1) People might think it was an abbreviation for Filofax and 2) It could sound like a dog's name.

PHINEAS. Only an adventurous parent with a sense of humor would dare choose this Old Testament name for his or her child. It is associated with Phineas Barnum, who started the Greatest Show on Earth and called himself (wonder why?) P. T., and was also the name of the hero of Trollope's novel about a young Irish lawyer, *Phineas Finn*. FINN, or more appropriately PHIN, makes a very good nickname. The guy who went around the world in eighty days was actually PHILEAS Fogg.

PRESTON. This surname that's been used as a first name for over a century was invested with appeal by the great screwball comedy director, Preston Sturges. Other surname names that begin with *P* and have been used for boys over the past decade or two include PEYTON (which sounds a tad feminine, achieving recent notoriety as the name of the evil nanny in *The Hand That Rocks the Cradle*), PORTER (originally an occupational name—it means gatekeeper—that now sounds eminently upscale, though its most famous bearer is country singer and former Dolly Parton–stage pardner Porter Wagoner), POWELL (a Paul offshoot currently appearing in the soap *One Life to Live*), PRENTISS, PRENTICE, and PRESCOTT. PHELAN is an Irish family name that's attractive as a first name.

PRIMO. Among the Latin birth order names—OCTAVIUS, for instance, and DECIMA—Primo, which means "first," is the one most likely to be used in these days of smaller families. Primo's jaunty *o* ending and Italianate flavor are appealing, though some may see its image as obnoxiously egotistical: You can easily imagine Primo as the name of a character played by Sylvester Stallone. Author Primo Levi is a famous bearer.

Q

QUENTIN. An offbeat name with a lot of character, Quentin, also spelled QUINTIN, QUINTON, and QUINTEN, relates to the Latin for the number five, and was at one time reserved for the fifth child born into a family. In any version, it is one of the rare boys' names that manages to be masculine as well as stylish and distinctive. Sir Walter Scott wrote the novel *Quentin Durward* in 1823, about a young upper-class Scotsman; Quentin Tarantino is a hot young Hollywood director (*Reservoir Dogs*, *Pulp Fiction*); one of the kids in the sitcom *Grace Under Fire* is called Quentin; and Burt Reynolds and Loni Anderson named their son Quinton, no doubt after the character Reynolds played in *Gunsmoke* in 1962—QUINT Asper. Trivia tidbit: Quinton was McHale's first name in *McHale's Navy*.

QUINCY. *Q* names are quirky, and Quincy is quirky veering toward wimpy, in spite of the fact that the talented and attractive musician Quincy Jones has done a good deal to counter that stereotype. Just bear in mind, if you are considering this name for your son, that it will take a powerful personality to counter its intrinsically limp image.

QUINN. Quinn, which means "wise" in Celtic, is an engaging Irish surname that has some history as a unisex first name. Writers Anna Quindlen and Sally Quinn both chose it, for obvious reasons, for their sons; Quinn Cummings was a child actress of the seventies. QUINLAN is another Irish surname with possibilities as a first.

R

RALPH. Ralph is one of the few names on which the two of us adamantly disagree, probably because it can be looked at in two diametrically different ways. At its most positive, Ralph is an upper-crust British favorite—think of actors Sir Ralph Richardson and Ralph Fiennes—sometimes pronounced as RAFE, and charmingly quirky when imported with that pronunciation to our shores. On the other hand Ralph is also (and to most Americans) Jackie Gleason's Kramden, the eternal blue-collar bus driver, bowler, and blowhard. Love it or hate it, Ralph is a name that's been around for a thousand years, was a favorite baby name in 1900, and could make a comeback somewhere down the line. Latin forms are RAOUL or RAUL, as in Raul Julia;

ROLF, ROLPH, or ROLFE (actually the Scandinavian form of Rudolph) may also be used.

RANDOLPH. Randolph is a name that had its last hurrah along with black-and-white westerns starring Randolph Scott. Nickname RANDY, which offered some aw-shucks appeal to baby namers of yesterday, including those of country singer Randy Travis, has gone the way of the parent name. The medieval form RANDALL has the slightly more stylish ring of a surname name.

RAPHAEL, RAFAEL. An excellent cross-cultural possibility, Raphael is a Hebrew name that is also well used in Latin countries. Raphael was one of the seven archangels who attended the throne of God and, as the angel of healing, is the patron of doctors (as well as of travelers, science, and knowledge). Another worthy namesake is the great Renaissance painter Raphael—and kids will love the fact that it's the name of one of the Teenage Mutant Ninja Turtles. RAFI is the popular nickname; RAFE is sometimes used as well.

RAYMOND. Another split decision here. To one of us, Raymond is the coolest of the cool, among the brightest stars in name style heaven, an opinion undoubtedly shared by Jack Nicholson, who recently used it for his young son. To the other, Raymond is as dull and dismal a prospect for a baby name as a name could possibly be, stuck back in the age group of Raymonds Chandler and Carver, Burr and Massey. The nickname RAY has long been a Southern ambigender middle-name favorite (Billy Ray Cyrus upholds this tradition, and Billy Joel and Christie Brinkley named their little girl Alexa Ray, after Ray Charles). St. Raymond is the patron saint of lawyers, and a memorable fictional Raymond/Ray of recent vintage is the autistic Dustin Hoffman character in *Rain Man*. Other Raymond relatives you might find more palatable: the sultry Latin RAMON and the Irish surname name REDMOND, used by Ryan O'Neal and Farrah Fawcett for their son.

REED. A slim, elegant, silvery surname name, Reed combines a brisk masculinity with an artistic air: A Reed might be an executive in the family firm, or an equally successful painter. Originally meaning red-haired, REID is a perfectly acceptable but somewhat less direct spelling, while READ may be too ambiguous.

REGINALD. Reginald sounds like the name of the chap in the smoking jacket in a thirties English comedy, though REGGIE manages a more modern, macho image thanks to sports greats Reggie Jackson and Reggie White. Several show biz personalities wisely dropped their given name of Reginald in favor of Rex (Harrison), Ray (Milland), and Elton (John). REYNOLD or REYNOLDS, medieval variations on Reginald, might be slightly better choices today.

REGIS. A venerable old saint's name meaning regal, Regis might have gone down in history as the name of a New York hotel, or one found on alumni lists of long-gone Catholic school students had it not been for the TV partner of Kathie Lee. Together ("Aw, Reeeege . . ."), they've almost made it sound cute.

REO, RIO, RENO. Three seductive ranchero place-names with an attractive Tex-Mex lilt. Rio was Marlon Brando's name as a young desperado in the 1961 *One-Eyed Jacks*; Rio Domecq is a character on the soap opera *Loving*.

REMINGTON, REMY. Even though Remington Steele was a made-up detective's name on that TV series, it soon became adopted by the suave and debonair Pierce Brosnan, who took on the identity of Steele. Since the eighties, then, the name has been in the public consciousness, sounding like the ultimate corporate title. Actress Tracy Nelson turned Remington around by giving it to her little girl. REMY (also spelled REMI) is a relaxed Gallic offshoot of REMUS (permanently terminated by the image of Uncle Remus), sometimes associated with the Cajun cadences of New Orleans (as in Dennis Quaid's character in *The Big Easy*).

REUBEN. One trend watcher we know (who gave her daughter an offbeat place-name more than twenty years ago) picks Reuben as one of the coolest names of the future—maybe even for girls as well as boys. And it does have all the ingredients for success: an Old Testament pedigree—Reuben was Jacob's only son by Leah and the founder of one of the tribes of Israel—plus the distinction of not ever having been heavily used and boasting a friendly, down-home image (anybody remember manager Reuben Kincaid on *The Partridge Family*?). So it's not hard to envision the current crowd of Jacobs growing up and following the lead of the biblical Jacob by naming their own sons Reuben. Panama-born salsa singer RUBEN Blades uses the Latin spelling.

REX. Rex Harrison prompted the epithet "Sexy Rexy," which has managed to stick to the name like Super Glue, and in a cartoony, glossy-haired, smooth-skinned way. (It does in fact belong to a cartoon character, Rex Morgan, M.D, who's been practicing since 1948, as well as to the soap opera star Rex Sterling on *The Young and the Restless*.) That said, there still is the charm of Rex's final *x* and an offbeat simplicity that you might find more than make up for its slickness.

RHYS. A common Welsh name, which means "hero" in Celtic, Rhys is sometimes Anglicized with the phonetic spellings REESE and REECE. It's been given a feminine twist these days via young actress Reese Witherspoon.

RICHARD. A classic male name popular for a thousand years and favored for kings (Richard Nixon was named after Richard the Lion Hearted) as well as the hoi polloi (every Tom, Dick, and Harry), Richard was at its peak in popularity here in the forties and fifties and has been considered unfashionable of late. But a new wave of favoritism for the name in Britain may inspire a revival on our shores. We predict that if parents do readopt the name Richard, it will be in its full and formal version—as reflected in most of the recent most high-profile bearers: Richards Burton, Gere, Chamberlain, Little Richard, *The Fugitive*'s Richard Kimble. The nicknames DICK and DICKY are too tricky and too subject to punning, RICKY too *I Love Lucy*, RICHIE too pre-1963 suburban baby boom. The Latin RICARDO may offer a more colorful variation. Trivia tidbit: *Poor Richard's Almanack* was published under Benjamin Franklin's pseudonym, Richard Saunders.

RILEY, REILLY. One of the jauntiest and least pretentious of the Irish surname names, Riley has been used as a first for more than a century. Appropriate for children of both sexes, Riley is the name of Howie Mandel's daughter; it is also the given name of blues singer B. B. King.

ROBERT. This classic has been among the American male Top 25 for an entire century, but today, Robert's rating has slipped to twenty-fourth place, still respectable but a significant drop when you consider that the name was number one in both 1925 and 1950. Back then, Robert was top dog because it had style as well as history. Today, history offers most of the name's appeal: A good percentage of baby Roberts these days are juniors or thirds. Numerous inspirational name-sakes include Kennedy, DeNiro, and E. Lee. Parents in search of a distinctive twist on the name might consider using the surnames ROBINSON or ROBERTSON, which mean "son of Robert," or the German form RUPERT. Nicknames BOB and BOBBY are stuck in the fifties; ROB and ROBBY or ROBBIE have an ever-so-slightly more modern appeal; ROBIN is another option. Perhaps it's time to go back and dig up some of Robert's old-time long-forgotten nicknames: DOB, HOB, and NOB.

ROBIN. Still as well used for boys in England today as it was from the time of legendary outlaw Robin Hood to childhood favorite Christopher Robin, this name is almost exclusively female in America. Even the popularity of actor Robin Williams has not been enough to inspire a generation of little boy Robins here.

ROCCO. Rocco seems like one those quintessential immigrant names that no modern parent long off the boat would consider using, but it embodies the quirky appeal of some other so-far-out-they're-in names—like BRUNO and Hugo and Homer.

ROCK, STONE, BRICK. The Rocks and Rockys—Hudson and Balboa, of course—have long since sunk as naming inspirations (if they ever were), but for parents who favor this sort of tough elemental name we offer two tough elemental substitutes: STONE and BRICK. Of course these are not really recognized as names, quite yet. But one recent TV character—macho, brooding—was named Brick, as was the hero of Tennessee William's *Cat on a Hot Tin Roof*, and Stone Phillips has gained recognition as a TV newsman.

RODERICK. A rather haughty, highfallutin name that has lots of literary allusions (including the novels *Roderick Random* by Smollett and *Roderick Hudson* by Henry James), but very little history of real-life usage in this country. ROD is the hyper-macho nickname; RODDY (as in actor McDowell, born Roderick) the boyish one. RODERIC is an alternate spelling, but the only way to squeeze any real pizzazz from this name is by using the Irish version, Rory.

RODNEY. A British place-name that was once considered the height of elegance and refinement by some parents—but then again, so was Seymour. For a long time it was associated with Rodney Dangerfield (born Jacob), and, in more recent headlines, Rodney King. ROD Steiger was a Rodney, Rod Stewart a Roderick.

ROGER. In the World War II period, Roger had nothing but the most positive associations, actually used by military personnel to mean A-OK, very definitely OK; and before that there was the Jolly Roger (which wasn't so jolly—it was a pirate's black flag with skull and crossbones). But despite several distinguished bearers—Rogers Maris, Moore, Daltry, Ebert, and Rabbit—the name is totally out to pasture for babies of this generation. And the spelling RODGER is even stodgier.

ROLAND. Roland is a chivalrous-sounding name made famous by the supposedly eight-foot-tall romantic hero and nephew of Charlemagne, celebrated in medieval poetry and song. After a long nap, it's one of the names that could, in time, sound possible again, as itself or, even better, in its Italian form, ORLANDO, or perhaps in its genial *o*-ending version, ROLLO (very fashionable in Britain right now). ROLLIN is another variant; baseball fans may like the association to the great relief pitcher ROLLIE (born Roland) Fingers.

ROMEO. How would you like to have people asking you where Juliet was for the rest of your life?

RONALD. As popular as President Reagan was in his day, he did nothing for the style status of the name Ronald, a mid-century favorite (it was number eight in 1940, number eleven in 1950) that's a dud today, made even more dated by nicknames RON and RONNIE. First used extensively in Scotland, Ronald is a traditional favorite of the McDonald clan, making the name of the Golden Arches spokesman all the more appropriate. The only variation on Ronald that offers any modern alternative: the surname REYNOLD or REYNOLDS, from which Ronald originated.

ROONEY, ROONE. Rooney is one of many attractive Irish surname names, but we think it's Roone (as in TV exec Roone Arledge) that's the possible winner—lively, distinctive, and strong—if you can get past its similarity to the word ruin.

RORY. This spirited Gaelic classic—that became popular in England via the illustrious twelfth-century King Rory O'Connor and legendary chieftain Rory O'More—is still fashionable in Britain today, as well as being a traditional boys' name in both Ireland and Scotland. In this country it is equally appealing as a girls' name—it was used for Robert Kennedy's youngest daughter. In Ireland the name has been associated with several surnames in particular (including McCann, McDonnell, McKinley, McGinley, Mulloy, O'Doherty, and O'Donnell), so if you happen to share one of those, Rory would be particularly apt. But stick with the Anglo spelling—in Gaelic it's the totally baffling RUAIDRI.

ROSS. A once-quiet, understated elegant name—Jane Pauley and Garry Trudeau chose it for their twin son a few years ago—that moved into an entirely different sphere when maverick tycoon H. (for Henry) Ross Perot ran for president. So even though it's had a conventional history as the surname (meaning "red,") of a famous Scottish clan, how you feel about the name Ross these days depends on how you'd feel about people assuming you'd named your baby after Perot. One of its other most famous bearers, mystery writer Ross Macdonald, was born Kenneth. ROSCOE is a variant form that is definitely in the so-far-out-it-almost-feels-redeemable category.

ROY. Roy is a down-to-earth, denim kind of name that's been consigned a country/cowboy image by such figures as Roy Rogers (born Leonard), Roy Acuff, and Roy Clark. Another in the list of *R* names related to the word *red* (the famous Rob Roy, for example, was a Robert nicknamed Roy because of his red hair), as well as to the French for "king," Roy hasn't been seen as a baby name for several generations, and isn't very likely to make a speedy return.

RUDOLPH, RUDOLF. Rudolphs have done lots of distinguished things: helped guide Santa's sleigh on a foggy Christmas Eve, portrayed the Sheik of Araby on the silent screen, been one of the greatest male ballet dancers of the twentieth century, and have even become mayor of New York City, but we don't consider this stiff, Germanic name (it was a favorite of the Austrian nobility) a very good bet as a baby name. And as for RUDY, it's hardly been heard of since the days of crooner Rudy Vallee (born Hubert). When the youngest Cosby daughter was called Rudy, it robbed the name of whatever masculine punch it had.

RUFUS. A rumpled redheaded name more suited to a pet than a person.

RUPERT. Publishing mogul Rupert Murdoch has helped keep this originally German (though now seen as quintessentially British) form of Robert alive and active. Though some may feel the name Rupert is too closely tied to Britain's classic cartoon bear, most Americans won't make that connection.

RUSSELL. Many of these *R* boys' names began as nicknames for redheads, and Russell is a prime example. It had some popularity in the first quarter of this century—one of the earliest heartthrob crooners was RUSS Columbo—but now sounds like one of the palest of the

many surnames available. *Make Room for Daddy*—period nickname
RUSTY is definitely just that.

RYAN. The energetic Ryan is among the Top 10 boys' names these
days and has been getting more and more popular every year, which
is kind of surprising since it's been around since Ryan (born Patrick)
O'Neal brought it to light in the mid-sixties. One explanation: Parents
like the Irish surname aspect of Ryan. Or they see it as a fresher take
on the now-enervated Brian. As long as you're prepared to face a posse
of other little Ryans, there's nothing wrong with using the name for
your child. But parents who want something more distinctive might
consider one of the many other attractive Irish first names or surname
names, from Conor to Cormac to Kieran to Rory, from Brady to
Sullivan to Quinn. Ryan O'Neal himself has one son named Griffin,
another called Redmond.

S

〜〜〜〜〜〜〜〜〜〜〜〜〜 ◉ 〜〜〜〜〜〜〜〜〜〜〜〜〜

SAMUEL, SAM. Not so long ago, Samuel was, like Jake and Max,
a cigar-chomping movie mogul name totally unthinkable as a possibility for an innocent, apple-cheeked baby boy, and Uncle Sam was
the white-bearded father of our country. Then some adventurous parents started to recognize the earthy attributes of these names, and
before you could say Samuel F. B. Morse, Samuel and Sam were
among the most stylish names around, as laid-back and enigmatic as
Sam Shepard, as up-front and funny as Sam Malone, as upstanding
and righteous as Sam McCloud. These days, Sam has lost a good deal
of its style edge, at least among trendsetters—though one Midwestern
friend of ours reports that it's still considered avant garde in Wiscon-
sin. In New York or L.A., however, Abraham or Moses would be
fresher choices; another is SAMSON, the superhumanly strong biblical figure betrayed by Delilah—the stuff of Cinemascope classics.
Among the celebrities who have been captivated enough by the candid

qualities of Sam to choose it for their sons are William Hurt, Bruce Boxleitner, Michael J. Fox and Tracy Pollan, and Sally Field.

SASHA, SACHA . This Russian pet form of Alexander and Alexandra is beginning to be used more and more on its own, for both sexes, chosen for its energy and ethnic flair.

SAUL. Jewish parents in particular may be attracted to this name of the first king of Israel, for its symbolic power above any questions of fashion or trendiness. A name that is both quiet and composed, Saul was also what St. Paul was called before his conversion, and is associated today with novelist Saul Bellow. A more unlikely association: Saul is the given name of the Guns N' Roses guitarist known as Slash.

SAWYER. A less usual surname name, Sawyer contributes a relaxed down-home feel to this upwardly mobile group. Steven Spielberg and Kate Capshaw have a son named Sawyer. Somewhat more formal is the Dutch SCHUYLER, which means "scholar" and boasts the winning nickname, SKY.

SCOTT. In 1965, Scott was the hippest name on the beach—the muscular, windswept surfer-lifeguard attracting all the girls. Even earlier it had an attractive image, attached as it was to the handsome, doomed writer F. (for Francis) Scott Fitzgerald; and then it seemed like the perfect astronaut name, as in Scott Carpenter. It originated, not surprisingly, as a surname for someone of Scottish descent but, although license plate frames still read, BEAM ME UP SCOTTY, the name is definitely on the wane.

SEAMUS. The Irish form of James, Seamus (pronounced shay-mus) once symbolized a fresh-off-the-boat Irish greenhorn, and later (at a time when most cops were Irish), spelled phonetically as *shamus*, became the generic term for a detective. But as such stereotypical racial epithets fade away, the perfectly fine names behind them— from Seamus to Jake to Jemima—come to light and back into use. Mia Farrow and Woody Allen's son Satchel is now being called Seamus, and it's also Peter O'Toole's middle name. Seamus Heaney is a noted Irish poet.

SEAN. This Irish form of John, always common in the Emerald Isle, has been au courant here for twenty-five years now, helped along by the popularity of Sean Connery and also, in the seventies, of Shaun Cassidy, and for some even the high-profile personality of Sean Penn. Several celebrities have chosen it for their sons, including Rod and Alana Hamilton Stewart, Tatum O'Neal and John McEnroe, Michael Keaton, and Jane Seymour. Alternate forms SHAUN and SHAWN are almost as widely used, though those spellings are seen more frequently for girls, and SHANE ambled along, in the movie of the same name, to put a cowboy twist on the name. (Shane actually goes back further than that—there was an Elizabethan-era Irish prince, Shane the Proud, who was the head of the O'Neill clan.) Today, however, it would take more than a spelling change to revive the tiring Sean, and less exposed Irish names—SHEA, SHAW, SHERIDAN, or Seamus, to name just a few—would make fresher alternatives.

SEBASTIAN. Parents considering this name often dismiss it as being just too flamboyant and ornate, and, indeed, it is a lot more dramatic than other British-inflected choices, such as Derek or Trevor or Oliver. But Sebastian is also a name with a substantial history, first as the third-century martyr whose sufferings were a favorite subject of medieval artists, then as the name of colorful characters in such varied works as *Twelfth Night* and *Brideshead Revisited*. Meaning "majestic" in Greek, it is associated with British Olympic runner Sebastian Coe, and was chosen for his son by actor James Spader. And although it may seem like a name with no possible nickname (a plus for some parents), in England SEB and SEBBIE are used.

SETH. Everyone thinks of the first family as Adam, Eve, Cain, and Abel, but few remember the third, postfratricide, child, Seth. (As a consequence, this gentle, muted name was often used by the Puritans for children born after an older sibling's death.) It was widely used in the American old West, as reflected in such vintage TV oaters as *Wagon*

Train, whose hero was Major Seth Adams. And what name was chosen for the awkward, shy scientist in *The Fly*? You guessed it.

SEYMOUR. Seymour is out playing shuffleboard by the pool at his condo in Boca Raton and won't be available for several generations.

SHANE. See Sean.

SHAQUILLE. With such a charismatic bearer as this name has, it's hard to believe it won't be picked up by many other new parents. And indeed, there were seventy Shaquilles born in 1993 in the state of Pennsylvania alone; 78 in California. We hope they all have as perfect a last name to go with it as O'Neal.

SHELDON. In a class with Melvin and Marvin, Sheldon is about as far outside the realm of possibility as a baby name as a name can get, even though there are very pretty towns in Devon and Derbyshire that inspired the name. SHELBY is a possible variation (country singer Reba McEntire used it for her son), but is used far more often for girls. Director Spike Lee's given name is SHELTON.

SHERMAN. Not quite as over-the-hill as Herman, but not far behind either.

SIDNEY. With Sydney rapidly growing in popularity as a name for girls, the boys' version has lost virtually all the testosterone it ever had. A contraction name (it comes from St. Denis and is related to DIONYSIUS, the Greek god of fertility and wine), Sidney is an aristocratic British surname (e.g., the Elizabethan poet, Sir Philip Sidney), and attained a considerable measure of dignity through its association with the self-sacrificing hero of *A Tale of Two Cities*, Sydney Carton, and with Oscar-winning actor Sidney Poitier.

SILAS. Until recently a folksy-sounding, farmerish, old fogyish name, killed off for many of us by having read *Silas Marner* when we were too young to appreciate it, Silas just might be up for reevaluation in this era of *Middlemarch*-fervor. Like the similar-flavored Caleb and

Abner, it has a funky feel appealing to parents who long to return to the soil. In the New Testament, St. Silus [sic] was one of St. Paul's companions.

SIMON. There is an appealing genuineness about this name, perhaps due to phrases like "simon-pure" and "Simple Simon." An Old and New Testament name (Simon was the second son of Jacob and Leah and the original name of St. Peter) that gained an English accent around the time Roger Moore was playing Simon Templar on *The Saint* then became part of the British invasion of names that hit our shores along with the Beatles and Mary Quant. Simon never reached saturation point here and can still make a stylish and interesting choice. We also like the original form of the name, **SIMEON**, although we must point out (before someone else does) its similarity to the word meaning *apelike*.

SINCLAIR. Sinclair might be just another of the scores of surname names clamoring to be heard today were it not for its connection to the writer Sinclair (born Harry) Lewis. A contraction of the Normandy place-name, St. Clair, Sinclair might be a novel way to honor an ancestral Clare or Claire in a boy's name.

SKY. One of the few seventies flower-power names that has managed to survive (for both sexes), perhaps because it was legitimized on the Broadway stage in the *Guys and Dolls* character, Sky Masterson.

SLOAN, SLOANE. Scarcely betraying its Irish roots, Sloan has the sound of a very upscale surname name, calling to mind Britain's socially conscious Sloane Rangers, so dubbed because they typically live near London's fashionable Sloane Square. (Princess Di, at one time, was the ultimate Sloane.) But those who aspire to Sloanedom should know that naming a child Sloan/Sloane is a very un-Sloane thing to do: Real Sloane boys, according to *The Sloane Ranger Handbook*, are given "plain English names" like Henry, Charles, Mark, Peter, Simon, Christopher, Richard, and William.

SOLOMON. A wise old name that, along with other patriarchal classics, is finally beginning to shed its long white beard and step from the pages of the Old Testament into modern nurseries. From the Hebrew shalom, meaning "peace," it was a favorite of Dickens, who used it for characters in three of his novels. The Arabic version is SELIM.

SPENCER. One of those names that have everything, Spencer is both distinguished sounding and perfectly accessible, dignified but friendly. It took on a noble air as Winston Churchill's widely known middle name, then was made more human and genial by Spencer Tracy. Robert Urich was the single-named private eye in the eighties series *Spenser: for Hire* and it's a name that pops up from time to time on soap operas.

STANLEY. Stanley is typical of the aristocratic English surnames (as in explorer Sir Henry Stanley, deliverer of the famous greeting, "Dr. Livingston, I presume?"), taken over by immigrant parents in the early years of this century, in an attempt to give their first generation sons an instant Anglo gloss. Although *A Streetcar Named Desire*'s Stanley Kowalski personifies brute force, most Stanleys have been portrayed as mild and meek, and the name, along with confreres Seymour and Sheldon, is in retirement. Stanley is the given name of rapper M. C. Hammer.

STEPHEN, STEVEN. Sometimes a name's likability is tied to its nickname, which may account for the fact that Stephen/STEVE has a more modern feel than, say, Richard/DICK or Robert/BOB. Already common in ancient Greece (it means "crown" or "wreath" in Greek), Stephen was the name of the first Christian martyr, one of the seven men chosen to help the Apostles spread the Gospel of Christianity, and a British king. In this country, it was in the Top 25 from the forties until just a couple of years ago, yet although its glory days as a fashionable name may be over for now, Stephen (especially in this older spelling, as opposed to the nouveau Steven) remains a name with a good measure of strength and dignity and appeal. There have been innumerable pop culture role models among its bearers—from Stephen Sondheim and Stephen King to Steven Spielberg and Steven Bochco to Steve Garvey and Steve Martin to Steve McQueen and Steve Allen to Steve Canyon and Steve Jobs to STEVIE (born STEVELAND) Wonder and Stevie Ray Vaughan.

STERLING. A surname name whose image had been fading since the fifties fame of actor Sterling Hayden and British racing driver Stirling Moss, only to be polished up again by hot young Green Bay Packer Sterling Sharpe. Certainly a shiny choice, though—like Crystal and Tiffany and other aggressively upscale names—Sterling could be one headed for a downmarket slide.

ST. JOHN. The only American St. John we know finally became so frustrated in trying to explain the pronunciation of his name that he simply changed it to the phonetic spelling, SINJIN. A British literary name (there's one in *Jane Eyre*), we think this would probably be too cumbersome for most American kids.

STUART, STEWART. An ancient surname tied to the royal family of Scotland, it had, in both spellings, a brief vogue in this country in the forties and fifties. Last heard from as the tax attorney character Stuart Markowitz in *L.A. Law*, Stuart is not quite as mired in that old-fashioned, upwardly striving, Britishy group as the terminally dated Stanley, Seymour, and Sheldon, but neither is it what anyone would consider a fresh choice for a baby boy.

SULLIVAN. A jaunty Irish last name as first, immortalized in the thirties movie, *Sullivan's Travels*. An equally jaunty but slightly muddied offshoot is SULLY.

SYLVESTER. Thufferin' Thuckatash! Sylvester might have forever remained a cartoon cat's name, had it not been for first SLY (Sylvester Stewart) Stone and then Rocky/Ramboman Sylvester (born Michael) Stallone. But although it was also the name of three popes, we don't see it being picked up on by many modern parents.

I

〰〰〰〰〰〰〰〰〰〰〰〰〰 ◉ 〰〰〰〰〰〰〰〰〰〰〰〰〰

TANNER. Tanner is a dark horse surname name that's been rapidly gaining favor for boys, one of several offbeat *T* names enjoying new-found popularity, joining Taylor and Tyler, Travis and Trevor. It's interesting the way stylish names seem to cluster around a few letters—and right now those are the strong consonants *T* and *K*, replacing the softer *J*, *S*, and *M*. In any case we suspect we'll be hearing of a lot more little boys called Tanner over the next several years. One stimulus to the name's success has been its visibility on a soap opera: the character of Tanner Scofield on *Days of Our Lives*.

TARQUIN and **TORQUIL.** Two almost unique options for the parent seeking a truly personal personal name. Tarquin was the name of two early kings of Rome, and was chosen by Laurence Olivier for his first child. Torquil, used mainly in Scotland, is actually an old Norse name related to the god Thor.

TAYLOR. Taylor is one of the most popular surname names for both sexes, solidly in the Top 50 across the country for boys, in the Top 10 for girls. Since it is so heavily divided, (see also Tyler), we see signs of a major gender-identity crisis in the offing for Taylor. But that aside, it still manages to sound classy and down-to-earth at the same time. Taylor's ongoing acceptability for boys has been reinforced by its use as such by the media (the son on *Evening Shade*) and by celebrities (e.g., Emilio Estevez) for their sons.

TERENCE, TERRENCE. A name that seems to hail from the old Irish neighborhoods of Boston, Chicago, and New York, Terence actu-ally dates back a lot of further, to the time of a famous ancient Roman comic playwright. Today, the original forms have little life, giving way to a battery of offshoots—TERRANCE, TERRELL, TERRILL, TYRELL—that are all immensely popular among African-Americans. The nickname TERRY has been used as an independent name—one of the first breakaway ambigender names—since the days of *Terry and the Pirates*, but has become almost exclusively female in recent years. Marlon Brando won an Academy Award for his performance as the sensitive Terry Malloy in *On the Waterfront*. Trivia tidbit: Terry is the off-the-mat name of wrestler Hulk Hogan.

THADDEUS. A distinguished, long-neglected name, Thaddeus (also spelled with one *d*) has an appealing three-syllable sound, plus a solid New Testament legacy—it was another name for the Apostle JUDE, patron saint of lost causes. We're not too crazy about the nickname THAD—a little too reminiscent of Chad and Brad. On the soap opera *All My Children*, Thadeus Martin is called TAD, but we much prefer the Italian TADDEO.

THEODORE. Although not yet as hot as its twin Theodora, this Greek name has succeeded in shedding some of its old dorky stereotypes—the nerdy Chipmunk, the real name of Beaver Cleaver. Its route to cool has been through its hip nickname THEO, first via the enormously popular *Kojak*, followed by the appealing Theo Huxtable of *The Cosby Show*. Theo was used on its own by Kate Capshaw and Steven Spielberg for one of their children. This pretty much leaves old standbys TED and TEDDY just that—old standbys.

THOMAS. Thomas came into being because there were too many Apostles named Judas; Jesus renamed one Thomas (meaning twin) to distinguish him from Judas Iscariot and Jude. At first used only for priests, but in modern times Thomas is one of the classic male names prevalent for men both highborn and low. Like many traditional names, Thomas has a new fashionability these days: In England it is currently the most popular boys' name of all, and its fashion stock is rising here as well. It is simple, straightforward, and strong, with more definition than names like James and John—in other words, everything the parent with a taste for the classics could want in a name. TOM is a similarly appealing nickname, as American as apple pie—or Tom Sawyer if we discount the negative stereotype of "Uncle Tom"—but TOMMY could sound like the son on a fifties sitcom, or else a rock opera. Thomas has some noteworthy foreign versions: the Scottish TAVIS and TAVISH and the multicultural TOMAS.

THOR, TOR. These powerful Scandinavian names, brought into the American experience by Norwegian explorer Thor Heyerdahl, relate to one of the key figures in Norse mythology, the god of thunder, rain, and agriculture. Two cross-cultural connections: In Hebrew, Tor is the name of a bird that symbolizes the arrival of spring, and the similar-sounding TORIN is an out-of-the-ordinary Irish family name.

TIMOTHY. While Timothy has teetered on the edge of stylishness for a few decades now, it's never tipped over into full-fledged trendiness and remains a classic name with a modern-feeling twist. A New Testament name—St. Timothy was St. Paul's companion, which might make the two appropriate and compatible twin names—Timothy was well used among early Christians but not popular in the English-speaking world until the eighteenth century. Its only real problem is that it somehow—maybe because of its -y ending—sounds youthful to the point of childishness: TIMMY is certainly a babyish nickname, and even TIM seems eternally boyish. Dickens's small hero, Tiny Tim, does nothing to give the name a more mature image, and several acting Timothys—Bottoms, Busfield, Daly, and Hutton—have a definite boyish charm.

TITUS. A rather forbidding old Roman name from Shakespeare's gory tragedy, *Titus Andronicus*.

TOBIAS. Tobias has the scent of a name on its way up. It's one of those Old Testament/Dickensian-feeling boys' names—akin to Caleb, Jonah, and Nathaniel—that hasn't yet become overused but has the same stylish flavor as now-ultratrendy brothers Benjamin and Jonathan, Jeremy and Zachary. It's a name with a distinguished pedigree—Tobias Smollett, for instance, was a major eighteenth-century English writer—that also has a contemporary feel. And if you'd like an update of that Jody-Cody kind of thing, you have the option of jaunty androgynous nickname TOBY. There is also the rarely used but still viable daddy of them all, TOBIAH.

TODD. Todd is a beach boy name of the sixties and seventies, a buddy of Scott, BRAD, Dean, and Duane. Even though it's already suffering from overexposure, let's continue to leave it out there on the beach, and not even think about it for our nineties children.

TONY. See Anthony.

TRAVIS. Travis's recent spurt of popularity has been fueled by its friendly, down-home country-western feeling (as in Travis (born James) Tritt), combined with some spark from long-running detective Travis Magee. It's already broken into the Top 40, and we fully expect to see it moving on up. One possible problem: Some people may still retain a nagging association to the extremely nasty Robert DeNiro character in *Taxi Driver*, Travis Bickle.

TREVOR. Trevor is one of those quintessentially British flyboy names that have been moving onto some U.S. most popular charts of late, following Ian and in tandem with Derek and Duncan. To many Yanks, Trevor may sound appealingly offbeat and classy at the same time, but true Anglophiles may realize it's more usually a working-class name in Britain these days.

TRISTAN, TRISTRAM. This intriguing pair of interchangeable names is known largely through the tragic medieval romance called both Tristan and Isolde and Tristram and Iseult. The dual name gained further fame from the Wagnerian opera it inspired, and from the eighteenth-century comic novel, *Tristram Shandy*. Both versions take on a slightly melancholy tone because of their relation to the French word for *sad*. Still, they can be thought of as a more original alternative to Christian, with TRIS a more unusual short form then CHRIS.

TROY. As a personal name and not an ancient city, Troy came to the attention of the American public via Troy Donahue (born MERLE) in the sixties, and has managed to hold onto its blond surfer image all these years, still being used for their babies by high-profile people like Leeza Gibbons. An outstanding current bearer of the name is star quarterback Troy Aikman.

TRUMAN. A presidential name that has just about shaken off its close identification with writer Truman Capote, Truman seems to radiate an aura of integrity and moral truth.

TUCKER. Tucker is a spunky last-name-first name that has a positive, comforting (could it have to do with being tucked into bed at night?) feel. It's been used for one of the Dan Quayle children and for a character on yet another soap opera—this time *All My Children*. A few other appealing surnames starting with *T* are THATCHER, TIERNEY, and TULLY.

TYLER. Tyler is now a hugely popular name, having ridden into favor on the wave of surname names as well as of old-fashioned-but-offbeat boys' names with a western flavor. With Taylor, it's rapidly become almost pandemic across the land and, to make matters even more confusing, both are used for girls as well. (As of this writing, the status is: Tyler more for boys, Taylor more for girls. In the state of Pennsylvania in 1993, for example, Tyler was number three for boys, Taylor number twelve for girls.) And to complicate the issue further, there is also TYSON, once reserved for boys, but appropriated for her daughter by singer Nenah Cherry. Boxer Mike Tyson's fall from hero status may make this a less attractive option.

TYRONE. The name of a county in Ireland, Tyrone emigrated into American popular culture in the person of Tyrone Power, who shared the name with his father. Some parents are now electing to use the short form, TY—that could be considered a nod to baseball great Ty Cobb—on its own, including Pam Dawber and Mark Harmon and hockey star Wayne Gretzky.

U

ULYSSES. A name far too weighty for a modern child to carry, Ulysses still might make a distinguished literary middle name. There are only two Ulysseses most people have ever heard of—one is the novel by James Joyce in which there is no character by that name but which is based on the Homeric epic of Odysseus, the Greek form of the name Ulysseus. Then there was General/President Ulysses S. Grant, who in fact was christened Hiram Ulysses Grant. The story that he changed his name around at West Point because he found his initials embarrassing is a thought prospective parents should definitely bear in mind.

URIEL, URI. This rarely used but evocative Hebrew name (it means "light") represents one of the four angels surrounding God's throne, and the one responsible for the inspiration of writers and teachers. It is a symbolic name given to boys born on Chanukah, and its nickname, URI (pronounced OO'ree) is often heard in modern Israel. But despite these attractive references, we do worry a little about unsavory nickname possibilities.

URIAH. This perfectly respectable Old Testament name seems to have been ruined forever as a result of its association with the odious Dickens's character Uriah Heep—even people who haven't read *David Copperfield* tend to shudder when they hear the name. The biblical bearer fared badly as well—Uriah was the cuckolded husband of Bathsheba, disposed of by King David.

V

〰〰〰〰〰〰〰〰〰〰〰〰〰〰〰 ◉ 〰〰〰〰〰〰〰〰〰〰〰〰〰〰

VAN. Van is not a name. If you're wondering how the well known Vans got to be called that, there are a variety of explanations. One of them used it as a short form of Evan—Van Heflin. Van Morrison was George Ivan, Van Cliburn was named Harry Levan, and Van Johnson was born Charles Van Johnson. So unless you are looking for a nonname, forget Van. VANCE is a proper name, but this book is full of far more attractive surnames than that.

VAUGHN, VAUGHAN. This Welsh name had a brief period, in the forties and fifties, when it was used more in the United States than it was in Wales, but it has been pretty much forgotten by now.

VERNON. Originally an artistocratic British surname, Vernon is now redolent of gas stations, tractors, and hot blacktop. The nickname VERN, especially as heard on recent west coast TV commercials, only serves to assure the name's inevitable fate.

VICTOR. One of the earliest of Christian names, Victor (in its Italian form, VITTORIO) was borne by several saints and Popes, but the name only made it big in the English-speaking world during the reign of Queen Victoria. Seeing it as one of the very few male names popularized by its female version, instead of the other way around, lends Victor some slight feminist élan, but we're afraid it would take more than that to lighten the stodgy macho image it has been saddled with for the past half-century. The Italian version, on the other hand, has considerable charm.

VINCENT. Although the name has a long and distinguished history, Vincent's image has definitely tarnished over the past few decades and probably at this point only the most Catholic of parents would name a child Vincent. If you commit the further sin of calling the baby VINCE or VINNIE, you might as well dress him in a little black nylon shirt with a plastic comb sticking out of the breast pocket. The Vincent with the most dignity of late was the sensitive furry-faced character in *Beauty and the Beast*. Trivia tidbit: Vincent is the real name of musician Alice Cooper, proof of how far a person will go to escape the name.

VIRGIL. The name of the greatest of Roman poets, as well as an early Irish saint, Virgil is rarely heard nowadays but retains a certain likable Southern twang. Virgil Tibbs was the character played by Sidney Poitier in two movies, and is the first name of astronaut "Gus" Grissom.

W

WADE. This is a surname name that stands out a bit from the rest: It's stronger, sharper, more direct than stuffier choices like PORTER and Parker, plus it packs more masculine punch than Jordan, Morgan, Taylor—names that are being increasingly taken over by girls. But it does have a stagey soap opera feel, as reflected by Wade Matthews in *All My Children*, and, worse still, could sound like Wayne with a cold.

WALDO. A German pet name that seems somewhat jokey to the American ear but also possesses a certain charm thanks to its final, jaunty *o*. The weighty reputation of Ralph Waldo Emerson adds a measure of backbone to the name, and older boomers may remember Robert Redford as *The Great Waldo Pepper*. But can any modern parent possibly give this name to a child, knowing the giggles that will ensue each time someone asks, "Where's Waldo?"

WALKER. One of the more popular of the surname names and one of the most appealing, perhaps because of its distinguished associations to writer Walker Percy and photographer Walker Evans. Walker was originally an occupational surname—like Taylor and Cooper—that referred to someone who walked on fabric to clean it. Really.

WALLACE. Wallace and its short form WALLY are names that have become so square that they could turn around sometime in the 21st century. But to use it now, you'd have to have a lot of confidence that your child could transcend having the same name as The Beav's big brother.

WALTER. Thanks to Sir Walter Raleigh and Sir Walter Scott, Walter was once seen as a name with nobility, and a few independent-minded parents are again taking it into consideration, seeing it as classic, yet nowhere near as common as a Robert, William, or Joseph. A favorite

Norman name, Walter was also extremely popular in this country from the 1870s all the way through the forties. And then there are all those great Walters and WALTs of the past to consider—from Whitman to Disney to Cronkite. The early British pronunciation of the name—Water—led to such surname names as WATSON, a possible consideration if you want to name your son after an ancestral Walter but dislike the original form; another is WALTON.

WARD. Like Wally, still a Cleaver name.

WARREN. Even when Warren Beatty was America's number one Lothario, his name did not sound very romantic. (Maybe he should have stuck with the original Henry.) Warren is a sober onetime surname still stuck in the stiff-collared image of President Warren Gamaliel Harding, and we can't imagine many contemporary parents considering it for their babies.

WASHINGTON. In the current search for names with meaning, parents are looking to honor heroes and heroines, including United States presidents. And with surname names in vogue, choices such as Washington—and Taylor, Tyler, Lincoln, and Kennedy—have a fashionable sheen as well as historical backbone. This one might not be as easy to handle as some of the shorter ones, but is certainly one of the most distinctive. Writer Washington Irving, author of "The Legend of Sleepy Hollow," provides a further illustrious reference for the name. Nickname: WASH.

WAYNE. It's 1966. A thirteen-year-old boy is walking down the street, wearing tight black pants and bulky white socks. His name is Wayne. Or maybe Glenn, but the point is that Wayne is a name last stylish when Mick Jagger was in his twenties. For further evidence, watch a rerun of *The Wonder Years* or think about Wayne Newton.

WILEY, WYLIE. This friendly, insouciant cowboyish name has an almost irresistible charm, and could make a more relaxed stand-in for the self-consciously stylish Wyatt.

WILLIAM. There has always been a constituency for a solid, established boys' name like William, but when the Prince and Princess of Wales chose it for their firstborn son in 1982, William rose from the ranks of stalwart classics to confirmed princely fashion. William has become the ideal name in the opinion of many American parents: conservative yet contemporary, traditional yet trendy, with the distinction of having been, for four hundred years, second only to John as the most popular name in the English-speaking world, represented in impressive numbers in royalty and politics (four American presidents), and literature (including Shakespeare). The trend these days is to call children by their full names: Elizabeth is Elizabeth and William is William. When nicknames are used, BILL and BILLY, the favored forms of our own youth, are decidedly out, while WILL (as in Will Smith, the *Fresh Prince of Bel Air*) and even WILLIE are very in (though be warned never to speak the latter out loud if you're visiting a British pub). Note, too, that WILLS, nickname of the princelet of Wales, is a bit too precious for an American boy. Riding on the William bandwagon is the Irish spin-off Liam and the Dutch form WILLEM, introduced to the United States by artist Willem DeKooning, adopted by actor Willem Dafoe (born William), and chosen for his son by rocker Billy Idol. A foreign cognate that might appeal to those of Welsh roots: GWILYAM. Aside from the presidential WILSON, (which has considerable appeal), other Wil names—WILFRED, WILBUR, WILBERT, WILLARD, and WILLIS—are gone and best forgotten.

WINSTON. There's a good reason why this name has been so tightly identified with the Churchill family: The original Winston Churchill, who was given his mother's maiden name as his first, was born in 1620. Over the years, it has been adapted more freely in Britain (it was the middle name of John Lennon) and, more particularly, in the West Indies, but Winston is rarely heard in this country, except among West Indian families. With the new trend toward using hero names, we hope to see this upstanding Anglo-Saxon name considered more often. Minor irritant: the connection to the cigarette brand. The nickname WINNIE came into the public consciousness with the *Winnie-the-Pooh* books, but is now thought of as almost exclusively feminine. More appealing is WIN, WINN, or even WYNN, which can also be reached via the somewhat haughty WINTHROP.

WOLFGANG. Wolfgang has become a sort of joke name, even though Valerie Bertinelli and rocker Eddie Van Halen did choose it for their son after our book *Beyond Jennifer & Jason* deemed it "so far out it will always be out." With that star stamp of approval—plus the high visibility of epicurian pizza king Wolfgang Puck—the name seems to be back in the realm of possibility again. Some parents may be attracted to its pedigree as Mozart's first name, though in the past most who wished to honor the composer with their child's name have opted for a variation of AMADEUS. The nickname WOLF—sometimes used as a name on its own—may have a certain lupine appeal.

WOODROW. To get to the popular nickname WOODY, you have to deal with its parent name, Woodrow, which sounds so formal and, well, wooden, that if you're considering using it to honor the president, it might be wiser to opt for WILSON. But Woody, which has a lot of good-natured, neighborly appeal, has been around for a long time. First there was bandleader Woody Herman (born Woodrow), folksinger Woody Guthrie (ditto), then Woody Allen (born Allen), and finally Woody Harrelson, who became famous playing a character named Woody Boyd.

WYATT. The name of the legendary gunfighter Wyatt Earp has recently become a hot item, even though it's been seen as cool, at least since the late sixties, when Peter Fonda played a Wyatt in the seminal film *Easy Rider*. Relaxed but still respectable, Wyatt has been used for their son by Goldie Hawn and Kurt Russell, and been visible in the soap opera *All My Children*.

X

∧∧∧∧∧∧∧∧∧∧∧∧∧∧∧∧∧∧∧∧ ◉ ∧∧∧∧∧∧∧∧∧∧∧∧∧∧∧∧∧∧∧∧

XAVIER. Xavier carries two divergent images: There's the Latin bandleader type, à la Xavier Cougat, who sports a pencil moustache and a shiny cummerbund, and then there's the ultra-Catholic name that invariably lies behind the X in all those Francis Xs. It's difficult to imagine any parent settling on Xavier as the one perfect name in all the world for their child, though that initial *X* is extremely attractive. If you are considering it, bear in mind that the correct pronunciation has it begin with a *Z* sound. The Spanish JAVIER is still widely used by Latino families.

Y

YAEL. Yael (pronounced with two syllables) is a Hebrew name that is popular in Israel, and also travels well across cultures. Spelling (and pronouncing) it YALE might seem to point to Ivy League rather than Hebrew roots.

YEHUDI. The Hebrew form of JUDE, Judah, or JUDAS, Yehudi's fame has been spread mainly through violinist Menuhin, though the name does not translate easily to American schoolrooms.

Z

ZACHARY. Zachary has a lot more zip and style than most other Old Testament names, which is probably one reason why it has become so fashionable over the past few decades. The seventh most popular name in Pennsylvania in 1993, it was chosen for their sons by such celebrity parents as Robin Williams and Cheryl Tiegs. Still, although Zachary, with its short form ZACK or ZAK, managed to retain a measure of strength and distinction despite its trendiness, more inspired choices at this point would be the name's older versions, ZACHARIAH or ZACHARIAS.

ZANDY. Zandy, like GANDY, is a rarely heard name (there was a seventies movie called *Zandy's Bride*) that has a lot more energy and charm than more common cousins ANDY, SANDY, and RANDY.

ZANE. What, we wonder, would have happened if famed western writer Zane Grey had written under his real first name of Pearl? We certainly wouldn't be looking at Zane as a viable name right now, since the author was pretty much solely responsible for this name's cool western image. Zane is, in fact, a name that may be too cool, if you believe such a state is possible. Any Zane would certainly have to grapple with people's expectations that he be sharp, sexy, and sophisticated in a way that a John or a George would not.

ZEBADIAH, ZEBEDY, ZEBULON, ZEDEKIAH. Yes, these are all mouthfuls, and might be too much for a small child to maneuver (let alone spell), but we're still not sure these venerable old biblical monikers should be dismissed out of hand. Just think of all those attractive western heroes known as ZEB and ZED.

ZEKE. This pleasingly innocent nickname for Ezekiel might make a willing substitute for the overused ZACK.

ZELIG. An alternate form of the Jewish SELIG, Zelig became known to a wider audience through the Woody Allen film of that name—even though Zelig was the character's last name. Unfortunately, the one Zelig we know changed his name to Alan as soon as he was old enough.

BIBLIOGRAPHY

〜〜〜〜〜〜〜〜〜〜〜〜〜〜〜〜〜〜〜〜〜 ◉ 〜〜〜〜〜〜〜〜〜〜〜〜〜〜〜〜〜〜〜〜〜

We have been engaged in onomastics, the study of names, for so long that a complete bibliography of references would be impossible. But the following are works that have been particularly helpful in formulating this book.

Amende, Coral, *Legends in Their Own Time: A Popular Biographical Dictionary*, Prentice Hall General Reference, New York, 1994.

Benaglia, Elena, *Il Nuovo Libro dei Nomi*, Giovanni De Vecchi Editore, Milano, 1992.

Browder, Sue, *The New Age Baby Name Book*, Warner Books, New York, 1974.

Coghlan, Ronan, *Pocket Guide to Irish First Names*, The Appletree Press, Belfast, 1985.

———, Grehan, Ida and Joyce, O. W., *Book of Irish Names: First, Family & Place Names*, Sterling, New York, 1989.

Dinwiddie-Boyd, Elza, *Proud Heritage*, Avon Books, New York, 1994.

Drabble, Margaret and Stringer, Jenny, *The Concise Oxford Companion to English Literature*, Oxford University Press, Oxford, 1990.

Dunkling, Leslie, *The Guinness Book of Names*, Guinness Publishing Ltd, Enfield, UK, 1993.

———, and Gosling, William, *The New American Dictionary of First Names*, Signet Books, New York, 1985.

Ellefson, Connie Lockhart, *The Melting Pot Book of Baby Names*, Betterway Publications, White Hall, VA, 1990.

Goulart, Ron, Ed., *The Encyclopedia of American Comics*, Facts on File, New York, 1990.

Hanks, Patricia and Hodges, Flavia, *A Dictionary of First Names*, Oxford University Press, Oxford, 1990.

———. *A Concise Dictionary of First Names*, Oxford University Press, Oxford, 1992.

Lieberson, Stanley and Bell, Eleanor O., "Children's First Names: An Empirical Study of Social Taste," *American Journal of Sociology*, Vol. 98, No. 3, November 1992.

McNeil, Alex, *Total Television*, Penguin Books, New York, 1991.

Monaco, James, *The Movie Guide*, Perigree Books, New York, 1992.

Nicholson, Louise, *The Best Baby Name Book*, Thorsons Publishers, Ltd., London, 1990.

Ousby, Ian, Ed., *The Cambridge Guide to Literature in English*, Cambridge University Press, Cambridge, 1991.

Room, Adrian, *Naming Names*, Routlege & Kegan Paul, London, 1981.

Rosenkrantz, Linda and Satran, Pamela Redmond, *Beyond Charles & Diana: An Anglophile's Guide to Baby Naming*, St. Martin's Press, New York, 1992.

————. *Beyond Jennifer & Jason: An Enlightened Guide to Naming Your Baby*, St. Martin's Press, New York, 1988, 1994.

————. *Beyond Sarah & Sam: An Enlightened Guide to Jewish Baby Naming*, St. Martin's Press, New York, 1992.

————. *Beyond Shannon & Sean: An Enlightened Guide to Irish Baby Naming*, St. Martin's Press, New York, 1992.

Salazar, Salvador G., *Los Nombres del Bebe*, Javier Vergara Editor, Buenos Aires, 1988.

Sidi, Smadar Shir, *The Complete Book of Hebrew Baby Names*, Harper & Row, New York, 1989.

Sleigh, Linwood and Johnson, Charles, *The Book of Girls' Names*, Thomas Y. Crowell Company, New York, 1962.

Stetler, Susan, *Actors, Artists, Authors & Attempted Assassins: The Almanac of Famous & Infamous People*, Visible Ink, Detroit, 1991.

Stewart, Julia, *African Names*, Citadel Press, New York, 1993.

Tuan, Laura, *Il Grande Libro dei Nomi*, Giovanni De Vecchi Editore, Milano, 1987.

Walker, John, Ed., *Halliwell's Filmgoer's and Video Viewer's Companion*, 10th edition, HarperCollins, New York, 1993.

Wilen, Joan and Wilen, Lydia, *The Perfect Name for the Perfect Baby*. Fawcett Columbine, New York, 1993.

Woulfe, Patrick, *Irish Names for Children*, Gill and Macmillan Ltd., Dublin, revised ed. 1974.